Springer Series on Social Work

Albert R. Roberts, D.S.W., Series Editor

Carole W. Soskis, M.S.W., J.D., is both a social worker and an attorney. She received her B.A. *magna cum laude* from Radcliffe College, her M.S.W. from the Simmons College of Social Work, and her J.D. from the University of Pennsylvania Law School. She had been a psychiatric and medical social worker in several hospital settings, and was Emergency Room social worker and Director of Social Work at Temple University Hospital, site of Philadelphia's busiest general emergency room. In addition, she served as Director of Health Rights Advocacy Program of the Pennsylvania Department of Health, and is currently Director of the Senior Citizen Judicare Project, a program of legal services for low-income elderly residents of Philadelphia. She is a Clinical Associate Professor in the Department of Psychiatry at Temple University School of Medicine and has published extensively in the fields of health-related social work and law.

Social Work
in the
Emergency Room

Carole W. Soskis, M.S.W., J.D.

Springer Publishing Company
New York

Springer Publishing Company, Inc.
200 Park Avenue South
New York, New York 10003

85 86 87 88 89 / 10 9 8 7 6 5 4 3 2 1

Library of Congress Cataloging in Publication Data

Soskis, Carole W.
   Social work in the emergency room.
   (Springer series on social work ; v. 5)
   Includes bibliographies and index.
   1. Hospitals—Emergency service. 2. Medical social work. I. Title. II. Series.
[DNLM: 1. Emergency Service, Hospital. 2. Hospital Departments.
3. Social Work. W 322 S715s]
RA975.5.E5S63 1985   362.1'8   84-20278
ISBN 0-8261-4410-1

Printed in the United States of America

Contents

Acknowledgments

Many people contributed to the ideas and materials in this book, but I want especially to thank the following: Marie Weissman, A.C.S.W., and Joan Hoffman, A.C.S.W., Allentown and Sacred Heart Hospital Center, Allentown, Pennsylvania, for material on occupation description, disasters, and working with families; Carol Kasoff, A.C.S.W., and Peggy Thomson, A.C.S.W., Hospital of the Medical College of Pennsylvania, for case examples and help with the chapters on the elderly, victims, and alcohol and drug abuse; the staff of the Social Work Department of Temple University Hospital, Philadelphia, for their support and example, and Clifford Bell, A.C.S.W., for case examples, suggestions, and major contributions to the occupation description; Vera Johnson, A.C.S.W., Children's Hospital of Philadelphia, and Thomas Bale, A.C.S.W., St. Christopher's Hospital of Philadelphia, for case examples and help with the chapter on children; Karil Klingbeil, A.C.S.W., and the social work staff at Harborview Medical Center, Seattle, for the example of an outstanding program and the use of their protocols; Martha Swartz, M.S.W., J.D., for review of the chapter on legal issues; David A. Soskis, M.D., for review of the chapters on psychiatric emergencies and on alcohol and drug abuse; and Joan Doroba, for patience and accuracy in typing.

1 The Place of the Emergency Room in Modern Health Care

Even the terms used for designating emergency rooms show clearly the changes in the ways they have been used and described throughout the past few decades. At first, as "receiving wards," they were set up to be the conduit through which patients had to come before being admitted to the hospital. Then, as "accident dispensaries," they were geared toward acute trauma care for those who survived long enough to get there. Now, as "emergency rooms," "emergency departments," "emergency units," and sometimes even "walk-in clinics," they serve as the provider of services not only for those with conditions needing urgent medical attention, but also for those who feel that they must have immediate attention to their problems, whether medical or not.

Changes in Emergency Room Usage

In the last three decades visits to emergency rooms have increased nearly one thousand percent, as a little-used service of hospitals became a major health resource for many Americans.[1] In 1980 there were over eighty-three million visits,[2] almost two visits for every five people in the United States.[3] The increase in use has been so spectacular that it has led to a new medical specialty: emergency medicine. It is already the thirteenth largest specialty, with close to 11,000 members in the American College of Emergency Medicine and fifty-five approved residency programs. The first specialty boards were given in 1980, so that for the first time there is a group of physicians trained specifically in emergency medicine and tested as to their learning and competence.[4]

There are many reasons advanced for the growth of the emergency room population, ranging from increased medical knowledge to changed socioeconomic conditions. The following, for instance, are major contributors to the current heavy use:

1. Medical advances stemming from World War II and the Korean War, leading to great improvements in trauma care, so that more people now reach the emergency room alive;

2. other medical advances in coronary care and other areas of ambulatory care;

3. more complex technology that makes office treatment less appropriate than hospital treatment for some conditions;

4. the concentration of resources in hospitals and their availability twenty-four hours a day, especially when physicians have restricted their hours and outside visiting;

5. growing specialization in medical care so that the patient without a primary care physician does not know whom to call;

6. lack of physicians in the inner city, where many large hospitals are located;

7. increasing mobility among the population which leaves many people without a regular family doctor;

8. insurance programs which cover visits to emergency rooms but not to doctors' offices;

9. the increasing prevalence of chronic disease needing regular or medical attention (particularly among the growing ranks of the elderly, who may be trapped in the inner city);

10. cutbacks in social service programs providing free health clinics, psychiatric assistance, and other help;

11. the de-institutionalization of psychiatric patients, many of whom are unable to maintain themselves;

12. the rising expectations of medical care, fueled by the media, which lead people to seek emergency room services for all kinds of problems.[5]

These dozen reasons suggest four conclusions. First, more people with severe trauma and serious illness survive until they reach the emergency department and have a better chance of staying alive once they get there. Second, in spite of the advances in care of the seriously ill and injured, most people coming into emergency rooms suffer from problems and conditions that are important to them but not urgent in medical terms. Third, a small but substantial number of people coming to emergency rooms use it as their regular source of primary care, even when efforts are made to provide alternatives. Fourth, a sizable proportion of people visiting emergency rooms have no major medical complaint or sometimes no medical complaint at all, and often few or no resources—social, economic, or otherwise—to help them cope with the problems that brought them in. This group comes to the emergency room because the emergency room is always open, because they can usually get there (by police, fire rescue, or similar transport), and because they know that they will be seen.[6] As one researcher has pointed out,

> [t]he hospital EU (Emergency Unit) is an especially accessible and acceptable helping resource, since there are a minimum of administrative and even physical barriers to reaching it, and it carries the aura of special expertise of the hospital. It should, therefore, be prepared to act as a major crisis intervention and screening agent for the broad range of problems brought to it. This requires official acknowledgment of this responsibility and transmission of this attitude to the staff. . . .[7]

Some emergency rooms, no matter how their functions are defined by their staff and by the hospital administration, are viewed by the surrounding community as primarily a social agency. Consequently, while the staff are geared to handle trauma, such as industrial, automobile and other accidents; gunshot and stab wounds and burns; and serious illness, such as myocardial infarctions and CVAs, they also find themselves struggling with transients, alcoholics, psychiatric patients, victims and perpetrators of abuse, confused elderly, and a host of others for whom their skill, training, and experience are not necessarily appropriate. Many emergency rooms tend to attract disproportionate numbers of "underprivileged, high-need, high-resource-use groups," including non-whites, newer immigrants, the unemployed, undereducated, and unskilled. A large number of these are suffering from recent life stresses, mostly psychosocial, which may influence their decision to seek help but which they may not report directly.[8]

While medical and nursing staff may be puzzled and angered by this group, they no longer routinely turn them away. Expanded legal duties attributed to emergency rooms and the fear of liability, together with Joint Commission on the Accreditation of Hospitals (JCAH) requirements,[9] mean that nearly everyone is seen, at least by a triage officer, and most probably by a physician. Being seen does not mean being treated; many are the nurses and doctors who have wondered what on earth to do next with someone whose acute medical needs, if any, are easily met but whose other needs seem limitless.

Changes in Emergency Room Populations and Settings

There is some evidence that the emergency room population may soon contain even a greater concentration of the most deprived and underprivileged. Emergency room visits declined from 83,393,625 visits in 1980 to 81,106,576 visits in 1981, the first such reduction since the American Hospital Association began maintaining such statistics.[10] There could be many reasons for such a decline, but one possibility is that people who could go elsewhere have started doing so, such as to "free-standing emergency centers," also known as FECs, urgent care clinics, emergicenters, "Medical McDonalds," or "Docs-in-a-box."[11] These centers have arisen to fill the gap in medical care between that which is offered by the primary physician and that which is available in the hospital emergency room. The private physician may see patients up to eight or ten hours a day, often much less, and usually by appointment only. The hospital ER has long waiting times, high charges, and often an unpleasant environment. In contrast, FECs are usually open up to twelve hours a day, seven days a week, and provide walk-in service with generally no more than a fifteen-minute wait. They are often located in the suburbs and/or shopping centers, places where people drive frequently, so that a patient may stop in on impulse. Hence, the FEC is likely to appeal to those who have no private physician or whose private physician is not available when needed, who prefer not to use hospital emergency rooms, and who are satisfied with episodic care (although some FECs do see patients by appointment and are apparently able to maintain the brief waiting time). The centers are able to limit reimbursement to cash, credit cards, or private insurance, screening out those with medical assistance, noninsurance, or an otherwise undesirable financial picture. In addition, "emergency" here is a misnomer, and the phrase "urgent care" is probably more appropriate. Treatment ranges from the provision of primary care to the handling of minor wounds and injuries; in 1982 only two percent of cases in these centers involved real trauma.[12] As the phrase "Medical McDonalds" indicates, FECs provide many of the same desirable features as fast-food restaurants: pleasant surroundings; convenient locations, usually with parking; minimal waiting time; and reasonable cost, usually 30–50% lower than in an ER and comparable to a visit to a physician's office.

Ownership and distribution of these centers varies considerably. Areas with rapidly growing populations sometimes have a large number; Houston, for instance, has at least twenty. Some cities have none at all and are apparently not seen as good markets. (Many inner-city areas already have primary care centers catering to medical assistance patients. These centers range from excellent to abominable, the notorious "Medicaid Mills." Even the best of these are rarely equipped for urgent care.) The FECs may be owned by physicians; owned by large corporate chains and leased to physicians, together with management services; or owned by hospitals eager to avoid competition. Sometimes hospitals cooperate in unusual and effective ways; in Dayton, Ohio, for instance, an underserved suburban area now has an FEC run by three hospitals who wanted to provide services without competing with each other.

Hospitals have greeted the development of these new centers with ambivalence. In spite of continued complaints about non-emergent patients who tie up staff time, some hospitals worry about the potential draining away of paying and well-insured patients. The hospitals would be left with major trauma, as is appropriate; night-time urgent care; and those patients without money, insurance, or other resources. Yet developers of the centers argue that patients with relatively minor complaints should not have to subsidize the care of the severely ill and injured, nor should they have to endure long waits and rude, impersonal treatment.[13]

The impact of FECs is still not known. Questions as to whether they should remain in underserved areas, whether they do take "business" away from hospitals, what kind of affiliation they do and should have with hospitals, whether they are a

permanent part of the health care landscape or just a passing fad
still remain to be answered. With all this uncertainty, however,
there are still three implications for the social worker. The first is
that social workers, along with other staff, have to put increasing
effort into making the atmosphere of the ER less aversive and
more supportive. It is one of the central arguments of this book
that the presence of a social worker does just that, and the
following chapters discuss how. Second, if freestanding emergency centers do drain off paying patients, there may be even
more pressure on social workers to discover and utilize resources
for those who are left and whom the hospital cannot turn away.
Finally, if FECs are the wave of the future, then they may
involve new employment opportunities for social workers. Physician groups with large practices have been known to hire social
workers to provide counseling and referral services to their
private patients.[14] Similar services for a small additional fee or a
slightly larger base service charge might be built into the programs of certain FECs.

Rural Emergency Rooms

This book is geared more for the social worker in the urban ER,
which tends to be accessible to many populations with very
different needs, not all of them medical. Much of the material is
relevant also to social work in the rural ER, although small rural
hospitals are unlikely to provide these social work services. Rural
hospitals can range from university medical centers to tiny hospitals serving a number of surrounding communities. Some have
full staffs; others have one, two, or a few workers to provide
certain well-defined services; and some have no professionally
trained social workers at all. Few social workers in these or any
other hospitals complain of lack of work, so additional responsibilities in the emergency room may have little appeal. Even so,
since a substantial proportion of admissions in rural hospitals
may come through the ER, the social worker needs to know
something about the patient population the ER serves and to
have some acquaintance with the characteristics of the surrounding communities.[15] Students can often get valuable and
satisfying experience doing studies and providing services in
emergency rooms. If there is someone available to supervise, a
graduate social work student, particularly one on a block plan,

might contribute substantially to efforts to evaluate what happens in the ER.

The patient population is likely to depend on a number of factors. One is the size and reputation of the hospital. Research suggests that in rural areas, even with closer medical care available, people will travel long distances to the emergency room of a respected hospital. Understanding patient expectations and their assessments and interpretations of the medical care they actually receive is crucial to better service. Other factors include the types, if any, of medical services available in the various communities, such as federally-, state-, or locally-funded health centers; foundation-sponsored health centers; private practitioners, including physicians and various physician extenders, as well as local efforts to recruit them; and ambulance services. Willingness of local private practitioners to defer payment or take medical assistance may also be important in some communities. The number of these is relevant, too, as some providers may be so busy and so overutilized for their resources that waiting times are long and the quality of care may be jeopardized. Other factors include socioeconomic status of the various populations; population density and distribution (are many households relatively isolated?), terrain, climate, road quality, and other characteristics affecting transportation. Distance to a large metropolitan area makes a difference, too, as city hospitals may draw a substantial proportion of patients willing to drive further or in need of specialized care. The social worker covering the rural ER, whatever his or her assignments, may have to contend with issues that are less frequent in urban settings. A number of rural hospitals are near state lines, and the social worker may be among those involved in sorting out the differences in insurance coverage and reimbursement requirements. Follow-up is likely to be more difficult when long distances and fewer resources are involved, and the need for linkages among the various social service systems and programs is critical. In one Pennsylvania experiment, people from five rural counties who worked with the elderly were gathered in a central location for training in advocacy for this population. The sessions were one day each during three consecutive months. Not only did the participants learn something about advocacy and useful techniques, they also met each other, exchanged information about programs, discovered resources they had not known existed, and in some cases began long-term collaborations. A nearby college, government program, or large institution can provide a setting and will sometimes provide funds and personnel for relevant programs. Professional isolation is demoralizing and exhausting and is likely to lead to less creative and effective patient care.

Another subject of concern for rural social workers is the increased likelihood of inadequate physical resources and facilities in poor rural communities, such as plumbing. Follow-up is made even more difficult by the lack of such things as solid waste disposal and running water. A social history has to include basic questions about living conditions and availability of various utilities. Still another area is the subpopulations served by the hospital, particularly those who tend to keep themselves apart and have well-defined and established beliefs and customs that may interfere with medical care and follow-up. It helps to be familiar with and respectful of the indigenous healers in the communities, such as "herb doctors" and others, and to have some understanding of the beliefs, fears, and folk medicine practices of the different groups. Presenting medical care as not inconsistent with these may increase the chances of acceptance and compliance.

Dental care may be expensive or in short supply in some areas so that emergency rooms will see people in considerable pain and in need of substantial dental work. If the hospital can provide nothing but pain relief, then it needs to work with other agencies to see what services can be made available. A social worker just beginning in an ER, in urban areas as well, might want to check on the availability of emergency dental care, both inside and outside the hospital. Another problem in some locations is maternity services (see Chapter 3). Women who live far from prenatal care, cannot leave their children, or who planned to have home delivery may come to the ER in the advanced stages of labor and may have complications. If possible, the social worker should work with other sympathetic staff to help the hospital develop a policy of admitting, without question, all women near delivery. That is not to suggest that pregnant women in the surrounding areas should be encouraged just to show up, with or without coverage, at delivery; obviously, arrangements are best made ahead of time. However, ten minutes before delivery is not the time to ask questions or to make an example of someone. This problem also occurs in urban emergency rooms but without the added difficulties of remoteness and long distances. These are just a few examples of problems that may occur in rural emergency room social work. Those with the most knowledge and experience need to share their knowledge with those who are still beginning.[16]

Other Issues for Social Workers

Hospital emergency rooms face two major problems: (1) how to keep the group of insured patients who can now choose to go elsewhere, and (2) how to deal with the larger proportion of those with severe social problems who are likely to come in. The potential financial drain is a frightening one.

And yet the emergency department offers the chance to provide good service to those who most need it, both the truly urgent cases and those who have nowhere else to go. As to the latter, there have been reminders in the literature about hospitals' traditional role as charitable organizations and the obligation they now have both to continue to minister to the public's health and also to find new sources of revenue to fund those efforts.[17]

The new stresses on social work resources make the role of the social worker even more invaluable than in the past. He or she is the one who remembers that factors such as stress, loss, adverse life situations, and low socioeconomic status can have a deleterious effect on physical health. The social worker often helps to evaluate the presenting problem and encourages the patient to translate it into one the medical team can deal with, then works on the socioeconomic aspects of the problem whose alleviation will contribute to physical relief or make compliance with a medical regimen more feasible. An important aspect of this function is that it takes some of the pressure off medical staff by coping with "difficult" patients and incomprehensible complaints. In addition, the worker serves as an advocate for those patients not receiving appropriate attention and care and in the process helps humanize the whole setting. He or she helps to keep down costs by referring for post-hospital planning those admitted through the emergency room, preventing repeat visits, and directing patients to resources more suitable to their needs. He or she watches for "quiet" crises, helps to defuse tension during long periods of waiting, matches resources to patients, and remains available for counseling, support, and comfort. These are only a few of the tasks of the emergency room social worker that will be discussed in the following chapters.

Hospitals who recognize the benefits of social work services have already set up programs in their emergency rooms, and others are now doing so or trying to assess their need. It is the thesis of this book that all emergency rooms should have social work services at least available, if not on-site. The next chapter, which discusses the role of the social worker in the emergency room, describes in detail the enormous contribution that social work services can make in that setting.

Notes

1. Joan Clement and Karil Klingbeil, "The Emergency Room," *Health and Social Work*, 6 (November 1981):835–905. The eighties, however, have brought about a decrease in visits, a 1.6% drop in 1981. See Emily Friedman, "Slicing the Pie Thinner," *Hospitals*, 56 (October 16, 1982):64.
2. *Outlook*, American Hospital Association, 3 (May–June 1982).
3. "Increase in ER Use Affects Health Care Delivery," *Psychiatric News* (March 19, 1982):8–9.
4. Gary Sollars, "The Challenge of Contempo," *Journal of the American Medical Association*, 245 (June 5, 1981):2181.
5. See, for a discussion of various reasons, Clement and Klingbeil, "The Emergency Room," 835–905; G. Gibson, "Patterns and Trends of Utilization of Emergency Medical Services, in G. R. Schwartz, *Principles and Practice of Emergency Medicine* (Philadelphia: W. B. Saunders, 1978); Leonard M. Riggs, "Emergency Medicine: A Vigorous New Speciality," *New England Journal of Medicine*, 304 (February 19, 1981, 480–483; David G. Satin and Frederick J. Duhl, "Help? The Hospital Emergency Unit as Community Physician," *Medical Care*, 10 (May–June 1972):248–260.
6. Carole W. Soskis, "The Emergency Room on Weekends: The Only Game in Town," *Health and Social Work*, 5 (August 1980):37–43.
7. Satin and Duhl, "Help?", 258.
8. David G. Satin, "'Help,' The Hospital Emergency Unit Patient and His Presenting Picture," *Medical Care*, 11 (July–August 1973):328–337.
9. Joint Commission on the Accreditation of Hospitals, "Emergency Services," in *Accreditation Manual for Hospitals* (Chicago, 1982).
10. *Outlook*, American Hospital Association, 3 (May–June 1982).
11. For a description of the typical FEC, see Janet Plant, "The Urgent Care Craze," *Multis*, 1 (American Hospital Association, June 1983):25–26, 28–31.
12. "AMA Guidelines for Freestanding Emergency Centers Cause Dispute," *Hospital Week*, 19 (July 22, 1983):2–3.

13. Daniel S. Schechter, "Note From the Publisher," *Hospitals*, 56 (October 16, 1982):10.

14. For instance, as described by Elaine S. Weatherly and Carol M. Bauman, "Social Work in an OB/GYN Setting: A View from the Other End of the Spectrum," Symposium on Social Work Practice in Sexist Society (Washington, DC: National Association of Social Workers, September 14–16, 1980).

15. For background, see Basu, Ramala, and Basu, "Use of Emergency Room Facilities in a Rural Area: A Spatial Analysis," *Social Science and Medicine*, 16 (1982):57–84; and Cecil G. Sheps and Miriam Bacher, "Rural Areas and Personal Health Services: Current Strategies," *American Journal of Public Health*, 71 (January 1981):77S.

16. See, for example, Julia M. Watkins and Dennis A. Watkins, *Social Policy and the Rural Setting* (New York: Springer Publishing Company, 1984).

17. Joseph Peters and Ronald C. Wacker, "Strategic Planning: Hospital Strategic Planning Must Be Rooted in Values and Ethics," *Hospitals*, 56 (June 16, 1982):90–29, 97–98.

2 The Role of the Social Worker in the Emergency Room

The role of the emergency department social worker, while not infinitely expandable, generally grows and changes according to both the views of the individual worker and the needs of the patient group. This role expansion takes place more in the emergency room than in other parts of the hospital because of the patients' expressions of urgency and the worker's conviction that he or she may be the last or only resource available.[1] The flexibility of the role and its functions are part of what makes the job so exciting and the service given so extensive, but the flexibility must be a function of the social worker's orientation and not of the medical/nursing staff's propensity to refer indiscriminately everything that is not strictly medical and to promise patients that all will be taken care of. It is critical for the social worker to train physicians and nurses to refer properly, that is, not to promise that "the social worker will take care of this" or "the social worker will see that you get an apartment," but to say "I will ask the social worker to talk with you" or "the social worker might have some ideas about your problem." The importance of this distinction cannot be stressed too much. There is nothing more demoralizing for a social worker than a stream of patients whose unrealistic expectations result from promises by staff. The social worker's anger and frustration may then be directed toward the medical and nursing staff and will seriously interfere with any efforts to function as a team.

This, then, is the beginning of staff education, which is one of the major functions of the emergency room social worker. There are three others: patient/family service, the most important one; crisis intervention; and what might be called "filling in the gaps." The latter, which can be discussed briefly, is one reason why doctors and nurses tend to make promises for social workers, who in the emergency room particularly, try to take up whatever slack exists in a given situation.

Time permitting, social workers carry trays, play with children, hunt for shoes and coats, and perform a myriad of activities that would not get done otherwise. Filling in the gaps, however, is not just a matter of concrete service, as the following example illustrates.

> A badly injured patient who had jumped out of a window was brought into the emergency room. Everyone gathered around to begin emergency treatment. The social worker noticed a nine-year-old boy in one of the treatment rooms watching the scene and shut the door, as the view was hardly appropriate for a child. When the social worker later asked why he had to be the one to shut the door, the response was that no one else had thought of it because it was not part of someone else's job.

Filling in the gaps can range from providing picture books to children sitting for hours in the waiting room to making sure that the spouse of a critically injured patient has a quiet place to sit—and before that, that there *is* such a quiet spot in the emergency room if it is ever needed. This is not a function that can be broken into components and taught very well; it depends on the sensitivity and perceptiveness of the worker and his/her ability to respond quickly to a variety of situations.

Patient/Family Service

Case Finding

The delivery of service to patients and their families can be broken down into a number of elements. One of the critical factors here is the way that the social worker gets his or her cases; a worker who waits in an office and takes only referrals will miss a substantial number of patients badly in need of social work assistance.

The earlier the social worker becomes involved with the patient, the better in most cases, particularly since the emergency department is often the patient's first contact with the hospital or even the medical system. Attitudes, compliance, and future behavior may be shaped by the positive or negative nature of this first contact. The worker must be visible and available and must spend considerable time doing his or her own case finding. One way of doing this is through monitoring the waiting room. Patients in great physical or emotional distress; repeaters; confused, angry, or frightened people all may be spotted by routine monitoring of the waiting room and given preliminary screening, instruction, and support. The medical staff can be provided with helpful information about these patients, whose use of the emergency room may then be more appropriate and satisfying because of the early social work contact. While monitoring the waiting room is an important method of case finding, it also serves a useful public relations function. Maintaining visibility, providing small concrete services such as water or toys, apologizing for delays, and similar activities help to allay patient resentment at long waits, uncongenial surroundings, and sometimes impersonal care. These activities may be ones that the social worker shares with an ombudsman or community representative, or they may already be provided by other staff.

Security guards and registrars or clerks also find cases for the social worker and send patients directly, bypassing triage and medical procedures, or give anticipatory hints of the waiting problems. Both these groups are key members of the team and can be of invaluable assistance to social workers, for instance, by screening out people who come inappropriately, identifying "regulars," or keeping a close eye on those who are potentially disruptive or hostile. The social worker may also want to check with staff to see if patients are still waiting from a previous shift or to refer to a log that lists patients to be picked up or referred.[2]

A visible and known social worker will also have patients asking to see him or her, either before, during, or after treatment. Some busy emergency rooms have patients who come in asking not for medical help but to see the social worker. (This can become a dangerous state of affairs when a community begins to view an emergency room as a kind of technological soup kitchen.) Finally, there will be many referrals from nurses and physicians, and as stated earlier, the social worker must caution them about making promises and must also teach them what constitutes an appropriate referral. Even then, the worker will often confront patients whose needs and problems, besides being urgent, seem limitless and unresolvable. Some workers may see the rest of the staff as dumping patients on them, but it is just as likely in a well-functioning system that the referral is based on appreciation of the worker's knowledge, experience, and ingenuity. Staff may feel that if anyone can help this person, it will be the social worker. These feelings are often justified and result in still more difficult referrals.

Specific Services

The social worker performs many services both *for* and *with* patients. The following sections list some of the most frequently needed services.

Providing Concrete Services

The services to be provided depend on the resources available. Some social work departments have special funds, provided by the hospital, by grants, or by community agencies, which pay for these concrete needs. If the hospital is not willing or able to provide funds, the social worker might develop a grant proposal for a small amount of money to be used for specific patient needs. In addition, hospital administrators who do not want to admit indigent or uninsured patients not really in need of acute medical care may be willing to provide funding if they understand the potential savings. United Ways, Community Groups, trusts, and local foundations all might be able to make small, specially earmarked grants, even in these penurious times. Such funds can be used to pay for paratransit and ambulances (and agreements might be made with certain ambulance companies for preferred rates in areas where there are several operators in competition); for taxis; for public transportation; and in some communities, for private drivers who make arrangements with nearby hospitals. Where taxi vouchers, subway or bus tokens, and other monetary equivalents are used, a rigorous control system is necessary which determines who holds these items, who can authorize their use, and under what conditions. Otherwise, they are likely to disappear with astonishing rapidity. Patients without food are often referred to community resources such as food cupboards, church groups, and missions. Many hospital departments have agreements with hospital dieticians whereby they can order trays for patients who are seen in the emergency department but not admitted. In instances in which the patient cannot pay or be billed, either the social work department or the hospital absorbs the cost. Ordering a tray, for instance, is often a very good idea for a marginally nourished elderly person who will be returning home. It is also helpful to have a small supply of food items available for emergency snacks, such as when someone is brought in and discharged in the middle of the night, a child has been waiting to be seen for several hours, or a patient really does not need much in the way of medical care but is just too hungry to be sent out. The following is a list of foodstuffs which are nutritious and/or keep well:

- coffee (packets), plus packets of creamer
- bouillon
- hot chocolate
- juice (small cans)
- oatmeal
- dried fruit
- packaged cheese and cracker combination

Generally these are best obtained through the hospital's dietary department, first, because they can provide them more cheaply and in bulk; and second, because they may be willing to share government surplus food materials that have been given free. Other ways of obtaining food are from cooperative local merchants who might be prevailed upon to make donations or through an emergency petty cash fund. Needless to say, food supplies must be controlled and monitored in the same way as taxi vouchers and subway tokens.

Clothing may be collected and stored in conjunction with patient relations and volunteer departments. Particularly in cold weather, some patients will need shoes and coats before being discharged. As with so many patient needs, running around looking for two matching shoes may not really be a social worker's function, but most emergency room social workers will take on the task rather than send the patient out to freeze.

Patients may need help with medications on a weekend when stores are not open, when they cannot afford to buy what has been prescribed (physicians may forget to think about cost when prescribing), or when they are not sufficiently mobile to obtain them independently. While actually obtaining medications is usually a waste of a social worker's time and should be done by a volunteer, a patient relations staff member, or a family member wherever possible, the social worker can often expedite the filling of prescriptions.

In certain cases the social worker will arrange payment of prescriptions through departmental, grant, or other funds between checks, for instance, or when prescription costs are very high. It is best to develop a good relationship with the pharmacists within the hospital and to ask for a "social work price" which should be the pharmacy's cost. It may be that certain companies will allow the purchase of medical supplies with a similarly reduced price or at least with a smaller profit margin.

Such concrete services, and referrals for concrete services, can be and are often given by people who are not social workers. The crucial ingredient supplied by the social worker is a redefinition of the problem as including, but not limited to, the immediate need. Thus, support, evaluation, counseling, referral, and/or teaching may all accompany the provision of food or money. It is part of the social worker's function to think with the client how he or she will deal with the need the next time it arises, if it is likely to, and to work toward meeting it on a less frantic basis.

Promoting Communication

This category includes several components, such as social work assessment, the goal of which is to learn more about the patient's social, emotional, financial, and demographic situation. Such knowledge is useful to nurses and physicians in understanding the nature and history of a patient's complaint and in planning the kind of follow-up regimen which is likely to be carried out. It is useful to the social worker in assessing the kinds of supports and services that the patient and his or her family are likely to use. Part of this task may include communicating with families or caretakers at home when no one has accompanied the patient to the hospital, in order to inform them of the patient's whereabouts, obtain more history, and assess their willingness and ability to help. Another function in this area is helping patients articulate their real problems to medical personnel when presenting complaints have been too vague or understated. This kind of help may also involve advocacy, for instance, pushing a seriously ill patient ahead when staff have not been aware of the nature of his or her condition. In one hospital, for instance, a child with a nasty puncture wound who came in without his parents would have waited a very long time for treatment if not for the efforts of the social worker. The communication that the medical staff had received had had more to do with his age than with the seriousness of his condition. The social worker's ability to communicate the emergent nature of the injury resulted in immediate and appropriate treatment.

In addition, the social worker must sometimes translate medical terms, diagnoses, and instructions to patients who might otherwise refuse treatment or leave without understanding follow-up instructions. The social worker may also find it necessary to develop a roster of translators for certain groups using the emergency department, particularly when other hospital departments have not done so. Finally, it is extremely important when a patient is admitted through the emergency department for the social worker to pass on to the next worker as complete a record as possible so that help and planning can begin immediately on admission.

Referrals

Of all people in the emergency department, and in fact, in the hospital, the social worker is most likely to be aware of community resources and services—and of the gaps. In fact, the social worker may be viewed as, and may function as, the liaison person to various community groups and organizations. Specific kinds of referrals, other than the ones mentioned in this chapter, are discussed later in the book. When the social work department is large enough, it is usually a good idea to appoint a small group of people as a resource committee to compile a list or book of sources of service/assistance, how to apply, and how they actually work. On occasion, the worker should be freed from his or her responsibilities in the emergency department to visit heavily used agencies and/or to join with others in identifying and comparing services and identifying and publicizing gaps.

Providing Support and Brief Counseling to Patients and Their Families

The anxiety level of those not used to emergency departments or those bringing friends or relatives for serious illness or accident is usually very high. Children and their parents, the elderly, those with conditions possibly related to sexual activity, and numerous other groups may be extremely anxious. Alleviating this anxiety by a word, a touch, an offer, a concrete service, or sometimes by the worker's very presence is an important part of the social worker's function. Besides explaining the workings of the emergency department, what to expect next, the long waits often involved, the worker can begin to help the patient and family cope with what is happening. He or she can counsel them on dealing with specific illnesses and their manifestations and can try to mobilize whatever family and other supports are available, as well as identifying and pointing out the patient's strengths and needs. He or she can help with emotional problems related to or exacerbated by illness or injury and can assist with psychosocial screening of patients whose emotional problems appear to be paramount. All this occurs in the context of a psychosocial assessment which will help the worker formulate with the patient and physicians a realistic plan for follow-up. In some hospitals social workers in emergency departments provide brief counseling to patients who come in for several sessions specifically for that purpose.

Providing and Promoting Patient Advocacy

The National Association of Social Work's Code of Ethics[3] points out that a social worker's primary duty is to his or her client. This obligation, however, is sometimes in conflict with the worker's responsibility to the hospital, particularly when financial considerations arise. No one but the social worker is likely to try to stand outside the hospital to look objectively at the services it provides and does not provide. Urging a hospital with a busy emergency room and long waits to provide a more comfortable and congenial waiting room is one kind of advocacy. Insisting that an elderly woman and her critically ill spouse not be separated is another. Refusing to arrange discharge for a patient returning to an intolerable and dangerous setting is yet another. Patient advocacy does not involve taking an obstructionist or adversarial stand against the hospital, medical staff, or emergency department administration. Such a position would be a self-defeating one and would not in the long run be particularly helpful to patients. It means, rather, first gaining enough credibility and respect so that one's suggestions and objections are heeded; second, trying to find out what patients and families want and, when feasible and appropriate, trying to get it for them; third, communicating patients' needs and feedback, together with constructive recommendations, to those who can make changes; and fourth, vigorously opposing policies and decisions that are needlessly burdensome, unpleasant, or dangerous to patients.

Crisis Intervention

While crisis intervention could certainly be considered a part of direct patient services, it deserves a category of its own because of the different ways that medical and social work personnel deal with crisis. A crisis in medical terms is a situation where immediate intervention is required to prevent further break-down, damage, and death in a patient. If the patient passes through the crisis successfully, there is enormous relief and some-times a lessening of interest. Although treatment may continue and follow-up efforts to prevent further crises may be instituted, the major work is done. In mental health, while some of the same tasks are necessary, the immediate life-or-death component is usually absent and the crisis may be viewed as much as a period of opportunity as of disintegration. Caplan[4] describes a crisis as an upset of a steady state and explains that psychologically, as well as physically, the human organism is always trying to main-tain homeostasis in what is usually a rather fragile balance. When this balance is threatened, the organism engages in problem-solving activities to restore it. If these fail, there may be an even more serious reaction, accompanied by feelings of hopelessness and confusion.[5] As one commentator has described it, ". . . a crisis exists when an individual is faced with a problem that seems to have no immediate solution. Many times the problem seems hopeless because the individual cannot resolve the crisis with his usual problem-solving skills."[6] In other words, there is an imbalance between the difficulty of the situation and the person's repertoire of problem-solving skills.[7] What is important for the social worker is that a crisis is a time of disorganization and vulnerability, a time when the person is most susceptible to change and to the influence of others. This is the time when appropriate intervention can make the most difference. By helping the person cope with the crisis and adapt old or develop new problem-solving skills, the social worker can help him or her strengthen internal resources, avoid breakdown, and stave off feelings of hopelessness and despair. The feeling of being able to cope with devastating events may sustain the person throughout future happenings. The word "person" is used here because the individual most affected may be either the patient or a friend or relative.

Generally, there are three steps necessary for crisis resolu-tion.[8] The first is cognitive: the person needs help in viewing what has happened realistically and accurately. The social worker must elicit his or her perception of the event and its meaning and gently correct distortions and exaggerations. It may be necessary to find out why the person has come for help at this time. This is particularly important, for instance, when the illness or injury is seen as worse than it actually is or as a punishment for actions or omissions. Without a reasonably accurate perception of events, the person will be unable to cope with future developments, to hear what is said and suggested, to weigh alternatives, and to take actions appropriate to alleviate the situation and the concomitant suffering. In addition, he or she may be unable to see connections between stress, physical systems, and emotional upset.

The second task relates to emotion: the person needs help in becoming aware of his or her feelings, acknowledging them, accepting them, and discharging them. While certain groups require and maintain a stoical demeanor (and feel that their values should not be tampered with), everyone needs to hear about the universality of certain feelings, their acceptability, and the different ways of expressing them. Blocked emotions can result in physical symptoms, unresolved depression, exhaustion, and maladaptive behaviors. Some people need to know that they will not "fall apart" if they express their feelings and, in fact, may eventually have more energy for resolution of the situation. Those with emotions they see as unacceptable—anger at a relative for not caring for himself or herself, relief that a burdensome relative has died—need acceptance and support. Anger— at doctors and nurses, at the patient, at the world—guilt, shame, fear—all may need expression, and the nurses and physicians dealing with the medical elements of the crisis are not usually prepared to handle the emotional aspect. Privacy is crucial here, and the social worker must make sure that there are places where people can talk in private and can be alone.

The third task is problem solving: the person needs to be helped to consider and weigh alternatives, to develop adaptive behaviors, and to identify and seek out appropriate sources of help. This task is made much easier by attention to the first two. The worker should begin exploring situational supports, coping skills, and the amount of disruption the crisis has caused. While the emergency social worker can only begin to focus on this task, what is done in the emergency room may have a significant effect on the use of other resources, such as referrals and follow-up medical care.

It is important to remember that perceptions of what is a crisis may differ. The derelict who arrives in the dead of winter, half-dressed, hungry, and homeless, may not be in a crisis at all. He has been through this before and knows that sooner or later someone will provide him with food, clothes, and temporary shelter. On the other hand, the mother who brings in a child with a minor injury may be in a state of considerable agitation because of guilt over real or fancied neglect. Other than disasters or major accidents which produce a state of crisis for all involved, including the healers and treaters, whether or not a situation or event is a crisis may depend on its meaning for the individual.

This discussion of crisis theory is a brief and uncomplicated presentation of a sophisticated and complex body of knowledge. The emergency room social worker might want to do some reading in this area and should be allowed some time off to attend occasional seminars on the topic.

Staff Education

Much of what an emergency room social worker does is staff education—imparting relevant material from psychosocial assessments; translating patients' complaints into acceptable medical categories; reminding physicians of the costs of treatments and medications. The perception and interpretation of a patient's presenting problem will always be partly a function of the background and experience of the evaluator; these perceptions and evaluations will then affect the subsequent handling and treatment. The effect of certain "moral and social evaluations" are greatest for those patients "whose illnesses and medical problems are not amenable to quick and immediate diagnosis and treatment [and who] are seen as threats to the routine order and mission of the hospital E. R."[9] The social worker is constantly trying to help nurses and physicians understand the needs of this group of patients and determine the most helpful approach. Even with more medically acceptable patients, the social worker strives to communicate the part that a patient's life-style plays in ability for self-care, compliance, and future use of medical care. In one emergency room, for instance, the very important distinction is made between the *presenting problem*—what the doctor and nurse see and treat—and the *primary diagnosis*—which is what the social worker learns is the real issue and which may or may not be primarily a medical one. For instance, a young woman's presenting problem may be a broken arm, but after talking with her, the social worker may make a primary diagnosis of spouse abuse. The approach of the whole medical team, not just that of the social worker, will be different because of this knowledge. A man coming in with pancreatitis may have the primary problem of alcohol abuse. Looking at only the pancreatitis would be inadequate.[10]

Even where the presenting problem and primary diagnosis are the same, the social worker needs to communicate what he or she knows of the different groups who use the emergency room. The expression of pain, the use of medication, the reliance on faith healers, certain child-rearing practices all may affect the presentation of the patient's complaint and his or her willingness or ability to follow the medical recommendations. In addition, physicians who are unfamiliar with the customs of a new immigrant group may be horrified at what is perfectly acceptable care. In one hospital, for instance, staff were taken aback to find infants dressed only in large towels. The social workers explained that custom, not ignorance, neglect, or inadequate means, was the reason for the lack of clothing. At the same time that they were educating the physicians, however, the social work staff were becoming acquainted with the new population, explaining without coercion local child care practices, and making available items of clothing whose names they had had translated into the language.

The more this kind of communication occurs successfully, the more likely it is that the emergency room staff will begin to function as a team. Administrators who judge professional functions in terms of cost-effectiveness sometimes overlook the increased efficiency and higher morale that come from the development of a smoothly running team. The social worker, particularly in the emergency room, may well be the one individual who most shapes the team. It has been noted that

> Good team relationships are essential to good patient care but are always difficult to achieve. Knowledge of both individual dynamics and group process has enabled social workers to unsnarl some of the team tensions as they occur. They have been able to respond to the training and style of the various individuals on the team, to minimize scapegoating, and to help the team sort out which problems belong to the system and which problems are engendered by patient pathology.[11]

The formation and integration of the team is just part of an educational process that may also include formal small group sessions and/or training programs on specific subjects. At one hospital, for instance, the social worker in the emergency room and the director of patient relations held a series of group sessions for all three shifts. Representatives from medical, nursing, administrative, clerical, and security staffs attended. While the stated goals included learning to view the patient as a whole individual, developing sensitivity to patient attitudes, and understanding disposition alternatives, implicit goals were to foster cohesiveness, to eliminate intrateam racial bias, and to educate each team member about other members' roles, conflicts, and stresses. These groups were especially successful with evening and night shifts, who sometimes felt neglected and unappreciated.

An important component of such programs, in the hands of a social worker with group experience, is roleplaying. Encouraging a triage nurse to change places with a security guard or a registrar to play the part of a patient may elicit some resistance but can eventually be an extremely effective teaching approach. Staff members who have been participants or observers in such roleplaying episodes are never again quite so critical of those with different jobs and can often talk with them more readily.

The formal presentations that the social worker could organize, either alone or with expert help, are numerous. Topics include stress; costs and methods of treatment; patients' rights; racial and ethnic problems; disruptive patients; and many others, depending on the patient population and staff needs and interests. In some presentations, staff education and patient advocacy become one and the same; in others, such as the group program just discussed, staff can enjoy something that is being presented for their own growth and learning and for no other purpose.

Record-Keeping

The activities just discussed would more than fill the time of any social worker, but somehow recording patient service must also fit into the schedule. Record-keeping for the ER social worker can be divided into four parts, whether the worker is based in the ER or is called when needed from other areas in the hospital. The first is the ER patient record itself. In many hospitals, the one-page record form provides little or no room for social work comment. In fact, where there are several consultations, there may not be enough space for all the necessary medical information. However, inadequacies of space notwithstanding, there should always be a social work note on the record. If the social worker sees the patient as part of a formal consultation, the written response is like any other consult, and in the appropriate space, reason for consult, assessment, actions, recommendations should be noted very briefly. Informal consults, self-referrals, and social work screenings can either be recorded in the space for consults or in any other appropriate place on the form. Where there is no system or consistency, it is advisable to have the director of the ER, the director of the social work department, and the director of medical records reach an agreement on exactly where on the record the social worker is to put his or her notes. The limited space makes brief and cogent recording particularly important. Complete and complex sentences, long descriptive passages, and elaborate analyses have no place here. The necessity for brevity, besides refining thinking and planning, has another advantage: there is less opportunity to record inappropriate and potentially damaging material. Emergency room-related malpractice suits occur frequently enough so that the record may become a much-examined and interpreted document. The note should be clear and readable, with no scratched-out words or phrases. Corrections should be made by a single line through the error, the word "error" and the writer's initials, and a new entry. Important information includes whether the patient was known previously, why the patient was referred or picked up, what the social worker's assessment was, what he or she did, what he or she recommended, and how the patient responded. The social worker should know all the abbreviations approved by the hospital and use them freely. The following are two examples:

Social Work: Family known to me. Referred now to ensure FU care. Pt missing clinic visits because son can no longer take him. Talked c̄ Sr. Citizen Transport and they will take application. SW will pay cab fare for clinic visit this month. Mr. X to call me next week.

(FU = followup; Pt = patient; c̄ = with; Sr = Senior. This note could be shortened even more.)

Social Work: Suspected child abuse. Mother insists child fell down stairs. Unable to get more info. Filed Form X, called DCW. Explained reports and consequences to mother. No prev. contact c̄ this family.

(Departmental records would undoubtedly include more information, but this is adequate here. DCW is Department of Child Welfare. Agency abbreviations vary from place to place.)

The purpose of the note here is to document social work contact and activity. Another purpose is to ensure continuity of services; a physician who looks at the record of a previous emergency room visit and sees the social work note is more likely to think about a social work referral this time. Communication and supervision, other goals of ER recording, are best met in different ways. The second kind of record-keeping, for instance, is a social work log in the emergency room. Every patient seen should be logged. Some of these contacts may not appear on the ER record, such as those in which the patient comes in only to see the social worker, those in which the service rendered is primarily support for the family, and those in which the social worker discovers after treatment that the patient has no way of getting home. All contact should be logged in a way that allows recovery of useful information, such as types of patients taking up the most social work time, busiest hours of the day, physicians who make the most referrals, and so on. The log is not only invaluable for supervision of the ER social worker, but it also provides information on patient groups, special problems, referrals and referral sources, inadequate resources, and other specific material that the social work department may be interested in evaluating. In addition, it provides a brief but convincing picture for the hospital administration of what the social worker actually does in the ER, and as discussed in Chapter 11, some of this information can be extrapolated to provide an estimate of cost savings due to social work intervention. An example of such a log and the accompanying instructions are provided in Appendixes A and B.

Another kind of log is the on-call log, used in the system in which social workers are called at home, usually during evenings and weekends, to consult with staff on particular problems. The on-call log is probably best kept in book form and should always be in the possession of the person whose turn it is to take call. It should include columns for date, patient name, staff calling, reason for call, social work recommendations, and action taken. Important phone numbers, such as those of the administrator on call, emergency shelters, and the director of the social work department, can be in a separate section in the front of the book. This log can provide information as to what prompts a physician or nurse to call a social worker and can be a useful educational tool in encouraging certain kinds of calls and discouraging others. It can also be used to show that social workers receive so many calls at certain times of the week that the hospital should consider a worker on-site.

The third kind of record, already mentioned in other parts of the book, is the card file on patients who come in frequently, are well known to staff or at least to the social worker(s), and may have major social problems. Some hospitals keep "problem lists" of patients who are known or suspected drug abusers, for instance; the social work card file could include additional information on these people. Repeaters; chronic psychiatric patients; patients with medical problems aggravated by emotional or environmental factors (asthma); patients with routine special needs; and noncompliant, manipulative, and especially vulnerable patients are some of the groups for which the card file is appropriate. Besides the routine identifying information, the cards could include names and numbers of involved family, friends, landlords, and agencies and a description of services found helpful in the past. Cautionary statements, such as what has been tried unsuccessfully and what the patient should not get (e.g., "do not give carfare; he always has money but will not admit it") can be very helpful to staff when the social worker is not there or to a new social worker. Descriptive material is sometimes invaluable to staff in their assessment of a patient and sometimes even in their identification of a patient. In one case, an elderly patient named Mary Brown was brought in, confused and unable to remember where she lived. Although she was familiar to some of the staff, they knew very little about her and despaired of trying to figure out which of the many Mary Brown charts might he hers. A search through the social work card file revealed a card that described her exactly and provided all the necessary family information. As a result, a relative was located who came and took her home.

The usefulness of the card file lies in its availability to nursing and medical staff as well as the social worker. On off-shifts it is there when the social worker may not be able to provide relevant and sometimes crucial information on patients. It should not be open to everyone, however, and it is best for the social worker or social work supervisor and the nursing supervisor to make some kind of arrangement about access. One possibility is for the file to be locked when the social worker is not in the office and for the charge nurse on each shift to have a key. The file itself should be kept in the office which the social worker uses in the ER.

Records in general often tend to be scattered around in the ER, and the social worker must try to keep them in order and maintain confidentiality as much as possible. The periods of crises and the inability to space patients and plan recording time contribute to poor recording practices and unfinished entries. Whenever possible, the social worker should leave the shift with all recording done; if not, incomplete records should be placed in a locked drawer and never taken home.

The fourth kind of record is the social work chart. Departments vary considerably in their record-keeping formats, with some requiring very full and elaborate recording. The trend toward reducing and streamlining records can well be applied in the ER. For most contacts, a very brief form, such as that in Appendix C, is adequate. Certain patients who are seen frequently and regularly may need a more complete social work record. Also, two forms can be available, first the initial assessment form and later a less detailed one for a series of contacts. Some social work departments require a copy of the form in the central office and/or a file card with patient information for the central file. Whatever the requirements, recording in the ER should be designed to be useful but not so burdensome that the social worker never gets it done. Better a brief form that is available when needed than a comprehensive recording scheme that no one ever wants to complete or to read.[12]

Those social work departments with a link to the hospital computer system can experiment with even more efficient methods of recording. The log, for instance, could be completely computerized, with information called in by phone or entered into the department's terminal.

A few other record-keeping issues come up from time to time in the ER. For instance, one woman may have several children with different last names (also see Chapter 6). The social worker is probably the person best able to get a complete list of all the children and make sure that there is adequate cross-referencing. Appointments, communicable diseases, immunizations, and related issues will be handled in a very fragmentary and ineffective way if the children are not known to be siblings in the same household.

Another problem area involves those who use I.D. cards of friends and relatives, usually to ensure payment. Those who have been stricken from the medical assistance rolls, for instance, may seek help with someone else's card, fearing, sometimes realistically, that help will not be available otherwise. The danger there is that treatment may be based on information gained from the record of the person whose name is on the card, with potentially serious results. The social worker who suspects that a patient is using someone else's card is in a difficult position. If he or she persuades the patient not to use the card, the hospital cannot deny medical care or the patient's fears will have been well-founded; if he or she allows the patient to use the card, he or she is taking part in the fraud and allowing the patient to face a danger that may not be apparent to him or her. Whatever the resolution, the situation must be approached with the utmost tact and delicacy, and some kind of warning should be given to the patient even in the absence of an explicit acknowledgment that the card belongs to someone else.

The grouping of functions articulated in this chapter is a general one and appropriate for emergency rooms of all sizes and settings. (Appendix D presents a recommended occupation description for emergency room social workers.) The nature of the patient population will determine specific tasks that the social worker must assume. Some of the typical emergency room patients and problems are discussed in the following chapters. In any emergency setting, however, whatever the demands, the effective social worker will find that he or she is indeed providing direct service, filling in gaps, doing crisis intervention, and participating in staff training. Supervision of emergency room social workers should include defining these functions and their components, promoting their development, and minimizing factors that interfere or compete with them.

Notes

1. Parts of this chapter are based on Carole W. Soskis, "The Emergency Room on Weekends: The Only Game in Town," *Health and Social Work*, 5 (August 1980): 37–43.

2. Allentown and Sacred Heart Hospital, Allentown, Penn., *Protocol for Emergency Room Social Work* (courtesy of Joan Hoffman, A.C.S.W., and Marie Weissman, A.C.S.W.).

3. National Association of Social Workers, *Code of Ethics*, passed by the Delegate Assembly, 1979; implemented July 1, 1980, *Social Work*, 25 (May, 1980): 184–187.

4. Gerald Caplan, *Principles of Preventive Psychiatry* (New York: Basic Books, Inc., 1964).

5. Larry L. Smith, "A General Model of Crisis Intervention," *Clinical Social Work Journal*, 4 (Fall 1976): 163.

6. *Ibid.*

7. Caplan, *Principles.*

8. For general principles of crisis intervention, see Caplan, *Principles*; Donna C. Aguilera and Janice M. Messick, *Crisis Intervention: Theory and Methodology* (St. Louis: C. V. Mosby Co., 1978), especially Chapter 5, "The Problem Solving Approach to Crisis Intervention"; Naomi Golan, *Treatment in Crisis Situations* (New York: Free Press, 1978).

9. James M. Mannon, "Defining and Treating Problem Patients in a Hospital Emergency Room," *Journal of Medical Care*, 14 (December 1976): 1004–1005.

10. Joan Clement and Karil S. Klingbeil, "The Emergency Room," *Health and Social Work*, 6 (supp) (November 1981): 835–905. This paper contributed much to the author's formulation of the ideas in this chapter.

11. Frances Nason and Thomas L. Delbanco, "Soft Services: A Major Cost-Effective Component of Primary Medical Care," *Social Work in Health Care*, 1 (Spring 1976): 299.

12. For general guidelines to social work recording, see Suanna J. Wilson, *Confidentiality in Social Work: Issues and Principles* (New York: Free Press, 1978).

3 Legal Issues in the Emergency Room

The increasing importance of the emergency room as a source of general medical treatment and as a filler of gaps not otherwise dealt with by our system of medical care has contributed to substantial changes in the legal obligations of hospitals. Such topics as admission and discharge, consent and refusal to consent, negligence, abandonment, medical records, reporting, payment, substance abuse, and transfer, among others, are now major issues in the delivery of emergency care. The emergency room social worker should be aware of the hospital's and the staff's legal responsibilities, of the patient's legal rights, and of his or her own potential role in assisting both.

This chapter will confine itself to a few subjects where the presence of a competent and assertive social worker in some cases can make a major difference in how the hospital fulfills its responsibilities to patients. Admission and discharge, negligence, and consent are the three areas that will be covered here, with examples to illustrate the social worker's role. Other chapters, such as Chapters 4 and 8, deal with some of the legal aspects of those situations.

Admission or Denial of Care

All jurisdictions have laws or regulations on the types, level, and availability of emergency services to be provided by hospitals of various types and sizes. Whatever the services, however, until quite recently the law regarding emergency care supported the common-law rule that "no duty would be owed to a stranger"; that is, a private hospital could turn away any person who had not already been accepted as a patient. Consequently, emergency rooms could pick and choose those whom they would serve, often on the basis of race, residence, or financial capability, no matter how serious the condition of the ill or injured person might be. As one case noted, "Harsh as this rule may sound, it is permissible for the private hospital to reject for whatever reason, or no reason at all, any applicant for medical and hospital services."[1]

In the late 1950s, however, the courts began to realize that the general public was increasingly beginning to rely on emergency room services and that people were often seriously harmed by visiting emergency rooms where they were refused admission and/or treatment. In discussing court cases, it is important to remember that when courts develop or recognize a new obligation, they do not necessarily make a finding on behalf of the plaintiffs (complainants). Thus, the courts in the following cases were redefining the duties of hospitals. These decisions did not always help the patients or families involved in the litigation, but did make a difference to those coming after.

Humanitarian Grounds

The famous *Manlove* case[2] illustrates the changing legal perspective and the reason behind it. In the *Manlove* case, parents brought a four-month-old child, ill for four days, to an emergency room for evaluation. In spite of treatment by their private physicians, the baby was no better and was still suffering from diarrhea and a fever of 102°. The nurse in charge told the parents that since the child was under the care of a private physician (who apparently could not be reached), he could not be treated at the hospital, the rationale being that medicines might be prescribed that could react adversely with those given by his own doctor. The child was neither examined nor treated and died later that day.

In a departure from previous legal reasoning, which might have emphasized that the hospital had no duty to accept the patient, the Supreme Court of Delaware pointed out that the parents had relied on the well-established custom of the hospital to render aid in such a case. This reliance could lead to possible worsening of a patient's condition because of the time lost fruitlessly seeking aid. Consequently, the court said, the hospital must examine the patient to see if an emergency exists (and then, of course, treat any emergency condition discovered). In this particular case, the court did not find an unmistakable emergency and sent the case back for further determination. However, the importance of this decision, considering past reasoning, can hardly be overestimated. It is "the first decision in which a state's highest court officially recognized the public's changing attitude toward the emergency room, and a legal as well as a humanitarian duty to treat persons needing assistance."[3]

The key word in the comment above is "humanitarian"; the Court decided that the law required that the hospitals do what most of us think is the right thing. Now hospitals in Delaware might be expected to take a more humanitarian stance toward patients coming to the emergency room and a less rule-bound and unsympathetic one. The court decision in *Manlove*, which technically bound only hospitals in Delaware, gave direction to other courts and other hospitals and helped to change the way that emergency patients were treated all over the United States.

Although the decision was a very welcome one for patient advocates, one could speculate that the presence of a social worker in the emergency room might have prevented the *Manlove* tragedy. A confident and assertive social worker in that setting, with a good relationship with the staff, might have been able to exert enough pressure on the nurse to convince her to summon the physician or even to examine the child herself. One of the most important functions of the social worker is to help the staff look beyond the rules to the patient. Rules that are consistently detrimental to patients are often struck down by courts sooner or later—but usually after death or severe damage to a patient and his or her family. It is the social worker's job to get around those rules for the good of the patient.

Financial Grounds

Some rules are purely financial and emphasize the conflict between the hospital's obligation to treat patients in need and the necessity to maintain a sound fiscal position. Hospitals in some urban areas lose many thousands or even millions of dollars a year in uncompensated care and do have to set up some guidelines regarding payment. Denial of emergency treatment because of inability to pay, however, is no longer acceptable. *Stanturf v. Sipes*[4] is an illustration of that principle. A man stranded all night in his car at zero temperatures was refused admission in the emergency room of the only nearby hospital because he did not have the $25 admission fee. When friends brought the $25, he was still refused care even though both physicians and hospital administration were aware of his severely frostbitten feet. Although the hospital's policy was to admit persons who offered the $25 fee, it was later speculated that worry about payment of the inpatient charges was the reason for the refusal. The patient was not admitted to any hospital for a week and eventually had to have his feet amputated; when he argued later that prompt care would have prevented the amputations, he lost on the ground that the hospital was not required to take care of him. The Missouri Supreme Court, however, reversed the case and said that he might have a claim, adding support to the growing body of law that required emergency rooms to evaluate all comers and treat real emergencies.

This case illustrates the rule that a patient's financial situation should be secondary to his or her condition and treatment needs in a true emergency. "Treat first and ask questions later"[5] is the rule of thumb here. Where death or severe damage would result from delay of treatment, then treatment should be instituted immediately. The hospital can do a financial evaluation later, can bill the patient, and may unfortunately even lose money, but emergency treatment is not just for those who can pay. The social worker in the emergency room plays an advocate role here and has an obligation to make sure that care is not delayed or refused for financial reasons. He or she can approach the problem in a number of ways. One is to emphasize to medical staff, repeatedly if necessary, the emergent nature of the situation and the probable consequences—both to the patient and the hospital—of delay. Another is to offer to look into the financial aspects while the patient is being treated, thus freeing staff from any conflict they might be feeling about treating a patient without obvious financial resources. Finally, the social worker can be active with members of the hospital administration and emergency room staff in developing and disseminating clear and sensible policies about acceptance and treatment of patients in the emergency room. In some hospitals, the social worker may have to push and prod and harangue even to begin discussion of such policies.

Defining an Emergency

Even though the law now requires prompt and adequate evaluation and treatment in emergency situations, there are still worrisome gaps in what is considered an emergency. A woman in labor, for instance, may not be considered an emergency, although the results of no care or inadequate care may be disastrous. Two cases illustrate the apparent reluctance of the courts to define labor as medical emergency requiring immediate attention. In the first,[6] a patient visiting another town began bleeding, thought she was in labor, and arrived at a local emergency room at 2 A.M. A nurse examined her and telephoned the physician on call, who suggested that the patient *call* her own doctor. Mistaking the message, the nurse instructed the patient to *go* to her own doctor, several miles away. En route the patient delivered her baby, which lived only twelve hours. For various reasons, neither the physician nor the hospital could be found liable, according to the court, although a jury could, if they wished, find the nurse negligent.

The second case[7] involved a woman who was visiting in another state and, on going into labor, felt she could not get home before her baby was born. She went to the local emergency room and was turned away without even an examination. That same night the baby was born, but the mother died, arguably through lack of medical attention. The court said there could be no recovery because, among other things, the "element of critical emergency [was] not apparent." While two cases do not necessarily change or support policies in emergency rooms throughout the country, they do suggest that some hospital emergency rooms may feel free to turn away women in labor. In fact, this is frequently done. In locations where a woman has had prenatal care at a hospital not close to her home but is taken by police or fire rescue squad or equivalent to the closest hospital, she may be refused admission. In times of economic slump, where unemployed and working poor women have no insurance, no possibility of any coverage, and no prenatal care, they may be routinely turned away in labor. Where there has been no prenatal care and/or the delivery may be a complicated one, the argument of "critical emergency" is a strong one. In each of the cited cases, for instance, a death resulted from refusal to give care. Since the law is so unclear, the social worker should assume that in certain hospitals it will take more than a fear of possible liability to get some patients admitted, particularly those without funds or coverage. One preventive step is to canvass other hospitals in the area to see if there are any who are willing to accept all patients (some hospitals, for instance, with heavily used and profitable maternity services, are willing to establish such a policy). Another is to become involved in planning with

administration, medical staff, business office, and others concerned with this problem. If the administration is adamant about
costs, perhaps a figure of one or two patients a month might be
acceptable, especially if other hospitals in the area are willing to
pool their resources in this way. The hospital might also be able
to develop a low-cost prenatal care and delivery package that
some families could afford.

In spite of all the planning, patients in labor will still present
themselves to the emergency room without funds, coverage, or
other supports. This is the time to play the advocate role and to
argue, pressure, cajole, and wheedle as skillfully and vigorously
as possible. Make sure any decision that is made will be a shared
one; the more people who become involved—such as administration, nursing, other medical staff—the harder it will be for
them to insist that someone be denied care. This is a prime
example of the social worker caught in the middle of conflicting
responsibilities to the patient and the hospital. A worker who
does manage to get patients admitted in this way also has an
obligation to become involved in planning and in the identification and development of additional financial resources so that
the hospital's losses do not become more than it can handle.

Discrimination

The cases discussed so far have dealt with denial of care to
patients because of rigid rules and financial issues (or perhaps in
the cases of maternity patients, nonresident status). Another
reason may be prejudice. In the past, patients might be denied
care solely because of color, race, or national origin. Federal
law, supported by state law, now forbids such discrimination.[8]

In a case in the Southwest in the mid-1970s[9], two Mexican
children, burned in a fire at their home, were refused treatment
and admission by the local hospital. Although the suit against the
hospital for additional injury to the children was originally dis-
missed, both the Appeals Court and the Arizona Supreme Court
found the hospital liable. Not only custom but also state laws and
licensing statutes indicated that the hospital could not deny
patients emergency care. Decisions such as this one are encouraging because they emphasize that it is the emergency and not
the person that controls the need for care. To deny or ignore the
emergency because of characteristics of the person is now a
risky business.

Negligence

There are many other reasons why patients are denied care in emergency rooms. The include prejudice against those known to be or labeled alcoholic or addicts, jumping to uncorroborated conclusions, failure to obtain a consultation, and pure callousness and slipshod behavior.

In one large urban emergency room, for instance, a young teenager was brought in acting in an agitated and disoriented manner. Because of his behavior and lack of cooperation, staff decided he was under the influence of some kind of drug and just let him sit. What they missed in their rapid and ill-founded diagnostic leap was a serious stab wound from which he bled to death, still in the emergency room.

As a monitor of such situations, the social worker can serve an invaluable function. In the following case,[10] for instance, an alert social worker might have prevented some of the damage caused by hospital and staff negligence and unconcern:

A 13-year-old boy suffered a head injury in a summer program and was brought to an emergency room. The intern who examined him recommended admission but was told—mistakenly —that admission was not possible unless the child was under the care of one of the hospital's private doctors. A staff pediatrician then happened to come in and was asked to examine the child. He did not do so but merely looked at the chart, which was missing some of the vital signs that should have been recorded, and advised that the child be sent home with his father. The child was sent home with his father, without the usual instruction sheet for head injuries which describes symptoms indicating need for immediate treatment. The child, in fact, already had certain of these symptoms and, on the advice of a doctor friend, was rushed back to the hospital that same evening. In spite of immediate surgery, the child is now almost totally paralyzed. The recovery for his injuries was over four million dollars.

In this case, a social worker familiar with the hospital would have known that the information about admission was wrong and could have explained the correct procedures to both the physician and the family. The social worker could have encouraged the intern to be more assertive about the child's possible injuries or could have expressed his or her own concerns very emphatically to the pediatrician, making it harder for him to leave without actually seeing the child. He or she could have supported the father's insistance on immediate and adequate care. If the child had still been sent home, the social worker would have made sure that the father had the instruction sheet and that he understood it and would have emphasized the need for attention if any of these signs became apparent. He or she would have given the father a number to call and would have given clear instructions about admission if it should become necessary. The most important intervention point, however, would probably have been with the intern. By asking pointedly, "Do you really think this child should be sent home?" the worker might very well have elicited the intern's conclusions about the child's injuries. Together they could probably have managed to have him admitted.

Negligence, or malpractice as it is called when committed by a professional person, is "the failure of a physician or surgeon to perform the duty which devolves upon him in his professional relationship to the patient—a failure which results in some injury to the patient."[11] The cases discussed earlier in the chapter, when patients were refused care, were also malpractice. Other types, besides those mentioned, include problems of triage, erroneous diagnosis, no diagnosis (when serious medical condition is present), inadequate or inappropriate treatment, and failure to continue hospitalization and/or treatment. One study of emergency room negligence has identified the failure to obtain "an appropriate specialty consult" as a major factor.[12] While the social worker may not have the medical expertise necessary to prevent some cases of negligence, he or she can try to keep doctors from jumping to conclusions, diagnosing according to their prejudices, and ignoring patients' expressed complaints. In addition, as is discussed in a later part of this chapter, the worker can intercept patients before they leave and take preventive steps at that point.

Consent

Other issues may also interfere with prompt and immediate treatment. Sometimes efforts to obtain an informed consent are misguided and not legally appropriate. The law requires that a person give consent before he or she is examined and/or treated in any way. Most emergency departments have blanket consent forms that patients are required to sign when they register. These cover the initial examination and diagnosis and relatively uncomplicated procedures like suturing, bandaging, medicating. For more extensive procedures, such as surgery, a separate and specific consent is needed. A true consent has three components: legal capacity, free power of choice, and clear and adequate information.

Legal Capacity

The first component, *legal capacity*, means that the person is in the category of those whom the law views as able to make decisions independently (i.e., is conscious; competent; not unduly under the influence of drugs, alcohol, or other substances; not so ill or injured or in shock so as to be confused or unable to think clearly; and of legal age to make treatment decisions). An unconscious person, in an emergency, where life or health are in jeopardy without immediate treatment, may be treated without first obtaining consent. The law implies consent in such a case, that is, it assumes that a person in such a state of critical illness or emergency would consent if he or she could, so that consent is given. Generally, patients must be competent. Competence is a legal term whose meaning varies according to content. Essentially it means ability to meet the cognitive requirements of a task, to be able to understand his condition, the nature and quality of the treatment proposed, and the consequences of a refusal to consent. Incompetence to consent to treatment has various causes, such as psychiatric disturbance; senility or other disorders of old age; the effects of certain illnesses; medications; substance abuse. Even a patient suffering the effects of one of these conditions or causes, however, may be competent to consent to treatment. Even a person who is confused, psychotic, dazed, or otherwise mentally clouded may still be able to understand simple information about treatment and consequences and should be given the opportunity, wherever possible, to hear the explanations and make his or her own decision. Such a process is usually time-consuming and frustrating and unpleasant for physicians. Often they jump to conclusions about a person's incapacity to make decisions and may refuse to treat, may force treatment, or may let family members decide. It is generally acceptable to let the closest family member consent for the patient who cannot do so himself or herself, although where the procedure contemplated is risky, experimental, very invasive, or otherwise complicated, legal proceedings may be instituted.

The social worker can be helpful in three ways where there

is a question of competence to consent to treatment. Although he or she cannot make a legal or a psychiatric decision, by giving the patient a chance to try to understand what is going on, he or she will undoubtedly end up spending more time talking to him or her. Consequently, the social worker may have a much clearer idea of what the patient really is able to understand. Asking the patient questions is sometimes a very good way of gauging this. In addition, where the language and/or concepts and/or treatments are very complex, the social worker can simplify and translate to help the patient understand. This kind of assistance will help to ensure that lack of comprehension is not misinterpreted as lack of decision-making ability. Finally, the worker can serve as the patient's advocate by emphasizing to the physician(s), and sometimes to the patient's family, what the patient wants and is expressing. If no one will listen to the patient, the social worker may have to speak for him. It remains the responsibility of the treating person (i.e., the physician, physician's assistant, or nurse-practitioner, etc.) to obtain the consent, but the social worker can certainly play an invaluable part.

Minors, in most states those below the age of eighteen, are often considered incompetent to consent for themselves. Most states, however, have statutes which allow minors to consent on their own in certain cases. The Pennsylvania statute, for instance, which is reproduced in Appendix E, allows anyone who is eighteen, has graduated high school, has been pregnant, has a communicable disease, or is in an emergency situation to consent to treatment without parental involvement. It also protects caregivers who provide treatment in good faith in reliance on one of the above claims. In addition, a minor who is the parent of a child can also consent to treatment for that child.[13] Every emergency room social worker should be familiar with the applicable statute in his or her own state.

The mention of emergency situation in the Pennsylvania act should be noted. Hospital personnel are often far too conservative when it comes to treating minors, fearing parental complaints. Any minor (or incompetent person) whose condition could be considered an emergency, when treatment does not result in some irreversible change, such as amputation, should be treated as necessary to alleviate the emergency whether parents are available or not. And a critical emergency, where death may be imminent without immediate treatment, needs an immediate medical response. If the physician is unsure of whether to act or not, he or she should consult with another physician, notify the hospital administration, and document fully all that has occurred.

In many emergency departments, it is the responsibility of the social worker to call parents, either to notify them of a child's presence or to obtain permission to treat (or enable the physician to do so) or both. Telephone permission, with a witness listening in on an extension, may be completely adequate. These efforts should be documented, and it is up to the social worker, when all attempts to reach responsible family members appear futile, to state clearly and decisively that family cannot be reached and a decision as to treatment must be made. When there is reluctance to act, or at least to come to some kind of resolution, the social worker may have to be the one who articulates the situation and the options. The options could include:

1. Instituting immediate treatment because of the dangers of delay, along with regular efforts to reach family;
2. giving only the amount of care needed to stabilize the patient and waiting for parental consent to begin post-critical treatment;
3. deciding not to treat until family can be reached (this decision may result in a child's being held for hours in an emergency room without treatment);
4. letting a "mature minor" or emancipated minor consent on his or her own and then beginning treatment.

A "mature minor" is one (usually aged fifteen or older) who is able to understand and consent to the proposed treatment. The concept is usually applied in situations where the treatment is relatively uncomplicated and not very risky, such as suturing a laceration. In such situations, the minor must be able to understand his or her condition, the proposed treatment, and any risks involved, and be able to act in his or her own interest. At times where a young person with a relatively minor injury is sitting waiting because the parents are nowhere to be found, the social worker may want to suggest that the patient be evaluated as a mature minor. The worker may want to help the physician interview the patient or report his or her own findings to the physician. Where a mature minor has consented to treatment in his or her own interest, complaints by parents about lack of consent have not been successful.[14] The social worker should try to become knowledgeable about the concept of mature minors as applied in his or her location and may even want the social work department to consult the hospital's legal counsel on the issue. This is not a concept to determine on one's own; many states and locations have developed their own definitions and applications. The same is true for the term *emancipated minor*, which refers to a minor no longer under parental supervision and control. Exact meanings, however, vary greatly according to location and in some places are not well defined at all.

Free Power of Choice

The second component of an informed consent is *free power of choice*, meaning that a person has to be allowed some latitude to make his or her own decisions and is not subjected to pressure to decide as someone else wishes. Sometimes coercion can be subtle, as when a patient who appears reluctant to consent is left unattended and ignored for a long time. Elderly patients may be persuaded by well-meaning families to go along with treatment programs that they really do not want. This component is not always obvious, especially in an emergency where speed and decisiveness are imperative. In less critical situations, however, the social worker can help by making sure that patients are given time to think and the opportunity to voice their objections and by trying to bring about better communication between the reluctant patient and the offended physician.

Clear and Adequate Information

The third component is *clear and adequate information*. How much information is appropriate will depend on the immediacy of the circumstances, the setting, the patient's education, comprehension, level of anxiety, and desire to know. Generally, the more risky, complicated, and unproven the procedure, the more complete the information should be. The following are the elements that the physician should try to transmit to the patient:

- Diagnosis
- nature of proposed treatment, including names of medications, methods of administration, duration
- possible side effects
- major risks
- alternatives to this treatment

- probable consequences without this treatment
- other useful information includes costs, length of in-capacity, and necessity for return visits.

The process of consent, particularly in an emergency room, can be a frustrating and time-consuming one. Physicians may be harried, impatient, and overpowering. Since most people tend to retain very little of what they are told in such circumstances, the best approach is to explain briefly and simply and then to *give the patient a chance to ask questions.* The presence of a relative, especially where a major procedure is being contemplated, is also helpful. Routine, minor procedures need little explanation.

Consent forms are useful to show that some kind of communication has occurred, but they do not constitute an informed consent. The information necessary for a true consent should be conveyed verbally, and it is for that reason that the social worker can be so important in the process. Although the person doing the procedure is supposed to obtain the consent, someone else can often do a more effective job of translating, interpreting, and explaining, so that the patient really does have some idea of what is happening. The following is a case where the social worker was able to help obtain consent and in the process discovered other needs of the patient.

Case

Ms. A, a young mother in the neighborhood, came in complaining of wrist pain. Examination revealed gonococcal arthritis, with a need for admission and intensive treatment to save the use of the hand. She refused admission and was referred to the social worker. The worker realized that the woman had no idea she was in danger of losing the use of her hand. In addition, Ms. A was resisting hospitalization because of worries about child care and her new job. After explaining her condition to her, the worker discussed child care arrangements and ways of dealing with the employer and asked the staff to arrange for admission two days hence. Telephone support during the next two days helped Ms. A mobilize her resources and admit herself to the hospital.[15]

The right to consent includes the right to refuse to consent. The trend toward recognizing patient rights and liberties in the medical setting has led to more of a willingness to let competent adults make their own decisions about refusing treatment. If a person understands his or her condition, the nature of the treatment being offered, and the consequences of not having that treatment, he or she is usually allowed to refuse. The reason may be desire for cessation of pain, religious scruples against blood transfusions, objections to amputation, or something even less clear. Exceptions may be made for a pregnant woman, the mother of small children, or a parent who is a sole provider. Some hospitals, uncomfortable with this trend, nearly always try to obtain a court order but often cannot do so. A psychiatrist may be called, or the social worker may be asked to talk with the patient. When the refusal is a result of poor communication or lack of understanding as in the example, the social worker can be extremely helpful. Otherwise, people should be helped to come to their own decisions, and those decisions should be respected and well documented.

Many regular users of emergency rooms have psychiatric histories and may or may not be able to maintain themselves adequately. Some, in spite of impairments, are quite able to make treatment decisions, either in favor of or against recommended treatments. A commitment for psychiatric care is not a finding of incompetence. Physicians may feel uncomfortable about certain patients, although technically they may be capable of deciding against a treatment, and will often ask for a psychiatric consultation. Psychiatrists differ in their willingness to make statements about competence, which is a legal rather than a medical concept. They will, however, comment on a patient's ability to accept and absorb information, to understand alternatives, to comprehend results, and to exercise judgment. A patient who is seriously deficient in these areas is probably incompetent to consent to—or refuse—treatment.

Where an incompetent patient refuses treatment that is not urgent, it should not be administered. The social worker can then help explore with the family, other concerned individuals, or agencies the possibilities of additional psychiatric treatment and guardianship. Sadly enough, many of these patients are no longer involved with families and are not seen as the responsibility of any agency. Social workers from a particular city or region may have to work together on a long-term basis to force some government entity to acknowledge responsibility for these people.

Where the treatment refused is urgent, or even life-saving, the emergency department staff should work with the hospital administrator on call, who will obtain an emergency (verbal) court order from the judge available on that day. Many localities have such a system, where a judge is always available by phone for judicial emergencies. The exact procedure has to be worked out well ahead of time in each hospital so that valuable time will not be lost in trying to figure out what to do. After treatment, the social worker or his or her colleagues in the hospital will remain involved in discharge planning for the patient.

In the case of children, whatever the parents' beliefs, a doctor will not be held liable for administering treatment in a true emergency. Here, again, documentation is extremely important. If the situation is urgent, but not an immediate life-or-death matter, the emergency room staff must notify the administrator, who will attempt to obtain a court order. The social worker can help here by soothing and supporting the conflicted parent.

States vary as to requirements for informed consent, but legal issues aside, it is important for a patient to realize what is going to happen to and be expected of him or her. Lawsuits for lack of informed consent are not common, because the patient must prove essentially that (1) he was not told of a certain risk, (2) that risk occurred, and that (3) had he been told of the risk, he would not have undergone the procedure.

As the third can be very difficult, it is not often stated successfully. People do sometimes recover damages, though, and most state or federal laws and cases do require some kind of consent procedure.[16] Also, since effective communication with patients may very well promote more positive attitudes and better compliance, this is an area that calls for social work understanding and involvement. Although negligence is a more troublesome issue in the emergency room than consent, a large portion of this chapter is devoted to consent because it involves communication. Poor communication between doctor and patient has been shown to be a substantial factor in patient dissatisfaction and malpractice claims.[17] Documentation is equally important.

Discharge

Several of the cases described earlier in the chapter involved premature discharge, that is, sending the patient out before he or she had received sufficient diagnostic and medical care or had stabilized enough to be out of the hospital, with resulting damage. Even with excellent medical care up to that point, discharge before the patient is medically ready can mean deterioration in his or her conditon and potential liability for the hospital. If the hospital lacks the personnel, equipment, or other facilities for the treatment of a particular patient, then it has the responsibility to transfer that patient—when his or her condition allows—to a place where adequate care is available. The receiving institution must agree to accept the patient, and the transferring institution is responsible for care until someone at the second location takes over.[18] Sending a patient in a taxi or ambulance, or via police, with the hope that another institution will not refuse a surprise admission, is not adequate care.

Premature discharge may involve a transfer and in some cases result from prejudice and jumping to conclusions. In one case, for instance, police brought an unconscious patient to a hospital. The doctor on call performed a cursory examination, did not do x-rays, decided that the patient was intoxicated, and approved his removal to jail. The patient died in jail and was discovered to have broken ribs which had punctured his chest.[19]

In this case, perhaps a social worker would not have made a difference, since there probably would not have been contact with the patient. The social worker might have been asked to help identify the patient and locate the family, however, and in doing so might have discovered information helpful to the physician in the medical assessment. Where the social worker can be helpful, however, is in watching for and talking with the following groups of people: those who seem dissatisfied with treatment and/or recommendations, those who appear extremely ill or incapacitated upon leaving, and those for whom help is requested in leaving.

Patients with abdominal pain, for instance, should have assistance in communicating their symptoms and clear directions about whom to call if they become worse since ruptured appendices are sometimes missed in the emergency department.

The social worker can find out if the examining physician was aware of all the patient's symptoms, can make sure that language difficulties did not prevent effective communication, can ask for an explanation of the disposition, can clarify and explain the recommendations for follow-up, and can make sure the patient and the family have what they need for follow-up, including access to medications and explicit instructions as to what to do and whom to call if the patient's condition should worsen. In an occasional case, the worker might even ask the physician to reconsider the disposition and admit or at least hold the patient. Those who are unable to communicate because of hidden injury, substance abuse, or other conditions should be kept and observed till their condition and comprehension improve. Such requests must not come solely from sympathy or concern but must present real observations about the condition of the patient.

Other difficulties in discharge arise because certain patients are considered "undesirable," and hospitals want to get rid of them as soon as possible. These groups include the frail elderly, mentally ill, and alcoholics and are discussed in later chapters. For example, an elderly patient from a substandard nursing home might be given minimal care and sent back immediately to the home responsible for the illness or injury. In cases like these, the social worker has to be an advocate and resist discharge or transfer vigorously, perhaps even by refusing to arrange transportation. Whether or not the hospital would be liable for further injury to the patient, if it is known that return to the home would undoubtedly cause great harm, then the transfer should not occur.

A clearer example of potential liability involves the intoxicated person who is allowed to leave while still intoxicated, gets into a car, and injures a third person. An argument can be made that the patient should stay in the emergency room until he is able to drive safely or should only be released to someone who can drive him home. Again, it is usually the social worker who attends to these issues. Someone like the intoxicated person, or a confused or delirious person, or one under the influence of drugs should be released only to responsible people, at least as far as an assessment can be made. Legal answers are not always clear in these cases, but sensible precautions are crucial.[20]

Sensible precautions in the emergency room, at least for the social worker, involve also monitoring the waiting room to spot patients in trouble. In a busy, crowded emergency room, the wait may be one of several hours, and the "silent emergency," such as a rather nonassertive person with chest pains, could deteriorate very seriously while waiting to be seen. It has been pointed out that "delay cannot be excused on the basis that others are being treated."[21] By bringing to the attention of the medical staff those patients whose conditions would be worsened by delay, the social worker can sometimes prevent tragedy, recriminations, and litigation.

This is a brief discussion of some of the many topics in emergency room law. The law itself is always changing in response to changing times and situations. Adequate and appropriate care of the ill or injured patient, however, is always a legal responsibility, though the meanings of "adequate" and "appropriate" depend on many factors. The social worker, with his or her special perspective toward, and interest in, protecting the health and rights of the patient, can be a critical element in helping the hospital meet this responsibility.

Notes

1. *Le Juene Rd. Hosp. v. Watson*, 171 So. 2d 202, 203 (Fla. 3d Dist. 1965).

2. *Wilmington Med. Ctr. v. Manlove*, 174 A. 2d 135 (Del. 1961).

3. Barry Gold, "Emergency Room Medical Treatment: Right or Privilege?" *Albany Law Review*, 36 (1972): 530.

4. Stanturf v. Sipes, 447 S. W. 2d 558, 35 A.L.R. 834 (Mo. 1969).

5. For a discussion of this maxim, and for the hospital's responsibility to the patient in an emergency, see George Annas, Leonard H. Glantz, and Barbara F. Katz, *The Rights of Doctors, Nurses, and Allied Health Professionals* (New York: Avon Books, 1981), particularly the chapter "Emergency Care."

6. Childs v. Weis, 440 S. W. 2d 104 (Texas Ct. Civ. App. 1969).

7. Hill v. Ohio Cty. Ky., 468 S. W. 2d 306, 309 (Ct. App. Ky. 1971).

8. See Title VI, Federal Civil Rights Act of 1964 (42 U.S.C. § 1971 *et seq.*)

9. Guerrero v. Copper Queen Hospital, 537 P. 2d 329 (Ariz. 1975).

10. Niles v. City of San Rafael, 42 Cal. App. 3d 230, 116 Cal. Rptr. 733 (1974).

11. Bernard J. Ficarra, "The Hospital Emergency Room and the Law, *California Western Law Review*, 12 (Winter 1976): 232.

12. Steven E. Pegalis and Harvey F. Wachsman, "Emergency Room Negligence," *Trial* (May 1980): 50–53.

13. In this and other states, new abortion statutes may abrogate some of these rights to treatment without parental consent. The status of these new laws is not clear.

14. Ficarra, "The Hospital Emergency Room," 232; see Younts v. St. Francis Hospital & School of Nursing, Inc., 469 P. 2d 330 (Kan. 1970).

15. Carole W. Soskis, "Emergency Room on Weekends: The Only Game in Town," *Health and Social Work*, 5 (August 1980): 37, 40.

16. For a discussion of informed consent in question-and-answer form, see Annas *et al.*, "The Rights of Doctors," Chapter IV, "Informed Consent and Refusing Treatment."

17. Department of Health, Education, and Welfare, *Report of the Secretary's Commission on Medical Malpractice* (Washington, DC: U.S. Government Printing Office, 1973).

18. Joint Commission on the Accreditation of Hospitals, "Emergency Services," in *Accreditation Manual for Hospitals* (Chicago, 1982): 25.

19. Bourgeois v. Dade County, 99 So. 2d 575, 72 A.L.R. 2d 391 (Fla. 1957).

20. Charles Frey, "Medico-legal Aspects of In-Hospital Emergency Care: the Surgeon," in *Proceedings of the First National Conference on the Medicolegal Implications of Emergency Medical Care* (Washington, DC:, American Society of Law & Medicine & American Heart Association, June 8–10, 1975).

21. Arthur Southwick, *The Law of Hospital and Health Care Administration* (University of Michigan: Health Administration Press, 1978). Those interested in a more comprehensive view of these and other issues should read James E. George, *Law and Emergency Care* (St. Louis: C. V. Mosby Co., 1980).

4 Helping Victims of Crime, Abuse, and Disaster

Some emergency rooms see victims of crime, accident, and disaster every day; others treat them more irregularly. Whether victims arrive frequently or not, however, how they are treated in the emergency room is of critical importance. The visit to the emergency room is usually, except for the police, the victim's first encounter with the system that may include medical facilities, government bureaucracies, insurance companies, and the courts. It is here that he or she receives his or her first and probably lasting impression of how the system works: helping, supporting, confusing, blaming, punishing, humiliating.

This chapter is a particularly significant one because the social worker may be the most important person the victim sees; the social worker's attitudes and actions may have a profound effect on the victim's life and future. The social worker's attitudes and activity here may make a tremendous difference in how the patient views and copes with what is happening to him or her. For even one patient a year, it is worth learning and understanding what is now known about the experience of being a victim of crime or disaster. (Use of the word "patient" can imply someone who actively seeks help rather than someone who is passively acted upon; the difference is a significant one.) Familiarity with crisis theory, as discussed in Chapter 2, and its applications, is an essential tool.

This chapter will deal briefly with crime victims generally and with victims of rape and spouse abuse. Then, because there are similarities in the situations, there will be a section on victims of accidents and disasters.

Crime Victims

In 1960 someone was robbed in the United States every six minutes; by 1977, it was every seventy-eight seconds. In 1960, someone was raped every thirty-eight minutes; in 1977, every eight minutes. The frequency of these crimes has increased considerably ever since then.[1] The risk of being a victim of crime is substantial enough so that many people live in constant fear.

For most people who have actually been victims of a personal crime, their experience has been that of "the deliberate violation of one human being by another."[2] Two things are destroyed: their sense of trust and their sense of control over their own lives. While the former takes a long time to regain, the social worker must immediately begin trying to build up the latter. First, however, it is necessary to try to understand as much as possible what the patient is going through. The intensity and duration of the reaction may have more to do with the degree of personal contact between victim/assailant than with the nature of any physical injury. In fact, it is never correct to assume—or to say—that a physically uninjured victim is "all right." The meaning of the crime in that person's life is not something immediately known or understood.[3]

Many victims are surprised at the intensity of their own reactions, particularly since in the immediate post-attack period they may be very calm and unemotional. Some may even be confused or have memory loss. Nevertheless, most victims go through a strong and long-lasting emotional reaction. One expert explains it as follows:[4]

Phase 1: denial, shock, disbelief
Phase 2: setting in of reality
Phase 3: 'traumatic depression'—'circular bouts of apathy, anger, resignation, irritability, 'constipated' rage, insomnia, startle reactions, and replay of the traumatic events through dreams, fantasies, and nightmares'; also self-recrimination[5]
Phase 4: resolution and integration—may include new defensive patterns and profound revision of values and attitudes toward possessions, other people, and the world in general

The social worker will be dealing with Phase 1 and perhaps 2 and can help prepare the patient and his or her family and friends for Phases 3 and 4. The social worker can be most helpful by following these six steps:

1.   Make sure that a patient who is a crime victim does not sit for a long time in the waiting room, in order to avoid increasing his or her feelings of isolation and powerlessness. If the medical staff are busy and a wait is necessary, bring the patient into the social worker's office or into a patient room so that he or she can get a sense of care and attention. A badly injured patient, of course, will not be waiting.

2.   Remember that few people "ask for" or precipitate the crimes that are perpetrated on them. In addition, no one knows what he or she would do when suddenly confronted by a criminal. "Victims do the best they can, and no one is in a position to judge their behavior."[6] It may be difficult to keep this in mind when the patient victim is an alcoholic, or a derelict, but it is true nevertheless.

3.   Remember also that the patient's immediate reactions include a sense of powerlessness and a sense of isolation. One way to deal with the latter is through friends and relatives, who may feel awkward and uncomfortable and may consequently withdraw. Explain to them that victims tend to be blameless; that the damage is not always visible; that delayed reactions, including flashbacks, fear, depression, and somatic complaints are normal; that support for the patient is very important. Accepting feelings without agreeing with perceptions is very helpful, for instance, much more helpful than arguing with feelings of guilt. Above all, encourage family and friends not to withdraw. When people do not know what to do, they often will withdraw, so that explaining to them exactly what they *can* do may enable them to rally around.

4.   Help diminish the patient's sense of isolation by providing "psychological first aid."[7] Reassurance, nurturance, and acceptance are major components of this help, as they diminish the recent experience of overwhelming hostility. Bard and Sangrey describe what it means to be helpful:

> People who really want to help must focus on the victim, listen carefully to the victim's expression of his or her needs—and then respond to that expression—without imposing their own suggestions or judgments or perceptions. The ideal helper is one who is able to create a climate in which victims will be able to ask for and get whatever help they want.[8]

They suggest saying, "You must feel terrible. I'm so sorry you've been hurt. What can I do to help?"[9]

Similarly, Symonds presents principles of psychological first aid for victims which includes restoring power to them (for instance, by asking permission to interview them); reducing isolation and guilt by providing reassurance and nurturing behavior; diminishing the victim's helpless, hopeless feelings by allowing him to determine his behavior; and accepting expressions of rage and resentment.[10]

Nurturance can take many forms. Allowing and helping the patient to clean up; providing privacy if he or she wants it; and putting off questioning by medical staff and law enforcement personnel are all ways of taking care of the patient who is also a victim. Conveying a sense of acceptance is extremely important, since crime victims are so often confronted with a new, negative identity in our society—that of the loser.

5. Help diminish the sense of powerlessness that stays with the patient after the crime. Anyone subjected to a brutal, violent crime has had the experience of being absolutely in someone else's power. The sense of the world as a predictable, trustworthy place is gone; in its place is a feeling of lack of control over one's own life. Research shows that anything that restores a sense of control is helpful.[11] As mentioned, letting the patient decide whether to be interviewed and when; listening to his or her attempts to make sense out of the experience; and explaining the likely psychological consequences are all helpful. Another way of encouraging a feeling of control is to help the patient take action to feel more safe, for instance, by calling friends, finding a place to stay, or calling a locksmith. Listing the concrete things that need to be done may also help, such as notifying credit card companies, replacing cards and licenses, and repairing damage to home or car, but the patient may be overwhelmed at the thought of these demands and not ready to begin meeting them. In addition, it is very helpful to prepare the patient and his or her family and friends for what will happen. The patient needs to know what is going on and what is expected of him or her. The social worker should make an effort to be familiar with criminal procedures in the area in order to explain how they work: registering the complaint, describing the incident, identifying the suspect—and then, if one is caught, the long, difficult, and often humiliating and unsatisfying process of arraignment and trial. It helps a great deal to be familiar with police in the area and to be able to ask for special care for a particular person or to

make specific recommendations about what needs explaining. If the patient has not reported the crime and is uncertain whether to do so, the pros and cons have to be discussed and encouragement offered for reporting.

   6.   Develop some kind of follow-up program. If the patient is seriously enough injured to be admitted to the hospital, explain as much as possible of his or her needs to the nursing staff and to the next social worker, if another one will be assigned. In some cases, it will be worth a visit to the floor to introduce the new social worker. The family may need this same kind of attention.

   The patient who is able to leave the hospital should be referred to any appropriate counseling and assistance programs and given a name, if possible. There are many kinds of crime victim assistance. Some communities, for instance, use trained elderly volunteers to provide counseling to their victimized neighbors and accompany them to court. If none exist, he or she should be encouraged to stay in touch with the social worker and to call for help or reassurance. In addition, the social worker should be minimally acquainted with the Crime Victim's Compensation Program, if it exists in the state, and should be able to refer him or her for help in filing claims. Some of these programs are exceedingly complex, and the difficulty of filing claims may discourage those who qualify for awards. Finally, the patient should not leave until plans for immediate needs have been made—cash, food, shelter—and some kind of longer-term program for replacing necessities that have been lost has been set in motion. The social worker can not always help with, but should be aware of, what the patient may be coping with in the future: physical disability, unreimbursed bills, fragmented services, and unavailing efforts to gain his or her "rights."[12] Although most people have considerable emotional and physical reserves to use in a crisis, some, such as the frail elderly, may not. Even so, those who are victims of crime suffer long-term effects that tend not to be understood and appreciated.

Victims of Rape

Rape calls for special treatment because it is the quintessential violation of a person, although one who is kidnapped, beaten, or robbed at knife- or gunpoint may also feel terrible fright. Rape involves the experience of primal terror, the overriding fear for one's life. It also leaves the victim feeling "taken, used, damaged . . . defiled"[13] and susceptible to overriding feelings of guilt and shame. While physical injury must be treated and thorough physical examination and specimen collection are necessary for both medical and evidentiary reasons, the psychological-emotional component of treatment is sometimes neglected.

The experience of rape is a life crisis for a woman, one for which her previous defense mechanisms and methods of coping have not prepared her.*,[14] Consequently, except when there is serious physical injury, the overriding concern in the emergency room should be the emotional state of the patient. The sooner the intervention, the less psychological damage she is likely to sustain.

It is easier to meet the patient's needs for structure and comprehensibility when the emergency department itself has a well-thought-out protocol for dealing with rape victims. Examples of such protocols are included in Appendixes F, G, and H. Besides specific medical and legal instructions, the following protocols should be included:

1. A reminder that a rape patient is never to be kept sitting in the waiting room.
2. Directions to use the term "patient" instead of victim whenever possible.
3. Instructions on transfer to the local rape crisis center, if there is one (many urban areas have designated one or two hospitals as rape crisis centers, and they should be called and consulted and told ahead of time of the pending transfer).
4. The number of the local chapter of WOAR (Women Organized Against Rape) or WAR (Women Against Rape) or similar organizations, and an explicit directive to call them. These groups, made up of highly knowledgeable staff and dedicated volunteers, have provided invaluable assistance not only to victims of rape but also to medical and law enforcement personnel. They provide support and advocacy to the victim, accompany her through medical and legal procedures (all the way to trial), explain what is going on and what is to be expected, and help to dissipate the feelings of isolation and loss of control with which the victim must struggle. They also do community and police education and lobby

---

*While men and boys can be raped, and sometimes are, this section deals primarily with women and their needs. (See Appendix H.) Child victims are discussed in the section on child abuse.

for changes in the law to protect the victim and make apprehension and conviction of the assailant more likely. The social worker should be well acquainted with the local group. If none exists, serious thought should be given to getting one started. The worker may want to suggest the idea at a local college or school.

4. Instructions to let family or friends stay with the patient, even during the medical examination, if she wishes. This is not the time to push close supports away.

5. Designation of one person as responsible for the patient so that there will be continuity to her hospital experience. If she has to be hospitalized, this person should continue to visit her if possible. The social worker will be the most appropriate person in many hospitals. If the worker is male, it might be better to designate a nurse. While it has been argued that men can be effective rape counselors,[16] in the immediate post-trauma period a woman might be more effective. The decision will depend partly on what the social worker feels he can handle and how people react to him generally.

It should be noted here that listening to rape victims is very stressful. Many people are painfully reminded of their own vulnerability and/or have trouble dealing with their own anger or with asking for intimate details. Somehow, blaming the patient for getting herself into the situation makes the uncomfortable feelings much easier to handle. The social worker or counselor, especially if she is not used to working with rape victims, has to be very clear in her own mind that no one asks to be raped and no one is to blame for having been raped.

In fact, every person who has survived a rape has coped in a way, and has accomplished a feat of great mastery just by surviving. While many patients will express feelings of guilt and shame for not having resisted or resisted enough, fear, the fact that everything happened so fast, a very clear sense of the danger of harm, or simply their own makeup and reactions may have made resistance impossible. The situation is certainly not one that others are in a position to pass judgment on, but even so, it is possible to listen supportively and with acceptance of the patient's feelings. The fact that she succeeded in making it through the experience has to be acknowledged.

Rape counseling has become a highly developed skill, and the worker should consider getting some training from WOAR or a similar group. Basically, however, the counselor needs to express support and concern, to help the patient through the initial period of shock, and to mobilize family, friends, lovers, or other supports. The patient should be assured of confidentiality as far as is possible and asked what she wants family and friends to know—if anything. When a young woman does not want her parents told, alternate payment arrangements may have to be worked out. Friends and family may be bewildered and upset and consequently pull away and must be encouraged to stick by the patient, to support her appropriately, and to expect and understand her short- and long-term reactions. Short-term reactions may include feelings of shame and self-blame, disorganization, and a wide variety of somatic reactions, including sleep disturbances. Over the longer term, the patient may experience flashbacks, phobic reactions, nonorgasmic sex, depression, and a wide variety of other reactions. There may be far-reaching changes in her life-style.[17] Interestingly enough, initial research efforts indicate that some changes may not be temporary. About two years after being raped, for instance, many women in one study still had pervasive feelings of suspiciousness of others, 41% still had continuous or intermittent depressive feelings about the rape, and about half had sexual difficulties. It may be that rape, rather than being a crisis situation as is the usual experience of crime victims, causes more psychic injury. The emotional difficulties following the rape, then, can be viewed as a "posttraumatic stress disorder" which may persist for years.[18] If this is so, then the worker's attempts to create a "corrective emotional experience" for the patient in the emergency room would be unrealistic. The goals should be (1) support; (2) explanations and guidance; (3) assessment and acknowledgment of coping skills; (4) mobilization of resources, including places to stay; (5) help in getting through the medical and legal procedures and systems; (6) interpretation of the patient's needs to the medical staff; and (7) appropriate referral. The patient should be allowed to make as many decisions as she can to help her in reestablishing her sense of control. No patient should be left without some follow-up possibilities. If there are no rape crisis programs available, the worker should present the resources available and follow up with a phone call to the patient some time later.

Although the hospital has a legal obligation to notify police that a crime has been committed if they are not already involved, some patients will be reluctant to talk with police. Police in some locations are now much more sensitive to the plight of rape victims and treat them with courtesy and gentleness. In other settings, experiences with police and courts compound the injury and embitter the victim.

The worker needs to know, at the least, what the situation is in her community and to encourage efforts to involve and educate police in helping the rape victim. As a final note, when a hospital routinely refuses to treat rape victims, as some still do, the social worker should be involved with those who seek to change policy.

Spouse Abuse

As in the previous section, this discussion will deal with women, who are the primary victims of physical abuse by husbands and boyfriends. While men do suffer such abuse, it is unlikely that a man presenting himself to the emergency room will complain of being beaten by his wife or girlfriend (though gunshot wounds and stabbings are apparently actions that *are* acceptable to blame on women). "Abuse" here means bodily harm, attempted bodily harm, or a believable threat of immediate bodily harm. Statistics on the number of women who are abused vary widely, but even the lowest include millions of women. About 25% of homicides in the United States are intrafamily, and half of those involve spouse killing spouse.[19] Police injuries are not unlikely in domestic disputes, so that reluctance to intervene in family situations may have been as much a result of sad experience as of paternalistic attitudes. In the past few years, however, spouse abuse has generated increasing attention, and its relationship to child abuse is recognized more and more. For instance, abused women are at high risk for abusing their children. Emergency rooms, however, often tend to treat the bruises and fractures and send the patient back to the same situation unless she takes the initiative in asking for help.

This is an area of great conflict to social workers, whose belief in self-determination is often at odds with their frustration at seeing women go back to the same dangerous situation time after time. Before even attempting to design any kind of program, it is important to understand some of the factors in the inability to leave the abusive situation and to acknowledge that some women are not ready yet and may never be ready. As one study put it, ". . . the battered woman must make the decision to make a change in her life. The decision cannot be made for her. . . ."[20] The same study points out that "violence is such a natural way of life in people's families that they do not recognize other ways to resolve conflict." In addition, for some women the abuse may be infrequent and "mild" enough so that it is tolerable for the time being, though it does tend to escalate both in frequency and severity with time. Some women accept beatings as their due; their experience and low self-esteem do not permit them to think otherwise. Others, especially those with small children, may be financially dependent and pessimistic about their own capacities for self-management. Some women maintain feelings of affection toward the abuser and manage to "forget" in between beatings. And some women are so isolated and so ashamed of their situation that they cannot acknowledge it publicly. The emergency room may be the first opportunity to confront both feelings and situation and may be one of many helpful contacts that contribute to the strength to make a change in the future.[21] An angry woman can be helped to use her anger for change. A depressed one may need psychiatric care. A passive, beaten one is hardest to work with but is greatly in need of concern and support. Sometimes mentioning children and possible effects on them can make a difference. Since pregnant women are frequently beaten in some families, the opportunity exists to discuss both short- and long-term effects on the child. The social worker, then, must bring up the subject of abuse if it has not been alleged, offer assistance of various kinds, understand and accept if it is rejected, and be ready to offer it again.

The hospital should have a protocol for suspected abuse which should include the following (see Appendix I):

1. Referral of all alleged or suspected cases to the social worker;
2. separation of the patient from the accompanying male, unless she specifically requests otherwise;
3. an offer of photographs of injuries.

The social worker, after gently and tactfully bringing up the subject of abuse, needs to assess the woman's safety—whether she can return home, and if so, whether she needs an escort; if not, whether she may stay or needs to be referred to a shelter. Shelters are often full and should be used only as a last resort. Future safety may depend on a number of things, including past history, alcohol, and weapons use. The worker needs to express concern and support; encourage ventilation; assess coping skills and mental status; elicit the patient's priorities; evaluate social, financial, and other supports; make appropriate referrals; and assess the need for continued services and follow-up. Other specific issues include whereabouts and care of children, transportation, and funds.

Those who refuse further medical care and/or follow-up care should be given the number of the local crisis center for battered women, if one exists.[22] These organizations, though financially strapped, provide services ranging from shelter, including shelter for children, to legal advice to group therapy, sometimes even for male abusers. Most have hot lines which dispense service and information to those in need of support and/or advice. In addition, there are about 150 programs which provide services to men who batter.[23]

Those who can go home but want further help can also be given hot line numbers, can be referred to sympathetic counseling programs and drug and alcohol programs where appropriate, and can be instructed as to their legal options. Several states have laws providing for both civil and criminal charges against abusers. Some laws permit eviction of a violent spouse or boyfriend from the home and/or orders of protection to keep them away. Custody and support are also covered in some of the laws. The social worker should be familiar with the applicable state law(s), with the legal resources available, and with hot lines or women's groups that provide help. In addition, local police can be encouraged to carry and distribute materials describing the rights of and resources for battered women. Police cooperation is essential in this, as in all work with victims, and the social worker can be among those who promote communication between police and hospital. Inservices at both places could cover laws, resources, client/patient groups, and job demands.

Women who cannot go home need to be helped, as discussed, in finding alternative places to stay. If a shelter is the only option, often someone from the shelter will pick up the patient at the hospital. Women who need to go home to pick up valuables and belongings, or to get their children, can ask for a police escort. Such escort arrangements should be worked out between the hospital and the police beforehand and should be an accepted part of a cooperative program.

Women who are admitted to the hospital may worry most of all about their children. Every effort should be made to mobilize friends and family in order to avoid placement. Discharge planning should begin as soon as the patient is able, though the worker handling the case should not be surprised or angry if the patient elects to go home.

A typical example of a well-functioning emergency room in a situation involving abuse follows.

Case Study

Ms. B. came into the emergency room with her boyfriend, complaining of injuries suffered in an accident. The triage nurse, concluding from the nature of her injuries that she had been beaten, brought her into an examining room and asked the boyfriend to remain in the waiting room. The social worker came in, told the patient that the staff suspected abuse, and offered help and sympathy. After being treated, the patient acknowledged that she had been beaten, expressed fear that her boyfriend would injure her again, and asked for help. She did not want police involvement but did want to go back to her apartment, where she felt she would be safe. The social worker took her out of the hospital through another door and sent her home in a taxi. She was instructed to call the social worker or the local hot line if she needed additional help or information. The social worker then talked with the boyfriend, explained the situation, suggested that he stay away from the patient and described the consequences of further abuse, and offered assistance.

Abuse of the elderly, both in the family and in institutions, is an issue sadly familiar to ER social workers and is discussed in Chapter 7.

Working with Police

Any emergency room that treats victims is likely to have police in and out.[24] It is difficult to make generalizations about the relationship with the police, because that relationship may be shaped and affected by forces outside the emergency room. However, there are a few rules of thumb for emergency room social workers.

   1.   Know the precinct(s) or district(s) in which the hospital is located and which it serves. Know the names of the commanding officers and talk to one of them or to a community relations officer about their services to the community, such as emergency transport. Introduce yourself and explain the functions of the emergency department social worker.
   2.   If the same officer(s) generally brings patients to the emergency department, get to know him or her. Get to know the

policeman or policewoman on the beat. Ask about their functions and explain yours. Get a feeling for what they might do if you asked them. For instance, in some communities police will deliver emergency messages to families without phones.

3.   Try to arrange some kind of work/telephone space that police can use during an emergency or just while they are waiting. Such space is not only helpful to them, it removes them from the waiting room and the anxious eyes of waiting patients.

4.   When alleged perpetrators are brought in under police guard, they are to be treated as other patients in that no information except general condition is to be given to the police or any other party. Police should never be allowed to read charts or medical results or be given verbal information without the patient's consent. If the records are needed for legal purposes, the district attorney can obtain them in the proper manner. Similarly, patients under arrest should not be threatened or abused in the emergency room, even though they may be under guard. Some hospitals allow serious mistreatment of certain groups of patients in order to avoid conflict with police. The social worker should be a moderating force here and attempt to cooperate with the police while also protecting patients' rights.

5.   Police are often trained and astute observers. If they bring someone in who may be going back home, ask for their impressions of the home. They may report, for instance, that an elderly patient had left the gas on or had rotting food on the table, or that a mother with a young child had no heat. They may be the source of valuable information that patients are too ill, frightened, or confused to volunteer.

6.   Remember that policemen and women have difficult and often thankless jobs. Have a cup of coffee and a friendly word available now and then.

Disasters

Victims occur as the result of disasters, too—plane, train, and motor vehicle crashes, floods, fires, explosions, and other catastrophies. Often the emergency room has little warning that victims with multiple and severe injuries are being brought in. The way to deal most effectively with disasters is through pre-planning, and emergency rooms should be prepared at all times and should have periodic disaster drills. JCAH, in fact, requires each hospital to have a disaster plan. Although in a real disaster the plan may go for nothing, still it provides structure and specific responsibilities. The social work department should have a well-organized system to get staff into the emergency room quickly. If the emergency room social worker is already there, he or she should only have to make one phone call to get in as many staff as necessary. If he or she is not there at the time, a social worker should be on the list of those called immediately, either the emergency room social worker or the director of the department. With a trauma alert, which warns of the patients' arrival, there may be more time to get everyone in.

The social worker serves four major functions in a disaster: helping with communication; supporting patients and families; meeting concrete needs; and taking care of medical staff. Although flexibility is a necessary component in meeting the overwhelming tasks in a disaster, people still need assignments and should have some familiarity ahead of time with these assignments or some knowledge of how to get the information they need. The organization of the social work department will determine the level of preparation and access to information. Even when one victim or one family comes in, as a result of an automobile accident, fire, shooting, or other incident, these same functions remain the primary obligations of the social worker, except that support can be more personal and more intensive.

Helping with Communication. Particularly when there are many victims, the emergency department becomes chaotic as family, friends, police, the press, and others rush in. The first thing to do is to prepare a list of those who have been brought in, if at all possible. When victims are taken to several different hospitals, families may have to rush frantically back and forth in their efforts to find out where their loved ones are. If there is a public relations office, they usually serve as intermediaries and disseminators of information, though social workers can and do play a major role by trying to reach family who are not yet informed, translating and explaining briefings, bringing out news on specific patients, informing families of admissions and locations, and reporting on all that is being done. The social work department should assign at least one person to communications for the duration of the crisis. The hospital should have designated space ahead of time where families can wait, with phone linkage to the emergency room. The families will need to be reassured constantly that the social workers or other specified persons will be the go-betweens and will communicate as much as possible. Several people are necessary for effective communication.

Supporting Patients and Families. Although it may be impossible to spend time with everyone, the social workers should attempt to speak briefly with members of every family/friend group. Patients who have been only mildly injured may still be in a state of shock and will need help in pulling themselves together and in getting home. Families may also be in a state of shock and unable to comprehend what is happening. Some may become so frantic and excited that the social worker or assigned volunteer has to hold onto them. Holding and touching can have tremendous meaning in these situations and may be highly effective ways of communicating. Letting the doctor know the family is there and encouraging him or her to say *something* to them with the social worker present can be very helpful.

Those whose relatives or friends are critically injured will need extra support and assurances that everything possible is being done. In addition, the disaster system should include a designated person who informs relatives of deaths. If it is, as customary, a physician, a social worker should be present, should stay with the family, offer to call significant others, and try to find a private space for the family to grieve. The issue of whether the family can actually see the body of the patient may come up at that time, and in some cases it will just not be possible. If the patient died without pain, it is often helpful for the family to know. If the family has to be called to come to the hospital, they should not be told on the phone that the patient has died. First, it is better to deliver such news in person and in stages; second, the family do not need to be burdened with the thought that they did not get to the hospital in time (also see Chapter 5).

Where the waiting period is a long one, the social worker(s) should consider mobilizing volunteers to provide coffee and food for those who do not want to leave the immediate area. Some people may need help with phone calls, child care arrangements, and other pressing things.

Meeting Concrete Needs. Long before the disaster occurs, social work staff should be knowledgeable about services provided by agencies (Red Cross, Salvation Army, and others), churches, and other resources. Homeless but unhurt or mildly injured people should be sent immediately to shelters or to meeting places (for families), and those in need of food or other essentials should be appropriately directed. The social work department should also have some knowledge of how to refer patients for long-term follow-up, such as disaster relief programs. Also, if there are a number of deaths, the social worker(s) can help survivors get in touch with each other later and with appropriate self-help groups.[25] Other concrete needs may involve patients themselves. Helping to identify victims, going through clothes, interviewing police for clues, all may become the responsibility of the social worker.

Taking Care of Medical Staff. Physicians and nurses often work round the clock under much more physical and emotional stress than other staff. The social worker(s) can at least make sure that coffee, juice, and food are available to them and can provide support, encouragement, and sympathy for their fatigue. After the disaster and the physical recovery of staff involved, the emergency room social worker can be instrumental in helping them work out their own feelings.[26] Especially where there has been multiple trauma or heroic efforts or the staff have been more stressed even than usual, a period of decompression is essential. A group meeting or series of meetings can start out as an evaluation of emergency room function and then develop into a more in-depth exploration of reactions to experiences. Such meetings are well worth having and contribute to cohesiveness and more effective teamwork in the future.[27]

Notes

1. Eleanor Chelimsky, "Serving Victims: Agency Incentives and Individual Needs," in Susan Salasin, ed., *Evaluating Victim Services* (Beverly Hills: Sage Publications, Inc., 1981):75.

2. Morton Bard and Dawn Sangrey, "Editor's Introduction," in *The Crime Victim's Book* (New York: Basic Books, 1979). This book contributed substantially to this chapter and is highly recommended for anyone working with or trying to help victims of crime.

3. Ibid., 17.

4. Martin Symonds, "Victim Responses to Terror: Understanding and Treatment," in Frank M. Ochberg and David A. Soskis, eds., *Victims of Terrorism* (Boulder, Col.: Westview Press, 1982):95–96.

5. Ibid.

6. Bard and Sangrey, *The Crime Victim's Book*, 85.

7. Symonds, "Victim Responses," and as discussed in Salasin, "Services to Victims: Needs Assessment," in *Evaluating Victim Services*.

8. Bard and Sangrey, *The Crime Victim's Book*, 37.

9. Ibid., 38.

10. Symonds, "Victim Responses," 101; Salasin, *Evaluating Victim Services*, 35.

11. Bard and Sangrey, *The Crime Victim's Book*, 62.

12. Salasin, "Editor's Introduction," in *Evaluating Victim Services*.

13. Soskis and Ochberg, *Victims of Terrorism*, 113.

14. Donna C. Aguilera and Janice M. Messick, eds., "Situational Crises," in *Crisis Intervention: Theory and Methodology* (St. Louis: C.V. Mosby Co., 1978).

15. See Sharon L. McCombie, ed., *The Rape Crisis Intervention Handbook: A Guide for Victim Care* (New York: Plenum Press, 1980); Ann W. Burgess and Linda L. Holmstrom, *Rape: Victims of Crisis* (Bowie, Md.: Robert J. Bundy Co. [Prentice-Hall], 1975), especially chapters 3, 6, 8, and 9; Maria I. Vera, "Rape Crisis Intervention in the Emergency Room: A New Challenge for Social Work," *Social Work in Health Care*, 6 (Spring 1981): 1–11; and protocols from Harborview Medical Center in Appendixes, F, G, and H. The Burgess and Holmstrom book, in addition to the larger issues, addresses smaller practical ones as well, such as payment of the hospital bill and useful supplies for rape victims in the ER.

16. Daniel Silverman, "The Male Counselor and the Female Rape Victim," in McCombie, *The Rape Crisis Intervention Handbook*.

17. Vera, "Rape Crisis Intervention"; see also Carol C. Nadelson, Malkha T. Notman, Hannah Zackson, and Janet Gornick, "A Follow-up Study of Rape Victims," *American Journal of Psychiatry*, 139 (October 1982): 1266.

18. Nadelson *et al.*, "A Follow-Up Study."

19. The Federal Bureau of Investigation provides statistics on various crimes each year; in some states the figures may be even higher. California, for instance, reported that in 1981, one-third of all female homicide victims were killed by their husbands. See *Response*, 5 (Washington, DC: Center for Women Policy Studies, November, December 1982): 3.

20. Patricia McGrath, with Phyllis Schultz and P. O'Dea Culhane, and assisted by Diana B. Franklin, "The Development and Implementation of a Hospital Protocol for the Identification and Treatment of Battered Women," (Rockville, Md.: National Clearinghouse on Domestic Violence, 1980). This is one of many useful publications on setting up a hospital program or learning to handle abuse situations more effectively. See also Karil S. Klingbeil and Vicki D. Boyd, "Emergency Room Intervention: Detection, Assessment, and Treatment", in Albert R. Roberts, ed., *Battered Women and Their Families* (New York: Springer Publishing Co., 1984).

21. Ibid., 6.

22. See Albert R. Roberts, ed., *Sheltering Battered Women: A National Study and Service Guide*, (New York: Springer Publishing Co., 1981), for a description of at least some of the programs providing shelter. See particularly Majory D. Fields and Elyse Lehman, "A Handbook for

Beaten Women," reprinted in Roberts as "A Guide for Beaten Women: How to Get Help if Your Husband or Boyfriend Beats You" on p. 111ff.

23. Zak Mettager, "Help for Men Who Batter: An Overview of Issues and Programs," *Response*, 5 (Washington, DC: Center for Women Policy Studies, November, December 1982): 1.

24. A comprehensive discussion of the legal issues involved in the police/emergency room relationship, particularly on substance abuse, can be found in "Emergency Care Personnel and the Police," in James E. George, *Law and Emergency Care*, (St. Louis: C. V. Mosby Co., 1980): 151–178.

25. Leona Grossman, "Train Crash: Social Work and Disaster Services," *Social Work*, 18 (September 1973): 38–44.

26. Ibid.

27. For a discussion of planning for a large-scale disaster, see Christopher Maxwell, "Hospital Organizational Response to the Nuclear Accident at Three Mile Island: Implications for Future-oriented Disaster Planning," *American Journal of Public Health*, 72 (March 1982): 275–277.

5 Families of Critically Ill or Deceased Patients

There is no higher priority for emergency room social workers than caring for those who receive bad news. People who learn that their loved ones are critically ill or injured, dying, or have died need help and support that the social worker is well equipped to provide. The social worker should have not only his or her own written or understood protocol on this subject but also support from the hospital and the emergency room staff so that nothing interferes with the complete attention necessary for these families.[1] If the social worker hears that relatives are on the way, he or she should immediately arrange coverage for other cases in order to be completely available. The registrar should be alerted to notify the social worker at the moment the family arrives, without asking routine questions and increasing the suspense. There should always be a private place to sit and talk, without having to worry about being heard or having to observe patients or treatments.

Even before an in-person meeting, however, the social worker may already have had some contact with the family.

Telephone Calls to Family

It often falls to the social worker to notify relatives by phone of their loved one's illness, injury, or condition. The people at the other end of the phone are likely to be shocked and frightened, so that communication must be effective, comprehensible, and as supportive as possible. When calling family to give news that a patient has been brought into the emergency room, try to remember the following guidelines:

1.   Identify yourself and where you are calling from.
2.   Explain why you are calling as briefly and as clearly as possible and describe the situation. Hearing that you are calling from the hospital will have already aroused considerable anxiety. "I am calling to tell you that your husband has just been brought in from his office where he suffered some kind of attack." Add what you know of the patient's condition if it will be reassuring, and if possible, try to see the patient before calling the family in order to give a first-hand visual (not medical) report. "He is being treated in the emergency room, and his condition is stable. I just saw him, and he appears to be resting comfortably." In a case such as this, if the diagnosis is known, the first part of the communication could be more specific. Another example: "Your son has just been brought in from school and is being treated for a sprained wrist. He is fine except for that and will be able to talk to you in a few minutes." It is important to communicate the fact of a *mild* injury, as people are likely to fear the worst from vague statements. In general, statements should be as specific as possible so that people will not need to fill in the gaps with their own imaginings. Terms such as "critical," "serious," "good," "fair," "poor," and others do not necessarily have widely understood meanings among the general public and should be explained if they are used. The social worker's description can be very helpful in alleviating anxiety and in helping family grasp just what has happened: "She is able to move all her arms and legs"; "He himself asked me to call you"; "He is in pain, but conscious." Medical information, however, should be given out very sparingly, if at all.[2]

Where a patient is critically ill or injured, the family should merely be told the seriousness of the situation and asked to come in immediately. "I'm calling to tell you that your son has been in an automobile accident and is seriously injured. We'd like you to come in right away." And in response to questions, "The doctors are working on him now. We hope to know more by the time you get here." In these cases it is useless and cruel to give uncertain or false hope. If the patient does not survive, the family will have had some preparation for the shock of the loss.

Do not tell family members over the phone or immediately on arrival that a patient has died. That leaves them with the guilty burden of not having reached the hospital on time. It is more humane to state the seriousness of the situation on the phone, as in the example, and to repeat it even more emphatically on the family's arrival. A physician should appear briefly to tell them of the gravity of the patient's condition and the fact that everything possible is being done. A few minutes later the physician should come back and say that the patient has died. The knowledge of having made it to the hospital in time, if not to see the patient, then to be there while he or she was still alive, is a tremendous psychological support for many people. The social worker can discuss with physicians and nurses during quieter times the merits of this kind and simple deception wherever it is possible.

3.   Use the opportunity to ask appropriate questions about past medical history and medications. Knowing quickly of a recent or chronic illness or a current medication may be of enormous help to physicians. Ask only specific questions that need to be answered immediately.

4.   Assume that shock and fear will cause many listeners to miss or distort much of what you say. Make sure that they understand you and ask them to repeat what you have said if necessary.

5.   Finally, make sure that people can actually get to the hospital. Do they have a means of transportation? Are they able to drive? Can someone drive them? Do they want you to call a taxi? Do they know where the hospital is? Where to park? If they are far away, is there anyone nearby they want you to call? Help with concrete and practical details should begin right here. Also, in some jurisdictions, where the family do not have a phone or cannot be reached by phone, the police will go out to notify them, alert the neighbors, or leave a note.

Lodging Arrangements

If the emergency room social worker is the only one in the hospital, for instance at night, or if the family of the ill or injured patient are traveling through or have come from a distance, he or she will be expected to help with practical issues such as lodging. In trauma centers with heliports, patients are frequently brought from far away, and if their families also arrive, there are questions of lodging, long-distance communication, and meals to resolve. The location of the hospital will affect the answers to these questions. Centrally located hospitals may have hotels nearby which offer special rates to families of hospital patients. Medical school hospitals may make space available in dormitories. Some hospitals have set aside suites for families who have come a long distance. Hospitals located in unsafe urban areas may need more constructive solutions: transportation/escort services, for instance, or approved neighborhood families willing to provide lodging at a reasonable fee. Hospitals in remote areas might provide space themselves or offer some kind of shuttle bus to commercial lodgings. Some hospital administrators feel that the question of lodging does not concern them and is the family's problem. That is an unrealistic view, since the social worker on duty will still be faced with a worried family who have no place to go. A kindly staff who allow families to spend nights sitting up in various waiting rooms will not replace an organized listing of places to stay, restaurants, transportation systems, and other resources. Pulling together this kind of listing can be a very successful joint project for several departments in the hospital, such as social work, patient relations, and public relations. Support can be solicited from medical departments that seek to attract patients from a wide geographical range for specialty procedures, such as complicated cardiothoracic surgery.

Waiting with the Family

When the family arrives, the social worker should pick one person to be the main focus of communication in order to reduce confusion and distortion. This person may not be the one closest to the patient, although that is preferable, but may be the one who is calmest or seems to be a natural family leader. It is important to give some information immediately, as much as is available, and not to try to minimize the seriousness of the patient's condition. A family who have rushed to the hospital will already be in a state of shock and anxiety and will have trouble grasping and remembering what they are told. It may be necessary to repeat everything several times and to remind them over and over that everything possible is being done. If the patient was brought in by a rescue squad who provided good lifesaving or stabilizing care, it can be very reassuring to mention that so that the family knows (if it was the case) that the patient was well taken care of from the first.[3] Offer to help with concrete details, such as notifying other family members or friends, arranging child care, or calling employers. Never criticize what the family has done or discuss how they might have done things differently or support their "if onlys . . ." or self-recriminations. Even if there has been some kind of fault or negligence, except in cases such as child abuse, it is not the role of the social worker to explore it. The family's need is for support and acceptance; besides, most of us are not in a position to judge other people's handling of illness or crisis—to help with it, yes, but not to judge.[4]

With all these interventions, the most useful one is just to sit and wait with the family, in silence if they prefer, or listening to them. Expression of feelings, including anger at the hospital and staff, should be encouraged, and the family assured that their stress is appreciated and their efforts to cope with it acceptable. The social worker, throughout all this period, will be assessing the family's coping skills and whatever support systems are available to them. He or she should again offer to call, or help the family to call, other important people—other children, best friends, and those whose presence would be comforting.

Before the family arrives, if it is known that they are on the way, or at least while they are there, the social worker can excuse himself or herself and try to find out what the condition of the patient actually is. If the patient is conscious, or talking, or sitting, that information should be reported with an assurance that the physician will be in as soon as possible. If the patient is looking bad, or is essentially already dead but still being worked on, the social worker should tell the family something like, "It doesn't look too good; one of the doctors should be coming in to talk with us soon." It is a very uncomfortable feeling to sit with an anxious, pleading family, knowing the patient has died, and yet not able to tell them. Informing the family is the province of the physician; yet there are two things the social worker can do. One is to make comments such as those above, which start to deflate the family's hopes and prepare them for the shock to come. The other is to work with physicians to help them learn to break bad news gently and sympathetically, in spite of their own feelings of frustration and anger. A physician who walks in waving an autopsy form, or one who comes in, says three words, and stalks out, just increases the family's feelings of isolation and loss of control. The physician should sit down, introduce himself or herself, give the news, and as much as possible *be* with the family, that is, answer their questions, explain as much as is appropriate what happened, repeat that they did everything they could, and express his or her own sadness and disappointment. What the physician does and how he or she does it in these settings depends on time and patient pressures, personality factors of the physician, and the nature of the patient's identity and condition (compare, for instance, telling family of the death of an 85-year-old woman from her third stroke and telling family of the death of a nine-year-old boy who was hit by a car). It is advisable for the social worker to have worked previously with all emergency room medical staff, including residents, interns, and students, on these issues. An inservice could include encouraging people to remember their own experiences, asking what they have found helpful in the past and what they think others find helpful, and reviewing some of the literature on people in crisis and bereavement. Physicians need to learn that if the death of a patient leaves them feeling utterly defeated, it is all right to share that feeling of defeat with the family and may in fact be helpful.

Helping the Family Cope

When the patient dies, and the family is told, the news is likely to be devastating. No one is ever truly prepared for the death of a loved one. The initial response may be shock, disbelief, and denial. The family should have the opportunity to see their loved one and to spend as much time with him or her as they need, unless the patient's appearance is such that the family is best protected from it—burn victims, for instance. They may not be ready to be with the patient immediately and may have to spend some time absorbing the news first. Again, the social worker can be most helpful by sitting with them, listening and accepting what they have to say, and answering questions as well as possible. It is important to remember that there is no such thing as a typical or normal reaction here:[5] people react in different ways, covertly and overtly, and all reactions, feelings, and expressions should be considered appropriate for the particular people involved. Some people will not show any response immediately and should not be pushed to do so. They need time, and their inability to express anything is not harmful unless it persists indefinitely. Expressions may range from tearfulness and hysterical crying to flat affect and emotional lability and vacillation. There may also be angry, hostile reactions, some directed toward the social worker. There may also be feelings of guilt, of hopelessness and of loss of control over oneself and the situation.[6] It has been speculated that the expression of guilt, self-blame, and feelings of failure serve many functions that are not always recognized. These functions include help in finding answers (the answer to "Why did this happen," for instance, being "Because I did or failed to do X"); help at some subconscious level in retaining some element of control (being able to explain why, even if it involves self-blame, means that the world works in a predictable and orderly fashion); and help in dealing with sub-conscious negative feelings (such as relief, or anger at the patient) by allowing their expression through guilt.[7] Thus, while the social worker should not contribute to the substance of any of these feelings and, in fact, should reassure a family rather than blame, still the expression itself should not be blocked or circum-vented. It may be a necessary and effective means of coping.

Some people have somatic symptoms and reactions which can involve any of a number of systems, can be quite severe, and can occur intermittently for long periods of time. The social worker should not be surprised to see breathing and swallowing difficulties such as sighing, a feeling of tightness in the throat or choking, shortness of breath, hyperventilation (rapid or deep breathing sometimes leading to faintness, tingling, or muscular rigidity); nausea or complaints of strange abdominal feelings; muscular weakness, faintness, muscle spasms, or headaches; and hypertension. People may also become restless or hyperactive or confused or unable to concentrate.[8] While those with existing medical problems or extremely severe physical reactions may need medical attention, it is not advisable to administer sedatives routinely in order to "spare" people their suffering. They need to grieve and to feel their grief fully, each in his own way and in his own time. Similarly, there should *never* be any attempt to present the death in a positive light, such as "It was all for the best" or "She would have lived in constant pain." This kind of comfort interferes with grief and is a judgment it is not up to an outsider to make.

It is important to remember that acute grief is a defined syndrome with psychological and somatic components.[9] It may appear immediately or be delayed. Its purpose is adaptational, although some people's reactions become maladaptive. Initially, however, what the social worker can best do is encourage adap-tive behavior with acceptance and support. For some people physical contact is welcomed and comforting; for others it is an intrusion into their space. The amount of closeness or distance a family needs is something else that has to be assessed, not only in relation to the social worker but in relation to each other. A new widow or widower, for instance, may want to be alone for a while and not with the rest of the family. Religion may be a consolation to some but not to others, and the social worker should not discuss religion but should offer to make a chaplain, priest, minister, or rabbi available. (This may already have been done if there has been any question of last rites.)

When Children Die

Children are a special case because of the emotional wear and tear that caring for a dying child has on the caretakers themselves. While most physicians and nurses are very sympathetic to parents and family, sometimes they have to focus so narrowly on the medical needs of the child that they ignore everything else. The social worker is in a position to give the family the attention they need and to explain and interpret medical information. The Compassionate Friends, a self-help support group for parents whose children have died, have a number of suggestions for helping parents.[10] They recommend that, as previously discussed, parents and family be reassured repeatedly that everything possible is being done. The social worker should not assume that they know that; they need to be told, and often. It is important for them to be with the child. Although this is also true for adults, no one likes to think of a child dying alone, and helping the family be together may be the most supportive intervention the social worker can make for the child as well. Being allowed to stay with their child is likely to make the death slightly more bearable for the parents and to prevent vivid imaginings of last-minute suffering. In an emergency room, resuscitation efforts and similar treatment often preclude the admission of parents to the patient's room, however, if it is at all possible, it should be arranged. If parents are with a child at death, they should be left alone with him or her for as much time as they need. The social worker should remain nearby so that he or she can be immediately available. If the child is a baby or fairly small, the parents can be encouraged to hold him or her, and a nurse or physician will disconnect tubes and other medical equipment.

Where parents cannot be with the child, questions about pain, fear, and similar issues should be answered as reassuringly and truthfully as possible. If a child is without pain, or seems relaxed and peaceful, that should be communicated even if parents do not ask. The social worker may excuse himself or herself periodically to check on the situation and will know ahead of time that the child has died or that there is no longer any hope. When the physician comes to tell the parents, the social worker is already prepared to help them cope. As mentioned previously in the discussion of physicians, it is very supportive of the family if the physician can express some of his or her own frustration and sorrow. As the Compassionate Friends say, "Don't hide your feelings to protect them. You are in a position of authority and your permission (and modeling) gives their feelings validity." The family should be encouraged to express themselves in any way that they can—exhaustion, anger, crying—whatever is appropriate for them. It is all right to cry with them if the crying is spontaneous and real, and certainly there will be times when the social worker—and perhaps many of the staff—will want to cry about a particular child. Some families protect themselves with a wall of reserve and need to be supported but at the same time allowed some distance. Others will be greatly comforted by a touch, a hug, an arm around the shoulders. Again they should be reassured that the hospital did everything possible and that *they* themselves did the best that they could for the child. Recriminations have to be handled with great care, since self-blame or blaming each other can have devastating effects on a marriage. Loss of a child can damage a marriage very seriously, and when a couple are involved, the social worker must help them grieve together as much as possible. They should be left alone together if they wish and given as much time and privacy as they need.

Among the practical details to be considered when a child dies is baptism, which may be very consoling for some parents. Another is the taking of a photograph. Parents may not have pictures of babies at all, especially very young ones, or may not have recent pictures of older infants. The social worker can take pictures to be made available to the parents later if they want them. These pictures may be of great importance in remembering the baby in the future and in sharing these memories with other siblings. In the following case example, taking pictures is only one of the ways in which the social worker helped a young mother deal with the sudden death of her baby:

Case Study

Miss C, aged 16, came into the emergency department with her mother, two-week-old baby, and a family friend. They were brought in by police who waited to see the result of the medical evaluation.

Miss C reported that the baby had cried frequently during the night but that they had both fallen asleep toward early morning. When she awoke, the baby was not breathing.

The social worker sat with the family during futile attempts to resuscitate the baby and while the doctor spoke with them, then accompanied the mother while she held the baby one more time. The baby was clearly well cared for, and the tentative diagnosis was SIDS. The social worker explained matters to the police, who left; made calls as requested by the family, and talked at length with the father's family, as Miss C was afraid that she would be blamed for the child's death.

Although her own mother expressed her grief more obviously and vocally, Miss C was deeply grieved over the loss of her baby and felt adrift and alone. The social worker kept in touch with her for several weeks and was able to perform several valuable services. First, she went to the morgue, had the baby dressed and took pictures, as the mother had none and wanted some very badly. (It is a far better idea to have a camera available in the emergency room.) Second, on discovering that the infant's death was due to a fatal and not easily detectable heart defect, she arranged for Miss C to have a conference with a gentle and compassionate neonatologist. Miss C emerged from this with a clearer understanding of what had happened, a resolution of her own guilt, and some appreciation of the dangers inherent in teenage pregnancy. Third, when Miss C decided to return to school, the worker arranged for her to get extra support and attention from the guidance counselor. Miss C emerged from this period with her self-esteem intact and a feeling that she was in control of her own future.

The baby mentioned in the case example was thought to have died from SIDS until the autopsy revealed another cause. SIDS (Sudden Infant Death Syndrome) is a particularly terrible cause of death because it is often neither recognized nor understood, so that parents suffer extra burdens of guilt, blame, and humiliation. SIDS is the largest killer in the United States of babies from two weeks to one year old and occurs, usually without detectable warning, in two out of every thousand live births, usually in the first six months. Boys are more at risk as well as premature and low-weight babies and those in multiple births. The infant dies suddenly and silently in its sleep, with no obvious injury or illness except an occasional upper respiratory infection. SIDS is the tentative diagnosis in such deaths until confirmed or disproved by an autopsy.[11]

When a baby dies at night and is undiscovered for several hours, for instance, there may be pooling of blood under the skin and the appearance of bruises. Such phenomena can be very frightening to parents and may cause police to think the baby has been beaten. The mistake is compounded when hysterical parents begin litanies of self-blame. There have been numerous occasions when parents have been arrested because of a SIDS death wrongly thought to be child abuse. Police are naturally upset and angry at cases of child abuse and would tend to treat suspected abusers harshly and unsympathetically.

Where parents and baby are brought to the hospital by police, or police appear soon after arrival, the social worker should immediately explain that this is a suspected SIDS case, that the baby appears well or adequately cared for (if indeed this is so) and, while the diagnosis is tentative, there does not appear to be any question of abuse or criminal behavior. Those policemen and women who have not heard of SIDS should be given a brief explanation, and at some point the social work staff may want to consider an educational program with police or the sharing of relevant brochures. The family then will need support and assistance similar to that described in the last section, with repeated mention of the possibility of SIDS and reassurances that they were not to blame for the baby's death. Mentioning evidence of good and loving care can be very helpful and appreciated.

Parents whose children die in the emergency room or in other parts of the hospital will generally get a tremendous out-pouring of sympathy, but the same support is often lacking to those families who experience a miscarriage or stillbirth. These are not infrequent in some emergency rooms, when there is not even time to get the patient up to a labor floor. A stillbirth occurs about once in every hundred live births, and a miscarriage even more frequently, so that nearly all emergency rooms will see them occasionally.[12]

The major problem that parents or would-be parents have in this situation is isolation. They have suffered a tremendous loss over which they will need to grieve for an extended time; however, since there was not a live baby, they are seen as grieving over a "nonperson" and often receive very little support, both from hospital staff and their own family and friends.[13] The social worker can help by recognizing and acknowledging the magnitude of their loss and encouraging others to do so. This may include brief private conversations with accompanying family members to prevent them from making comments that are meant to be positive but actually are not, such as "You can try to have another one right away." In a stillbirth, the parents can be encouraged to see, hold, and name the dead infant, and to spend the time necessary to say goodbye. Again, the social worker should have a camera ready in the emergency room to take pictures which can be made available to the family at a later time.

The father is likely to be less invested in the pregnancy than the mother and so may grieve less and for a shorter time. It often happens that the man completes his grief work and then becomes impatient with the woman, whose changing physical condition and greater attachment make the loss more acute and harder to recover from. A word from the social worker about the differences in perspective, intensity, and length of time may be appropriate and helpful for some couples. Referral to a self-help group for additional support is of tremendous usefulness to some families. Groups with names such as SHARE, UNITE, and Empty Arms are for those who have suffered a loss through miscarriage, stillbirth, infant death; these groups *do* recognize the intensity of the loss of a child yet unborn.

Other support groups include the Compassionate Friends, mentioned previously, which is made up of parents who have lost a child through death and are willing to help other parents in their group. There are chapters all over the country. Another group is HOPE (Helping Other Parents Endure). For the parents who have had the shattering experience of losing a child to murder, there is POMC (Parents of Murdered Children). In addition, the national SIDS foundation and its local affiliates offer services to bereaved parents. All these organizations are full of people who have been through the same experiences as the newly bereaved and can share and understand their feelings. Some, like Compassionate Friends, are country-wide; others are local. The social worker should be well acquainted with the relevant self-help groups in the area and how to get connected with them.[14]

Practical Issues

At some point, when the family, or at least one member of the family, are able to tolerate such discussion, the social worker will begin to go over practical issues with them. The physician will take some part in this discussion or may initiate certain aspects of it, depending on the hospital routine. The first step is to explain to family what happens now: autopsy and/or burial, notification of various people, and so on. The social worker can again offer to help make calls and to draw up a list of people who should be informed either immediately or at least very soon, such as other relatives, attorney, employer, life insurance company, church, synagogue, or other religious group, close friends. If the family has no previous plans in regard to funeral arrangements, the social worker should explain the need to get in touch with a funeral director of their choice. The patient's personal effects will be available for the closest relative to take home, but the social worker might want to go over them first to prevent the shock to the bereaved of taking blood-stained, cut-away clothes, or other unpleasant reminders from the package.

There are several issues that arise at this time that are painful and difficult but must be resolved quickly. The first is the necessity or desirability of an autopsy. In certain situations, such as violent or unexplained death, an autopsy is usually required and becomes the responsibility of the coroner or medical examiner. In some locations this responsibility can be delegated so that the autopsy may be done at the hospital itself. If the autopsy is required, the physician or social worker or both will explain the legal necessity and the steps to follow, such as release of the body for burial. If an autopsy is advisable, the physician or social worker or both will seek to get consent from the legally appropriate person (generally there are state statutes listing who can consent and in what order). They should explain the reasons for the request, such as, for instance, eliminating unsuspected causes and helping to learn more about the patient's condition for application in the future. Since families often worry that the body will be disfigured, the social worker can explain that the procedure is done by a specialist and that viewing in an open casket will still be possible.[15] Whatever the usefulness and desirability of an autopsy, where it is not required by law, families do have the right to refuse, for whatever reasons. If the family agrees to an autopsy, they should understand that the results do not automatically go to them and may in fact be difficult to obtain. Some hospitals offer to make the results available either to the family or a physician of their choice. The hospital physician calls when the report arrives or when reminded by the social worker, who keeps a tickler file for the purpose. This is an "extra," a service that takes little effort but shows an added dimension of caring for an interest in the family. In most places the family will be able to obtain copies of the death certificate, which will be needed for insurance and other purposes. The social worker should know how to do so and be able to explain. Some families will want and be ready for this information; others will not.

Another issue which has to be dealt with quickly is organ donations: specific internal organs, eyes, skin, or whole body. The social worker should be familiar with the applicable state law on the subject. The patient may have previously filled out a donor card which is available. If the condition of the body allows, his or her wishes are likely to be carried out, but not if close family members object. The patient's family may spontaneously express a wish to make a donation or they may be asked, very gently and noncoercively. For some, such as the parents of a young child, the donation may represent the opportunity to make some sense out of their loved one's death. Others may feel it is what the deceased would have wanted. Again, they need to know that the body will be treated with dignity, will not be disfigured, and will be released to them for burial (except in the case of the donation of a whole body for medical research).

Before the family leaves, they should be asked if they have any more questions or if there is anything more the social worker can do. They should be urged to call the social worker and given his or her name and number. In addition, some people will find the names and numbers of local support and self-help groups of great value. Besides the ones mentioned for parents, there are numerous others, for instance those geared to the widowed such as TLA (To Live Again) and the programs sponsored by the NRTA-AARP Widowed Persons Service.[16] It is helpful to explain to them that they may not be interested in these groups now, but may find a great deal of solace later in sharing their feelings and experiences with those who have also had to deal with them.

A group that is often neglected are relatives of those who come in DOA (dead on arrival). The relatives may have accompanied the patient or may arrive already knowing he or she has died. The registrars should always alert the social worker when relatives—or close friends in many cases—come in under these circumstances. The social worker should postpone or delegate everything else and begin working with the family. Many will want to leave the emergency room as soon as possible, as will families discussed above, but the social worker should state that there are things he or she might help them with and try to get them to stay. If not, they should still get the social worker's name and number and assurances of assistance. It is also a good idea to give a follow-up call to all families to provide additional support, answer questions, and make requested referrals.

Finally, the social worker can direct attention to the staff of the emergency room itself. Although they are used to sudden and violent death, occasionally nurses, doctors, and others will be particularly upset about a case. It may involve a child, a needless death, an especially gruesome crime, an almost-save, or someone known to them. The social worker is often most aware of the "feeling tone" of the place and may want to express sympathy and frustration, encourage discussion in a quiet moment, or spend some time with one or two staff after work or away from the hospital. This kind of sensitivity and support not only helps medical staff to function more effectively and openly as part of a team but also enhances the social worker's role on that team.

Notes

1. This priority is best stated very explicitly. See, for example, Lin Holland and Lee Ellen Rogich, "Dealing with Grief in the Emergency Room, *Health and Social Work*, 5 (May 1980): 12–17. They stress that ". . . the social worker's first priority in the emergency room is caring for the family and friends of critically ill and injured patients, including those of patients who die in the emergency room. Sudden critical illness or death is a catastrophe that has an impact on a patient's family or social network for months or years after the event. Immediate intervention and the beginning of work with the family's grief are the social worker's goals" (p. 12). See also the protocol accompanying this paper, to which the author owes several points in this chapter.

2. For a discussion of telephone notification, see M. A. Robinson, "Telephone Notification of Relatives of Emergency and Critical Care Patients, *Annals of Emergency Medicine*, 11 (November 1982): 616–618.

3. For the point of view of an EMT, see Therese M. Floren, "Death and Dying in the Emergency Setting," *Emergency Medical Services*, 8 (August 1981): 38, 40, 42, 45.

4. Ibid.

5. Floren, "Death and Dying"; Holland and Rogich, "Dealing with Grief." The latter is a useful source of information on how people are likely to respond and how best to be helpful.

6. Holland and Rogich, "Dealing with Grief."

7. Floren, "Death and Dying."

8. Holland and Rogich, "Dealing with Grief"; Erich Lindemann,

"Symptomatology and Management of Acute Grief," *Journal of the American Psychiatric Association*, 101, (September 1944): 101ff. This is the classic article on the subject and still very timely.

9. Lindemann, "Symptomatology."

10. The Compassionate Friends, "Suggestions for Doctors and Nurses," (1981).

11. Pennsylvania SIDS Center, Children's Hospital of Philadelphia, "Sudden Infant Death Syndrome in the Emergency Room," (1982). See also J. DeFrain, J. Taylor, and L. Ernest, *Coping with Sudden Infant Death*, (Toronto: Lexington Books, 1982), which discusses the special problems of SIDS families.

12. Jean G. Stringham, Judith Hothan Riley, and Ann Ross, "Silent Birth: Mourning a Stillborn Baby," *Social Work*, 27 (July 1982): 323–327.

13. Ibid.

14. For a listing of the self-help and support groups in his or her area, the social worker can check with the National Self-Help Clearing House in New York City. They will direct him or her to the regional clearing house serving the area.

15. Pennsylvania SIDS Center Protocol, "Sudden Infant Death Syndrome."

16. NRTA-AARP refers to the National Association of Retired Teachers-American Association of Retired Persons.

For a very helpful discussion of many of the issues discussed in this chapter, see also Robert E. Clark and Emily E. LaBeff, "Death Telling: Managing the Delivery of Bad News," *Journal of Health and Social Behavior*, 23 (December 1982): 366–380.

6 Working with Children and Their Parents

The social worker in a pediatric patient emergency room (children's hospital) is likely to have a very different case load from that of his or her colleague in a general medical emergency room, but the latter may still include up to 20% children.[1] As with adults, use of emergency rooms for children by their parents is often inappropriate, with studies of pediatric emergency rooms showing from 33–73% nonurgent cases.[2] Many families use them for regular care even when other more appropriate sources are made available; hence, the social worker may have a regular group of families to follow. Greater use of emergency rooms is projected for the future, as 661,000 children lost medical assistance just in the year ending October 1982.[3] Not only is the emergency room the only place available to them in some locations, but also the delay in preventive and routine care will mean that sicker children are brought in to the emergency room.

The role the social worker plays in the emergency room depends primarily on his or her location and on nurse/physician view of the social work function. While this is true of social workers in emergency rooms generally, the complicating factor here is the parents: they may not be the patients, but they need just as much care and attention as the patients. The social worker who is on-site can work readily with triage nurses to identify parents who need assistance. The social worker on call can try to set criteria for referrals, making them broad enough so that the on-call situation is manageable. (Evidence that it is not manageable, however, particularly from the medical staff, may help to get an on-site worker.)

The reasons for emergency room visits by children, for both urgent and nonurgent medical care, include the following:[4] respiratory distress and upper respiratory tract infection; acute otitis media (earache/infection); pharyngitis/tonsillitis; gastrointestinal illnesses; fever; seizures/convulsions; viral illnesses; cardiac emergencies; allergic reactions; crises in chronic illnesses; trauma from falls; accidents; abuse; and poisoning. This is not an all-inclusive list but gives an idea of typical uses. The social worker, even in pure medical situations, can look for gaps in services at the hospital and try to fill them. Accidental poisoning, for instance, claims the lives of 300 to 500 children a year.[5] Besides waiting with and supporting distraught parents, the social worker can provide concrete preventive aids. If the child is doing well and will be able to go home, the parents can receive not only instruction in the handling and storage of dangerous substances but also a sheet of the "Mr. Yuk" seals distributed by the Poison Control Center at the Children's Hospital of Pittsburgh and other poison control centers. These seals show a sickly green face with a grimacing expression. Children looking at them do not have a positive response. Recommending to the parents that they put Mr. Yuk seals on all containers with dangerous substances, whether or not they think the child can get hold of them, may make them feel more in control. Many children can understand the explanation that containers with Mr. Yuk seals have stuff inside that tastes bad and is bad for you. It is just this ability to combine small, concrete interventions with knowledge of a wide range of resources and sophisticated clinical thinking that makes social workers so valuable in the emergency room.

Not all presenting problems are as clear-cut as those just listed. Parents may come in with vague concerns that initially seem innocuous but upon explanation are not unfounded at all. Or the obvious complaints may mask something else quite serious, including major physical problems, family dysfunction, or psychiatric illness. Evaluation is a more complicated process than is often realized, especially by residents. Besides, while medical personnel may not see their child's problem as needing urgent care, to the parent it may be a real emergency, and he or she may need a great deal of support. The social worker's role is discussed in detail throughout this chapter, but there is almost always one thing he or she can do, even if unable to help in other ways, and that is to stay with the parent, just to *be* with him or her through the waiting, the treatment, the anxious questioning. Interpreting medical information and answering questions is another helpful function, as are counseling and assisting the parent in negotiating various medical/social service systems, both inside and outside the hospital. The social worker may also provide concrete services, such as transportation and medications, and may want to make sure of little amenities such as toys and books in the waiting room.

If the emergency room is a general one, not used to treating children, there may be added stress for both staff and parents because of the staff's lack of expertise with children and the ineffectiveness of the usual methods of approach. In a pediatric emergency room as well, staff may experience continuing stress. In many large children's hospitals, the emergency room social worker has regular meetings with residents and emergency room nurses in order to help them deal with their own conflicts and to exchange useful information.

Parent Referrals

Certain parents tend to be referred quickly by alert and sensitive triage nurses, as well as physicians. If the social worker is on the spot, the referrals are likely to be more frequent and the worrisome characteristics less dramatic, but even a social worker on call will be summoned for some of this group. Many parents, for instance, react badly to triage and respond to the designation of their child as a nonurgent case with hostility, anxiety, or inappropriate behavior. They need attention, support, and corroboration that their child is important. In addition, in some cases the social worker will try to evaluate the source of inappropriate anger or anxiety to make sure there are not situational or behavioral factors that are directly relevant to treatment and follow-up. Disorganized parents will be referred, too, as well as those who seem incapable of giving any kind of history. The social worker may be charged with making some kind of sense out of the presenting complaint and dredging up as much history and background as possible, a time-consuming task that takes considerable skill and delicacy. If the child's presenting problem is not a true emergency, it is advisable to watch the mother/child interaction for clues to what is going on between them in the family. During and after treatment the interaction can also provide guidelines as to what kinds of help the family may need. A mother who stands on the other side of the room while the physician sutures her small son's laceration may react violently to the sight of blood, may be unable to deal with her child's pain, or may just not be adequately connected to the child. The first two situations require comfort and reassurance; the latter is a more complicated problem and suggests more observation and evaluation to decide on whether the mother/child relationship appears impaired enough to suggest help.

A parent is the primary source of comfort for most children and should be encouraged to be just that, even in unpleasant situations, but when the parent just cannot take it, he or she should be allowed to leave without guilt, knowing that someone else is caring for and concerned with the child.[6] Again, a mother who cannot tolerate the sight of anyone else holding her child may be feeling anxious or guilty or may have real problems in differentiating between herself and her child. Nurses and physicians become increasingly sensitive to these interactions, but experienced social workers can point them out and act on them for staff who are unable to see or understand behavioral communications. Another important kind of interaction has to do with trust and suspicion. Parents who have had experiences of feeling betrayed are likely to expect the same in the future and may be inordinately suspicious of the staff. Others may be perpetuating similar patterns and may lie to their children, promising, for instance, that treatment will not hurt. All staff must cooperate in correcting this behavior and modeling appropriately for parents so that eventually they may make some changes at least in their presentation of medical behavior. They may also be able to see for themselves the difference in reactions between a child who knows what to expect and one who does not.

Intoxicated parents are also readily referred, with the immediate question being that of what contribution the parent has made to the child's current problem. Where neglect or abuse do not appear to be present, what the social worker does will depend on whether and how well he or she knows the parent(s). At the least, a comment on the state of intoxication, an offer of help, and an expression of concern about the family unit are probably appropriate. These are more easily proposed than said, as some people are likely to greet such statements with rage and/or denial. Even so, ignoring intoxication in a parent, including where the child seems generally well cared for and is going home, is not advisable. A parent who appears publicly intoxicated with his or her child is either out of control or communicating something that needs to be received.

Several other kinds of families tend to be referred, not at triage, but usually after repeated contacts. One is the family where the parent has trouble with compliance and follow-up. The youngster may be seen repeatedly in the emergency room without continuing medical care, required immunizations, basic screening tests, and so on. The family may be loving and concerned but unable to get it together. Going for regular appointments may just be beyond their capabilities. Sometimes hooking them up to a patient and flexible physician or nurse-practitioner in one of the hospital's clinics is the best answer. Parents who feel a sense of loyalty or relatedness to the hospital may manage to get their children to clinic, if not for specified appointments, at least with some regularity. Another approach is figuring out how to take care of the parent, so the parent can take care of the child. The following is an example of such an approach:

Case Study

Ms. D, a deprived, impoverished mother, had brought her child to several hospitals because of his seizures. When displeased with the recommendations at one hospital, she tried another. For the past few months she had been using one particular emergency room but had had little success in following the treatment regimen. The social worker, becoming acquainted with Ms. D, sensed that she wanted to do right by her child but needed some attention and nurturance for herself. The worker began expressing interest in Ms. D and her life and discovered that she had enrolled in an educational program and was not doing well. With permission, the worker called the school counselor, told her briefly about the child's medical situation, and asked for extra help for Ms. D. The counselor responded very positively, and Ms. D's grades began to improve. In addition, the social worker explained to her repeatedly the need for consistency in her child's medical care and the importance of observation over time at one institution to see which medications were most effective. Eventually the child began going regularly to the hospital's neurology clinic and following the prescribed treatment regimen. His seizures decreased and have stayed down. His mother now feels much more in control of her own life, and her boost in self-esteem has had clear positive results for him.

Again and again social workers will encounter situations where taking care of the parent is what will help the child best. Abuse, neglect, disorganization, noncompliance can all be expressions of low self-esteem and impoverishment in parents and caretakers.

Another group who tend to be referred are those who seem to have difficulty with basic parenting skills. Overinvolvement is one example, as in a mother who consistently overfeeds or overdresses her baby (here, too, diagnostic and evaluative skills are important: does she overfeed him because she is too involved, because she is ignorant, or because she wants him to sleep all the time? The approach will depend on the answer). Young, isolated parents may have had no opportunity to learn even the rudiments of child care. Mildly retarded parents may not have been able to figure out solutions to certain child-care problems. In such situations the child often will not respond as the parents expect and may be punished for normal childish behavior. The social worker can support the parent's good intentions and provide information, not only in practical matters but in child development, but it is also important to find educational and supportive resources outside the hospital. In-home services, parenting programs, partial child care—whatever is available and will teach the parents without undermining their confidence —are likely to be of some help. If no programs exist or have vacancies, the social worker may choose to encourage emergency room visits until he or she can locate an appropriate program. All these parents may be part of "multiproblem families," where emotional, intellectual, physical, and economic resources are persistently inadequate. Dealing with one or two of these families can be very stressful; a whole caseload is overwhelming. An emergency room social worker cannot take on the responsibility of managing these families. The first priority is an assessment of the child's safety and the general adequacy of his or her care. Such an assessment is useful but not determinative, since an opinion that a child is receiving inadequate care is frequently communicated to child welfare authorities with no response and no result. The next priority is helping the family negotiate the system to get whatever services they can obtain and use. Third, in his or her own work with a multiproblem family who continue bringing their children to the emergency room, the social worker needs to decide to focus on one issue at a time and suspend work on the others. Getting the mother to give the two-year-old his medicine on a regular basis or send the six-year-old off to school every day may be a major achievement. Nurses, physicians, and social workers need to work on these problems together and reinforce each other and the parents for every achievement.

In working with these families, someone needs to keep in mind that one mother may have several children with different last names. Coordination of appointments and other plans for the children is likely to be impossible without an approach to the family as a unit. The social worker may want to maintain a roster of certain families by mother's name, with the various children listed beneath.

Another group of parents who are likely to be referred are those who cannot accept a child's illness. Denial can be useful and even healthy in situations of serious illness, but not when it interferes with treatment. A parent who is unable to cooperate with treatment because to do so would acknowledge the fact of the illness or the prognosis is endangering the child and needs understanding and skilled counseling. Where there is no hurry, a lapse of time may bring about some change, as the parent slowly absorbs the reality of the situation. If the illness is one with frequent crises that necessitate emergency room visits, or if inconsistent care results in emergency room visits, the social worker may see one or both parents regularly and can try to assess their capacities to cope with the situation. While respecting their need for denial he or she can help them to look at the problem bit by bit, at their own pace. As long as the child is getting the necessary treatment and affection and nurturance from his or her parents, their denial should be respected and even seen as adaptive. Support groups can be very helpful in this kind of situation, and information on their availability should be given to the parents. See Chapter 5 for a sampling of such groups and a discussion of families with dying children.

These are "problem" parents, but nearly all parents can use some kind of help. Those who have a child with a newly diagnosed or chronic medical condition may need concrete help with finances and services but may also have many questions that they need encouragement in asking. Parents generally want to know what has happened, whether it will recur, whether it can be treated medically and how, and what else will help. Parents should always be asked if they have any questions before leaving and urged to write down any further questions before a scheduled visit to the clinic, doctor, or hospital.

Deprivation, Inadequacy, or Conflict in the Family

In addition to the "routine" problems listed at the beginning of the chapter, children come in for a variety of other reasons which may involve the social worker. One is failure to thrive (FTT), a condition in infants which reflects inadequate growth and development. The causes can be organic, environmental, or mixed, and the retardation in growth is so marked in many of these babies that they are hospitalized for evaluation and treatment. The social worker can make a major contribution in terms of the history and psychosocial evaluation and can also suggest that other children in the family be located, brought in, and examined to assess their growth and development.

Older children, too, may be developmentally delayed or learning disabled. A three-year-old who is not talking will cause concern in the evaluating physician, who is likely to refer him or her for social work services if they are perceived as available and effective. Again, evaluating, counseling, and referral are the appropriate social work services. They are often difficult to deliver even when the family is able to be cooperative, but too many children, with this and other problems, are lost to view until the next crisis.

Other babies are abandoned or brought in by parents who say they can no longer care for them. Some of these situations are resolved by finding support, respite, and concrete services for the overburdened mothers, but frequently there is an infant who must be placed quickly. This kind of problem requires coordination among family, hospital, social agencies, and police. In fact, police can be extremely helpful in such situations by trying to find family, by ferreting out information, and by providing transport when appropriate. Decisions must be made as to whether the baby should stay with relatives, be placed by the local child welfare agency, or go to a shelter. Many communities do have shelters, some very good ones, just for babies and small children, with or without their mothers. For some hospitals this is an atypical problem; others, unfortunately, deal with it all the time.

Environmental conditions, including family dynamics, are a major factor in children's illnesses. Lead poisoning is a single example, although dealing with it may be anything but simple. Terrible housing is another example, such as the case of the one-week-old baby brought in with heat prostration. The family had been forced to spend the summer with the windows closed because of raw sewage seeping from the condemned house next door, which continued to be inhabited. The fumes were so overpowering that the family were not able to open the windows and endured the suffocating heat. Other children were also not doing well. Since finding new housing was a long-term and difficult process, the social worker had to concentrate on emergency shelter. The infant's illness, however, was in some ways a help to the family, since is increased the possibility that they would get help in locating housing.

Parent against parent is yet another "environmental" problem. A typical scenario involves separated parents sharing custody of a baby, perhaps with one taking responsibility for weekends. On the return of the child, the custodial parent brings him or her to the emergency room in order to prove neglect. Sometimes the neglect is there, sometimes not. If there is a social worker immediately available, he or she can step in and begin the process of assessment and referral. This is exactly the kind of situation where having a social worker on-site makes a difference. It is unlikely that a person on call would be summoned, and yet social work intervention can lead to a major improvement in family functioning.

Children's Reactions to Medical Treatment

Children themselves will not respond uniformly to situations of deprivation, conflict, injury, and illness. There are, however, certain stages that children go through that do affect their experience of and response to medical treatment. Put very simply, they are as follows:[7] from infancy till about age two, the chief reaction is separation anxiety, and every effort should be made to keep the child with his or her mother, or alternatively, father or mother substitute. Just the presence of that person will negate some of the worst elements of the situation and provide consolation and comfort for the child. Of course, this is true for nearly all children but sometimes forgotten for the smallest ones. From about two to six, the child is struggling with issues of mastery. Being restrained, pinned down, overpowered can be a tremendous threat, and even the most mildly intrusive procedures, such as ear examinations, can be extremely frightening to some children. Explaining as much as possible to them, letting them look around the examination room and touch various instruments, emphasizing that being sick has nothing to do with being bad—all these can be very helpful and reassuring to both child and parent. Nurses and physicians specializing in pediatrics tend to be very alert to these issues, and residents and students learn quickly the usefulness of this kind of approach. Parents, too, especially those who put pressure on frightened children to be good, that is, quiet, and who discuss doctors and medical treatments in punitive terms, can sometimes learn to adjust their own behavior when helped to understand what the children are feeling.

Older children, from about eight or so, are able to think about the future, comprehend to some extent and be afraid of dying, and worry about their own physical and psychological integrity. At this age and beyond, children need the opportunity to ask their questions; to have them answered, as well as some of the unasked questions that are expressed in other ways; and to get a limited idea of what the near future holds for them. Each child will have a different level of interest, comprehension, and tolerance, and communication should be slow and respectful. Again, modeling by social workers, nurses, and medical staff can be helpful and reassuring to parents.

How the children deal with these age-related tasks and stages, as well as with their injuries and illnesses, depends a great deal on factors which will be an important part of any psycho-social evaluation. These include not only age and developmental stage but also personality and coping style; prior experience with medical treatment and in hospitals; the nature and severity of the child's condition; the procedures to be undergone, now and in the near future; and the amount and kind of support from families and hospital personnel.[8] All these will help determine the social worker's recommendations and approach to the family. For children who respond abnormally or present psychiatric disturbances, see Chapter 8.

Adolescents

Adolescents bring their own problems to the emergency room and may come frequently to those in children's hospitals where they have received long-time care. They may have a sense of the hospital as "their" place and may have developed attachments to particular individuals. In addition, long-time users know the system in terms of waiting time, payment and nonpayment, and ways of presenting themselves, and sometimes prefer to use it when other more appropriate sources of treatment are available. Issues of consent and parental involvement are discussed in Chapter 3, but even the rules that do exist are not always adequate. Consent, confidentiality, parental involvement, and related issues depend not only on chronological age but also on maturity in decision making. A purely legalistic approach may ignore the needs and capacities of the patient and is not likely to be in his or her interest. A decision concurred in by all the treatment team based on an evaluation of the patient is usually a sound one. The social worker should be able to make a major contribution to this evaluation and in doing so can also be a great source of support for physicians.

Besides trauma and acute and chronic illness, teens come in because they are alone, pregnant, psychiatrically disturbed in some way, or under stress. Adolescents alone may be runaways (see Chapter 10) or may have been ejected by their parents, in addition to those living independently.

Case 1

E, for instance, a 16-year-old boy, came into a general hospital emergency room and said he had been thrown out of his home. Friends had helped him but were running out of resources. The social worker doubted his story but decided to check it out anyway. The worker from the local child welfare service whom she called had no doubt whatsoever about the story, as the family had a long history of abuse. They talked further with E and were able to arrange a suitable placement.

Teens under stress often somaticize their difficulties, and the social worker interviewing an adolescent whose physical complaints have an uncertain basis needs to remember to probe with delicacy and sympathy for the particular source of stress. Sometimes there is a problem or situation that needs to be shared with others or just acknowledged.

Case 2

F, a 16-year-old boy, came in alone, complaining of abdominal pain which appeared to have no origin. Interested questioning elicited that he was gay and in need of some kind of support system; he was referred to a local center specializing in counseling of gays. Only because he knew the hospital and had been coming for years was he able to use the emergency room in this way.

A typical example of the pregnant teenager coming into the emergency room usually involves communication of the pregnancy, as in the following case:

Case 3

G, an obviously middle-class adolescent, came into the emergency
room with her mother. She complained of persistent headache, but
examination revealed nothing but a positive pregnancy test. The
physician found himself unable to discuss this result with them and
hurriedly summoned the social worker, saying, "You tell them!"
The social worker, after only a few minutes with mother and daughter,
realized that both already knew of the pregnancy but needed help
in bringing it out into the open so that they could begin to deal with
it. She encouraged open discussion and helped them to start the
necessary process of planning and decision making together. The
social worker's skilled handling of the communication enabled
the mother to support her daughter and feel more a part of the
decision making.

Pregnancy and parenthood are stressful experiences for adolescents and may lead to psychiatric illness and a need for
psychiatric intervention. Psychiatric emergencies generally are
described in Chapter 8. Although adolescents attempt and commit suicide in growing numbers, their use of suicidal gestures to
express anger or disappointment can provide important clues for
the social worker or psychiatrist. Asking an adolescent *why* he or
she attempted suicide usually elicits the truth—"My boyfriend
left me;" "I failed geometry." These responses, which are not
uncommon, are in contrast to those of the seriously depressed
teenager who needs intensive treatment. Any gesture, however,
should be taken very seriously.

Adolescents may come to the emergency room, with or
without their mothers, not only during pregnancy, but after-
ward. Staff in many inner-city pediatric emergency rooms find
themselves caring for children with their own children—fourteen-
and fifteen-year-old mothers coming in for their own medical
care and for their babies' care. The mothers may be overwhelmed
and depressed by their new responsibilities and enmeshed in
competitive, angry relationships with their own mothers. As long
as the babies are receiving reasonably adequate care, the need
becomes one of counseling, in-home, and supportive resources.
These situations are very stressful for staff because they often
feel helpless and exasperated, and physicians are only too happy
to refer cases to the social worker if he or she is available. The
following are typical situations:

Case Study

Two sisters, H, aged fifteen, and I, sixteen, had brought their babies in to the emergency room at different times. H's one-month-old baby had "rolled" off the couch but suffered no injury. I's infant twins had gone down concrete steps in their stroller but were also unhurt. Investigation revealed that the two girls were home all day with the three babies while their mother went to work. Although she supported them, she was furious at them and had withdrawn as a source of help and reassurance. The two girls had been diligent about providing good child care and were doing their best but were unable to handle the many demands on them. The social worker helped the girls get into a part-time school program and fortunately was able to provide some in-home services for them. As the situation stabilized, the social worker began thinking about the possibility of offering support to the grandmother.

Case Study

Ms. J, a thirty-three-year-old grandmother, brought in her daughter's five-month-old baby, who had been "accidentally" sprayed with insecticide. She herself had an eleven-month-old baby. Mother and daughter were in fierce competition, and mother was extremely critical of her daughter's irresponsibility and neglect of the baby. Whether the daughter just could not compete with her mother or just did not choose to continue being responsible for the baby is not clear; she eventually left home without him. The social worker had at first contacted various referrals, including child protective services, who arranged for Ms. J to gain custody of her grandchild.

The contrast between these examples is a reminder that, whatever the parent's stresses, the safety and well-being of the baby are paramount. Sometimes the social worker can reassess the presenting problem, locate and coordinate helping services, and enhance parental functioning, as in the first example; other times family breakdown has already progressed to such an extent that very little can be done beyond attempting to ensure the child's safety. Adolescents who have known the hospital and have seen it as a place for help during pregnancy can be encouraged to come for support and assistance with the baby. The social worker, besides providing these, can work to dispel the stereotyped thinking among medical professionals about adolescent mothers.

Evaluating Physical and Sexual Abuse

Estimates of the incidence of child abuse in our society vary widely, but even the most conservative figures show millions of children abused and neglected yearly, some killed or maimed for life. For babies one to six months old, the mortality rate is second only to SIDS (Sudden Infant Death Syndrome); for children one to five years old it is second only to accidents.[9] The schools may be the critical location for identification of abuse and neglect in older children, but for infants and toddlers, it may well be the emergency room. This group is nonverbal, demanding, and defenseless[10] and in some families is the frequent target for violent expressions of frustration and anger.

The major categories of abuse and neglect are physical abuse, physical neglect, emotional abuse and neglect, and sexual abuse.[11]

Physical Abuse

Physical abuse is nonaccidental injury or injury that cannot be explained to the physician's satisfaction by the parents. Often there are unlikely or contradictory explanations that do not coincide with the medical facts, and sometimes there has been a delay in seeking treatment. Bruises, welts, fractures, burns, and head injuries are some but not all of the ways in which children are hurt. Photographs should be taken of the injuries, with or without parental permission, although the major goal after treatment becomes not so much documenting the injury as keeping the child safe. If possible the child should be interviewed privately and other children screened. Parents should be asked about disciplinary practices, since some abuse is clearly the result of overharsh discipline, or about previous injuries, although children may have been taken to a different hospital each time. The physician will be looking for signs of earlier injuries and should be someone who is knowledgeable in this area.

Just about every state has a law on child abuse, each of them requiring reporting to the local child welfare agency or equivalent. Although there were laws previously, in 1974 the federal government gave grants to states to set up reporting systems and investigational and follow-up programs.[12] Reporting is mandatory for those professions which come into regular contact with children. The reporting should be not only of cases involving extreme injury but also of suspected injury and of *children at risk*. The latter category may sound vague, and there will be further discussion later, but the rule of thumb is to resolve doubts in favor of the child. *Report all children who may be at risk*, but only after investigation bears out the possibility of risk. The law provides immunity for those who make reports, even erroneous ones, in good faith, and upsetting as an erroneous report can be for the parents, it is still better than ignoring a truly abused child.

As an observer has pointed out,

> The failure to identify a given episode of abuse can have dire consequences. Without intervention, abuse recurs in approximately 50 percent of cases. In 35 percent of these cases, the child ultimately is severely injured or killed.[13]

In addition it is possible to sustain criminal and/or civil liability in some locations for not reporting a child who is then injured again. Even so, much child abuse is never reported. Generally, the report can be called in, with a form to follow later. When calling in the report, make sure the case is picked up. Some child welfare agencies are so overburdened that cases are screened out over the phone as they are reported. Do not allow this to happen; make sure it will be investigated.

Laws sometimes allow a child at risk to be kept in the hospital, usually for 24 hours before any legal process has to occur. Even if the child's injuries do not warrant admission (or transfer to a children's hospital), if there is any question about his or her immediate safety at home, the physician should be urged in the most vigorous terms to admit. Parental permission is not required, although it is usually necessary to explain to them why the child is being admitted, even over their objections.

Physical Neglect

Physical neglect is the failure to provide the necessities of life,[14] including medical care, adequate nourishment, appropriate clothing, supervision of activities, and other needs. Neglect will not often require admission and, in fact, will not usually be seen in the emergency department except in combination with something else, such as injury. (It is not uncommon for several kinds of abuse and neglect to exist together.) It, too, must be reported, although families in poverty, who simply cannot manage to provide for all their children's needs, should be *supported*, not reported. They should be connected to whatever resources are available to them.

Emotional Abuse and Neglect

Emotional abuse and neglect are essentially the failure to provide a "loving environment in which the child can thrive."[15] It is difficult to diagnose, especially in a short-term contact, but may contribute to failure to thrive, learning difficulties, behavior problems, and other conditions. It is important to be aware that it may exist in combination with other kinds of abuse and neglect. Some states do include it in statutory definitions of abuse and neglect.

Sexual Abuse

Sexual abuse is not only rape, but any sexual activity between adult and child (the age definition of "child" depending on the jurisdiction), whether assaultive or not. As much as three-fourths of sexual abuse[16] involves incest, mostly between fathers or stepfathers (or "surrogate" fathers, that is, mother's boyfriends) and daughters. Sexual abuse is also difficult to establish in many cases, but it should always be suspected in a child presenting genital complaints of any kind. Children very rarely tend to lie about these things, so that a child's description of someone "bothering" him or a direct report of sexual attack or involvement is likely to have some validity.[17] Behavioral changes may also appear, depending on age: anxiety, fear, depression, rocking, thumbsucking, clinging, nightmares, fatigue, insomnia.[18] The child may need help in explaining what happened, with dolls, with simple language, and with someone who is relatively comfortable with the situation, either the social worker or a nurse, but not the physician who does the physical examination. (See Appendix I for a protocol on sexually abused children and adolescents.)

The identity of the abuser may have a profound effect on the family's response to the situation. If he is a relative, the family may have trouble believing the child's story and may need help in accepting it. Ejection of the abuser from the family circle may create guilt in the child and anger in the family at the child for being the cause of all the trouble. The situation is even more complicated when, as frequently happens, the other partner knows about the abuse and at some level even condones it. Even without the family anger, the child may feel guilty and rejected, especially if he or she also received affection from the abuser. The social worker should reassure the child, even if he or she has been foolish, that he or she did nothing wrong and should encourage the parents to do so. In addition, the parents need to hear, repeatedly if necessary, that children are not to blame for being victims of sexual abuse. (It can happen, however, that one child is sexually abused by another child; even then the victim is not to blame.)

In some jurisdictions, sexual abuse is reported as child abuse; in others it is simply a crime to be reported to police. In any case, it must be reported. Intrafamily abuse is generally reported to the local child welfare authorities but may also be reported to the police. When a less intimately related person or a stranger has abused a child, the police are generally called. Often parents are reluctant to report abuse, even a brutal rape, to the police, feeling that the resulting investigation and possible prosecution will be too hard on the child. The social worker needs to point out that such reporting may be necessary not only for the protection of that child but for others.

Child abuse is very hard to deal with, particularly for people unused to violence, but its incidence cannot be ignored. In many families, violence is a way of life, a way of expressing frustration, and a way of communicating for those with limited skills. The indicators mentioned in this chapter should alert the social worker to the possibility of abuse.[19] Not only parents but increasingly foster parents and baby-sitters may be responsible. History-taking should include efforts to learn about alcohol use, traffic accidents, history of family violence, expectations of the child, financial pressures, military history (there is some speculation that a higher incidence of child abuse occurs on military bases), and fundamentalist religious beliefs (again, harsh disciplinary practices sometimes accompany certain religious beliefs).[20] Young, immature parents, especially those who are isolated, with low self-esteem and few outlets generally, may be at great risk. Even where abuse is suspected or even just the possibility of abuse, the social worker should attempt to bring up the subject in a gentle and tactful way, such as mentioning how difficult it can be to cope with a child of this particular age. A comic book distributed through the U.S. Department of Health and Human Services and sponsored by the National Center on

Child Abuse and Neglect is useful to have available in the waiting room for parents to pick up and take with them. It is called *Dennis the Menace: Coping with Family Stress* and is available in both English and Spanish (*Daniel el Travieso: Como Manejas La Tension Familiar*).[21] In addition, even parents at risk can be encouraged to use local support systems. Parents Anonymous, for instance, begun in California in 1970, has at least 750 chapters throughout the United States. Its purpose is to help abusive parents obtain support from each other to change their behavior toward their children.[22]

A primary goal of intervention in cases of child abuse is to maintain children in their own homes without the risk of repeated abuse. Parents need to be told explicitly about referrals and reporting and the reasons for them. Although children must be protected, parents need not be censured and shunned and, in fact, should be helped and supported wherever possible, even when it is clear they cannot keep their children. The social worker must work with the emergency department staff to develop the most helpful attitudes and approaches, as well as with social agencies to make sure that adequate resources are available. In some locations, the social worker will also have to check up on the abuse referral to make sure that the case has actually been picked up and, because of limited resources, is being adequately monitored.

Questionable Abuse Cases

A social worker who does not do his or her own screening, that is, functions through an on-call system or through referrals, is most likely to be summoned for help with cases involving questionable child abuse. The obvious cases, while stressful and unpleasant for staff, are relatively easy in terms of decision making. The tough situations are those where the injury might be accidental or it might not, or where a mild incident of abuse seems to be an anomaly, or where child protective services are so limited and inadequate that reporting will only alienate the family from the hospital without bringing about any improvement. The latter situations sometimes involve physical neglect or emotional abuse, which many child protective agencies are just too overwhelmed even to consider handling, whatever their mandates. While the child should receive the benefit of the doubt, as the law requires, the reporting should not be completely automatic without benefit of any evaluation. In one case, for instance, a small child was brought into the emergency room with severe scalding injuries. The mother's explanation, that he had overturned a pot of boiling water she had been using to heat the house, turned out to be true. Instead of reporting the injury, the social worker helped the mother obtain heat and other home improvements. Another case involved a thirteen-year-old girl who came in with bruises she claimed were inflicted by her aunt. Investigation revealed that the "aunt" was fourteen and almost like a sibling and that the two of them fought constantly.

The purpose of these investigations by the social worker is not only to try to discover the origins of the injury but also to answer the questions of the existence and extent of risk to the child. The cases above do not illustrate the kind of continuing risk that makes reporting so necessary in true cases of abuse. Social workers who are on call may have to be ready to come in to the emergency room occasionally when physicians request help in assessing this risk factor. In addition, since child abuse is so often related to specific stresses, social workers need to be ready to offer other services as well as child protective ones. Reporting abuse may be presented as a helpful act but is not seen as such by the parent; referrals, concrete services, and other kinds of assistance can also be made available to abusive parents. Assuming that the child welfare agency will do it all is usually a considerable overestimation of their capabilities. In these situations, as in most cases involving referral of parents and children, the referral is not complete unless the social worker knows that the family is receiving services.

Notes

1. Ellen M. Meier, "The Pediatric Emergency Patient," *Emergency Medicine*, 13 (August 15, 1981): 29–32, 36.
2. Richard Halperin, Allen R. Meyers, and Joel L. Alpert, "Utilization of Pediatric Emergency Services: A Critical Review," *Pediatric Clinics of North America*, 26 (November 1979): 747–757. This whole volume is concerned with pediatric emergencies.
3. Emily Friedman, "Access to Care: Serving the Poor and Elderly in Tough Times," *Hospitals*, 56 (December 1, 1982): 83–90.
4. John P. Geyman, "Pediatric Health Care in Family Practice," *Journal*

of Family Practice, 15 (December 1982): 1047–1048. The social worker interested in pediatric emergencies can look at Stephen Ludwig, Gary Fleischer *et al.*, eds., *Textbook of Pediatric Emergency Medicine*, (Baltimore: Williams & Wilkins, 1983).

5. David Driggers, "Pediatric Poisoning—The First 30 Minutes," *Postgraduate Medicine*, 72 (August 1982): 52–59.

6. The Compassionate Friends, "Suggestions for Doctors and Nurses," (1981); Meier, "The Pediatric Emergency Patient."

7. Meier, "The Pediatric Emergency Patient."

8. Bascom W. Ratcliff, Elizabeth M. Timberlake, and David P. Jentsch, "Pediatric Social Work," in *Social Work in Hospitals* (Springfield, Ill.: Charles C Thomas, 1982).

9. Margaret C. McNeese, "When to Suspect Child Abuse," *American Family Practice*, 6 (June 1982): 191. See also Harriet R. Bakalar, Jacqueline D. Moore, and Donald W. Hight, "Psychosocial Dynamics of Pediatric Burn Abuse," *Health and Social Work*, 6 (November 1981): 27–32. (This article presents criteria for identifying children at greatest risk of nonaccidental burn injury.)

10. Ibid.

11. Ibid.; see also Margaret C. McNeese and Joan R. Hebeler, "The Abused Child: A Clinical Approach to Identification and Management," *CIBA Clinical Symposium*, 29: 5 (Summit, N.J., 1980); Jason Tanine, "Epidemiologic Differences between Sexual and Physical Abuse," *Journal of the American Medical Association*, 247 (June 25, 1982): 3347. One of the classic works is R. E. Helfer and C. H. Kempe, eds., *Child Abuse and Neglect: The Family and the Community*, (Cambridge, Mass.: Ballinger Publishing Co., 1976).

12. Child Abuse Prevention and Treatment Act, PL 93–247, June 1974.

13. McNeese and Hebeler, "The Abused Child," 190.

14. Ibid.

15. Ibid., 191.

16. Ibid., 190–191; see also Jerilyn A. Shamroy, "A Perspective on Child Sexual Abuse," *Social Work*, 25 (March 1980): 128–131. It has been estimated that as many as one in ten American children are sexually abused, most by people that they know.

17. Child sexual abuse is vastly underreported. See C. P. Shah, C. P. Holloway, D. V. Valkil, "Sexual Abuse of Children," *Annals of Emergency Medicine*, 11 (January 1982): 18–23.

18. Vivian Drayton, "Some Diagnostic Indicators of Sexual Abuse," in *Issues and Updates* (Family Resource Center, Child Psychiatry Center at St. Christopher's Hospital: Philadelphia, Penn., October 1982).

19. Observers point out the necessity of "a high index of suspicion for child abuse" in an emergency setting and emphasize that even if all the reports are correct, there still are too few of them. See Norman Rosen-

berg and Gerald Rottenfield, "Fracture in Infants: A Sign of Child Abuse," *Annals of Emergency Medicine*, 11 (April 1982): 178–180.

20. McNeese, "The Abused Child," 192.

21. *Dennis the Menace: Coping with Family Stress*. Field Newspaper Syndicate, Field Enterprises, Inc., 1981.

22. See Sally Holmes, "Parents Anonymous: A Treatment for Child Abuse," *Social Work*, 23 (May 1978): 245–247.

7 Problems of the Elderly

The elderly represent a special group with needs that are often different from those of the rest of the population. Although this chapter defines those 65 and older as "elderly," that division is a demographic rather than a descriptive one. Many people in their 60s and their 70s are healthy, fit, and active, requiring only routine medical care. Those who work in health care settings sometimes tend to see the elderly as a group with limited capacities, failing health, and few supports. It is important, however, to remember two basic features about the elderly in order to avoid susceptibility to stereotypes that interfere with helpful approaches and treatments. First, aging is not a disease. Though there are certain physical changes that are part of the aging process, the rate of these changes is different for everyone; and various genetic, environmental, and other factors contribute considerably to the ways in which people age. Thus, not everyone over seventy has impaired hearing or difficulties with memory and comprehension. Even so, it is not at all uncommon to see a nurse or physician or social worker or registrar shouting at an elderly person as if he or she could not hear or talking in a style that would be demeaning to a first grader. Although staff know intellectually that physical disability does not mean mental disability, their approaches often suggest the opposite. The temptation to lump elderly people together and to regard them solely as ill and impaired is so strong in settings such as an emergency room that countervailing forces must be brought to bear against it. One of those forces can be the social worker, who is often in a

good position to learn more about the elderly person as an
individual and may be able to spend a little time discussing past
achievements and current interests. A typical example of lack of
respect for and interest in older patients involved Mr. K, a
dignified elderly former professor of philosophy, who was in-
censed when an emergency room registrar shouted to him, "Just
sit over there, John." Although he had come in for a condition
that required immediate attention, he left rather than face further
indignities. He later complained bitterly to his private physician
in the institution, who worked with the emergency room social
worker to see that some changes occurred in the attitudes of the
registrars. Scenes like this take place constantly and reflect a real
failure of our system of medical care to adjust to the growing
number and changing needs of the elderly and to tailor care and
approaches to the individual patient.

The reality is that many older people care for themselves,
including those with low finances, and may find life satisfying
and pleasant. Although the majority suffer from chronic illnesses,
they see themselves as basically well and value their independence and their capacities.

Social Support and the Elderly

Many elderly people in our society do have support systems and
need help only in using them more effectively and in supple-
menting them. The major source of support is, of course, the
family. It is a widely held myth that families in the United States
do not care for their aged members. Many do, and at great
sacrifice to themselves. One study, for instance, found that of a
group of children caring for aged parents in their own homes,
forty percent spent the time equivalent of a full-time job in
custodial care.[1] The implications of this for social workers are
primarily the need to encourage and reinforce family members,
the need to find respite services when they are available as well
as additional helping resources, and the need to share information about medical treatment and patient tasks with helpers as
much as is feasible and appropriate. This is not to say that many
older people are not independent and not capable of handling
their own medical care, but where concerned family are involved, reinforcement and assistance are far more suitable than
criticisms, recriminations, and guilt-evoking lectures.

When working with families of the aged, the social worker must try to define what are the appropriate tasks for them, which can be shared, and what must be taken over by others. The answers will depend on a number of factors, not the least of which is the age of the children themselves. A 65-year-old woman taking care of a 90-year-old mother has to deal with issues of her own aging and the possibilities of reduced income, strength, and resilience. In addition, both the elderly and their aging children do lose valuable sources of support when their peers eventually start to become ill and die. Those who live to an advanced age outside an institution may have no peer group at all.

The Elderly's Use of the Emergency Room

The use of emergency rooms by the elderly is only beginning to come under scrutiny, and in fact there is some debate as to whether those over 65 do actually use them more than younger groups. Studies in some areas show that elderly patients use emergency rooms heavily; other research suggests that the use is different, not greater. Certainly inpatient use is heavier; from 1967–79, for instance, the rate of hospitalization for those under 65 years grew 11%; for those over 65, it grew more than three times that, 35%. Ninety-four precent of the increase in patient days represented care for the elderly; by 1989 that figure is expected to be still very high, close to 90%.[2] Obviously, some of these will come in through emergency rooms, and the social worker will provide support and services to them and their families and will make appropriate referrals to the social workers on the floors. There may be even some who come through the emergency room without being admitted and need services that they cannot always articulate and may be too proud to accept. Whatever the numbers, they are bound to be substantial since nearly 20% of our population is expected to be 65 or over by 2030.[3]

The elderly who use emergency rooms do actually have different problems from the rest of the emergency room population.[4] First, they often have limited mobility, which makes access to medical care and obtaining of food and medication very difficult. In some areas susceptibility to crime makes them reluctant to venture out, and extremes of climate add to the obstacles they must face. In addition, lack of resources may make the emergency room the only feasible source of care for some elderly, who may have no adequate transportation system, no pharmacies that deliver, no physicians who take Medicare assignment. Keeping these factors in mind, the social worker can try to see that the medical recommendations, which may be entirely sound and reasonable, are not totally impossible for the patient. Questions such as how the patient will get to the physician or clinic, who will take him or her, and what transportation systems are available, are crucial to follow-up. If the patient is depending on a relative for transportation, it is advisable to talk with that person to clarify the times, frequency, and importance of the appointments, and to make sure of his or her availability. If the patient is not sure how to get to an appointment, it is safe to assume he or she will miss it. Many localities have public or private transportation systems for the elderly, handicapped, and others in need of special transportation services, including some that pick people up at their homes, drop them off at the health care setting, then come back for them later. These services generally cost money; sometimes grants can be generated, hospitals contribute small amounts, or the social work department can raise some of the funds. Reduced taxi fares may also be available in some communities. Whatever the transportation facilities, the social worker should not underestimate their significance and should do whatever is possible to make existing resources available and to develop new ones. Similarly, prescriptions need to be checked, not only for clarity and comprehensibility, but in terms of actually obtaining them. If physicians can call prescriptions into a nearby pharmacy that will deliver to the patient's house, that arrangement may be more appropriate for someone who is not able to stop on the way home. Finally, if referrals are made through the emergency room to physicians on the hospital staff who are also in private practice, the social worker should have some knowledge of which ones do and do not accept Medicare assignment. (That is, do not accept payment from Medicare in full but rather bill the patient for the whole charge. The patient is then compensated by Medicare but often not for anywhere near the size of the bill.) He or she can explain the importance of this issue for those without additional coverage to the referring physicians. All this must be done, like the activities described in the next sections, without undermining the pride, independence, and capabilities of individual patients. Delicacy and sensitivity are part of the social worker's contribution to the treatment of the elderly patient.

Common Presenting Problems

Another area in which older patients are different is in the types of illnesses and conditions that they present. Even those who are functioning well may have a variety of health problems, including one or more chronic ailments that complicate whatever acute illnesses or flareups are the current focus. In addition, the normal aging process may produce different physical responses. Some diseases and illnesses, for instance, may present very atypically in the elderly. Chapter 8 discusses some of the confusion involved in diagnosing various conditions in the elderly, particularly when initial symptoms seem to be primarily psychiatric ones. An appreciation of these interrelationships is important for a number of reasons. The many physical influences (susceptibility to temperature, chronic disease, diminishing faculties, and others) affecting an older person's functioning make his or her equilibrium rather fragile, so that what may seem to be the smallest change or pressure can upset it completely. Looking for major changes or obvious stresses may not be appropriate or useful. Physicians and nurses versed in geriatric medicine often understand this; others do not. The social worker can help by working with the patient, family, and other helpers to reestablish the equilibrium. Support, encouragement, and realistic expectations can make a considerable difference. On the other hand, sometimes a little detective work can be extremely important, and a social worker who has taken a good history can make a major contribution to diagnosis. Finally, the combination of multiple conditions, lessened capacity, and diminished energy may make compliance with any regimen difficult and, to some patients, not really worth the effort. Even those who have had full, productive, admirable lives may feel exhausted, depressed, and ridden with failure when they feel they can no longer cope even with their own self-care. Recognition of the difficulty of this for some people is the first step to helping.

A listing of common medical disorders of the elderly is beyond the scope of this chapter. Examples, however, include diseases of the bones and joints such as rheumatism, arthritis, osteoporosis; hypertension; diabetes; congestive heart failure and cardiopulmonary difficulties; pneumonia; adverse drug reactions; increased susceptibility to climate, such as hypothermia; neurological problems, including CVAs and dizziness; and increased falls and fractures.[5] This is by no means a complete list, and it is obvious that many conditions occur in other segments of the population but are more frequent or serious or take a different course in the elderly. The specific conditions seen in a particular emergency room will depend on how it is used by the aged population near it. Whether it is used for regular and preventive medical care, episodic care, or only for true emergencies depends on the characteristics of the population and the neighborhood and the type and location of the hospital.

A third major difference in the elderly is their isolation. Of the three most vulnerable groups of elderly, two, the old-old (over 75) and women alone, are likely to be isolated, and the third, minorities, often have little available to them in the wider society. In fact, because women live longer than men, and because not marrying was at one time more common than it is now, two groups are often combined as the old-old woman alone, and in some communities it is all three. Smaller and more spread-out families also contribute to this isolation, as do a variety of physical and neighborhood characteristics. Isolation, when it is not wished for, can lead to depression, malnutrition (from not wanting to cook for oneself), and exacerbation of existing illnesses. Some more mobile people may in fact visit emergency rooms regularly just for the company. Combating isolation is always a priority for the social worker, but lack of resources does not make it easy. For immigrants with different customs and languages, especially when they are separated from the larger group, it can be very difficult. Besides, they may be used to much more attention, deference, and respect than we tend to show our elderly in this country. The social worker with a little time can try to spend some of it just in conversation with the elderly person, conveying a sense of respect and interest and willingness to learn about the past. Some elderly people do not understand the concept of entitlements and do not differentiate them from unacceptable charity. The social worker should understand and be able to make clear the distinction, emphasizing that an entitlement has been earned. Painstaking explanations may be necessary for things that the medical staff take for granted. Sometimes coping with isolation can call for very creative thinking, as in the following example.

Case Study

Ms. L's apartment was broken into, and she was robbed, beaten, and tied up. When she was discovered and brought to the emergency room, the social worker began to follow her in a respectful and nondominating way. Ms. L was a proud, independent woman who refused to move out of her deteriorating neighborhood. The social worker arranged for her to get bars on the window and got her connected with local community agencies. In addition, she persuaded the policeman on the beat to stop by for coffee every day. The obvious presence and interest of the policeman has discouraged any further interference with Ms. L. In addition, she looks forward to the policeman's visit and appreciates being able to provide him with something.

Without the social worker's involvement and initiative here, Ms. L would undoubtedly be living in fear and danger or would have long since moved out of the home she loved.

Abuse of the Elderly

Few laws protect the elderly, either at home or in institutions. It is not unusual for seriously abused or neglected elderly people to be left in emergency rooms, particularly on weekends when staff may be busier and less likely to take action against the offending institution or family. A social worker who sees multiple examples of such abuse can work with other interested parties toward passage of a mandatory reporting law.[6] Certainly every suspicious death should be reported as possible neglect or abuse. Photographs should be taken routinely where there are any suspicions, with the consent of the patient if he or she is able. The local town, city, or county welfare agency should acknowledge its responsibility for the abused elderly and should develop systems for receiving and evaluating reports and for emergency placements of those who cannot return home. No agency wants to take on this responsibility, and those who have it often do not deliver services, but in the long run it is a project worth considerable effort. Cities large enough to have an emergency social workers' group may benefit from an organized approach. In addition, where hospitals are forced to admit a large number of abused elderly patients, administrators may be willing to exert pressure on the appropriate agency to meet its responsibilities or even acknowledge new ones. All this involves long-term effort, however; an immediate and concrete change could involve the development of an area-wide hot line through which hospital social workers inform each other of the worst nursing and boarding homes, with the understanding that no one will refer patients to them. Such a project can be difficult to maintain where there is a shortage of resources and consequently must be supported by all the social workers in the area.

In the emergency room itself, the worker has to make the decision as to whether the patient can return home. The decision is not necessarily a medical one but rather an assessment of risk. Some patients cannot go home. Mrs. M, for example, was sent home weak, bruised, and malnourished in spite of the social worker's efforts and returned in two or three weeks DOA. This is the time to beg, plead, cajole the physicians; to refuse to make transportation arrangements if that is the worker's responsibility; and to use whatever channels, resources, or influence are available. The admission of such a patient reflects the inherent conflict between the patient's and hospital's interests, with the social worker in the middle; the stay may be an uncompensated one, and additional placements may be unavailable. In order to insist on or plead for such an admission, the social worker must have credibility in the institution and a willingness to work with colleagues to find additional placements.

If the offending home is one that the worker knows and considers relatively adequate, he or she should discuss the situation with the proprietor and explore ways to correct the deficiencies. If the home is known to be a poor resource, it should be put on the hot line and reported to the appropriate authorities. Even this step can be difficult when the hospital depends on inadequate boarding and nursing homes to take patients for whom there are no other places. Protection of these resources may mean turning a blind eye to what goes on in them, and a social worker with compassion, energy, and zeal for change may find himself or herself out of a job.

Where the patient is brought in by a family, the first step is to explore the situation to see if there are possibilities such as respite care, homemaker services, or day programs, to make the arrangement more bearable for all. Whether the incident is reported will depend on severity, legal reporting requirements, the family's interest in working out a new program, and the worker's assessment. If the patient is admitted, there is a little more time; if he or she is sent home, follow-up arrangements must be made immediately, with the guarantee of a home visit by *someone*. As in all abuse cases, other explanations may be offered, such as a fall, and the worker will have to decide whether to confront the caretakers directly or to discuss tactfully the inadequacies in the patient's care and the difficulties in providing it. The latter approach promises sympathy, support, and the offer of some kind of help. If the offer is rejected, confrontation may then be necessary.

Occasionally the social worker becomes involved in cases of abuse through the merest chance. Examples such as the following show how the opportunity to intervene can be thrust onto the worker in surprising ways.

Case Study

Mr. N was seen in the emergency department, and it was agreed by the physicians that he should be transferred to the V.A. Hospital. He was reluctant but was given no real choice. The social worker, attempting to notify his wife, reached a neighbor. The neighbor expressed great concern about the patient's wife and said that the local rumor was that she was seriously abused. The social worker arranged for representatives from the local welfare (adult services) agency to visit the house. There they found the wife and her sister tied to the bed with nothing available to eat but dogfood. They were both admitted to the hospital with severe dehydration and malnutrition. Further investigation revealed that the patient had pistol-whipped his daughter and terrorized everyone around. Adult services personnel had previously been unable to get in because they were afraid of the patient, and for some reason they had not called the police. If not for the patient's illness and the social worker's efforts, the two unfortunate women would have remained prisoners.

The Special Problems of Diet and Compliance

Among the concrete areas social workers can help with are medication and nutrition. Studies suggest that the elderly understand both their medical conditions and the reasons for their medication less well than younger people.[7] Compliance, however, does not always seem to correlate with comprehension, so there must be other factors which affect how correctly older people take their medications.[8] Family or other helping people are one, of course. Another is the number of the medications, as compliance appears to decrease as the number increases. It may also be that pills of similar colors, sizes, and shapes are confusing to people whose visual acuity is also impaired. An elderly patient with two pills or capsules that are similar to each other may have trouble telling them apart—even if a younger person could without any difficulty—unless they are in very different containers.[9]

The social worker can just alert physicians of this problem, especially in regard to patients who exhibit some confusion about medication. In addition, he or she can remind physicians to note in prescriptions that child-proof caps are not necessary. Patients may forget to mention this to the pharmacist and then may have difficulty opening the bottles. The social worker can go over the prescription with the patient, can make sure the instructions are clear, and can review them repeatedly with the patient if necessary. Sometimes writing out a schedule of when to take which medications, to be posted on the refrigerator or bathroom mirror, will promote compliance. The social worker may want to have some inexpensive divided plastic pill containers available, to show people how to put one day's worth of pills in the box in the morning and empty out the compartments one by one throughout the day. At bedtime the box should be empty and the right number of pills ingested at the appropriate intervals.

Another very important area is nutrition. Chapter 8 includes a section on the elderly and discusses how malnutrition, anemia, and similar conditions can lead to symptoms of psychiatric disorders. In addition, they can exacerbate existing illnesses and further weaken an already frail and limited person. Several factors contribute to the nutritional status of elderly patients. One is medications. Some drugs may cause loss of appetite, while others may interfere with the absorption of various nutrients by the body. It is helpful for the social worker to be alert to these possibilities in order to discuss how to add certain foods or how to cater to a flagging appetite. In a setting where the social worker, nurses, and physicians are relatively constant members of a team, information about possible drug-related nutritional problems can become part of routine communication. Some patients with ill-fitting or uncomfortable dentures have trouble eating many kinds of foods but will not necessarily admit to it without skilled questioning. Again, there may be many low-cost, appetizing, manageable substitutes that the social worker can suggest. Social workers on inpatient units and in outpatient clinics are likely to be working with similar populations, so that collaboration or an inservice with the hospital dieticians on the nutritional needs of the elderly is an invaluable part of building up skills and knowledge. Some patients, in fact, may need to be referred for nutritional assessment and counseling to whatever nutrition services are available.

Other factors related to inadequate diet are poverty, lack of mobility, and loneliness. Insufficient money to pay for the necessary foods; inability to get to the supermarket or store (because of physical infirmity, inclement weather, or dangerous neighbor-hood); and lack of desire to prepare a meal for one person and eat it alone all can mean that an elderly person will eat poorly and his or her health will suffer as a result. Meals-on-wheels programs, which provide home-delivered meals and a few minutes of companionship; food cupboards and similar programs which make food available to those in need; daytime activity programs for the elderly which provide a hot meal at noon and sometimes even transportation; and the matching of elderly people who live near each other and can plan and eat meals together are all among the possibilities for the social worker to explore. Response to heat and cold may also be related to adequate energy intake through meals. The same interview that inquires about eating should elicit information about the effects of weather conditions on the living quarters and consequently the well-being of the patient. The elderly have increased sus-ceptibility to hypothermia and heat exhaustion, and the discovery of an apartment with no heat in the winter and no ventilation in the summer may require quick remedial action or a change in disposition. The older person living in a dangerous neighbor-hood who is afraid to open his or her windows in the summer is at high risk for a serious heat-related reaction.

After determining what is available at home, and what is not available and must be put into the system, the social worker needs to assess first what are the possibilities for assistance, and second how quickly can they be put into place. It is not unusual to find that home care services needed immediately have a waiting list of three or four weeks. Among the services to be explored are home nursing; home health aid; occupational therapy; physical therapy; friendly visitors; various alarm systems, including some attached to the telephone; telephone reassurance programs; hot meals; transportation; and many more, depending on the loca-tion. The social worker needs to know what programs he or she can call on and how well and quickly they work. A particularly skillful intervention in the emergency room, provided that the resources are also there, may mean that an elderly patient's life at home is better, more satisfying, and healthier.[10]

Notes

1. Judith Treas, "Family Support Systems for the Aged: Some Social and Demographic Considerations," *The Gerontologist*, 17 (1977): 486–491; citing Newman, "Housing Adjustments of Older People: a Report from the 2nd Phase" (Institute for Social Research: Ann Arbor, 1976).

2. Emily Friedman, "Access to Care: Serving the Poor and Elderly in Tough Times," *Hospitals*, 56 (December 1, 1982): 83–90.

3. Lowell W. Gerson and Lynn Skvarch, "Emergency Medical Service Utilization by the Elderly," *Annals of Emergency Medicine*, 11 (March 1982): 610–612.

4. See, for instance, Mary Lloyd, Laura Bleiweiss Wilson, Sharon Simson, and Mary Duncan, "Emergency Nursing and the Growing Elderly Population," *Journal of Emergency Nursing*, 7 (July–August 1981): 162–166; Laura Bleiweiss Wilson, Sharon Simson, Mary Duncan, and Mary Lloyd, "Emergency Services and the Elderly: The Role of the Social Worker," *Health and Social Work*, 7 (February 1982): 59–64.

5. David C. Kennie, "Good Health Care for the Aged," *Journal of the American Medical Association*, 249 (February 11, 1983): 770–773; Gerson and Skvarch, "Emergency Medical Service."

6. For an opposing view, see Lawrence R. Faulkner, "Mandating the Reporting of Suspected Cases of Elder Abuse: An Inappropriate, Ineffective, and Ageist Response to the Abuse of Older Adults," *Family Law Quarterly*, 16 (Spring 1982): 69–91.

7. Lawrence E. Klein, Pearl S. German, Stephen J. McPhee, Craig R. Smith, and David M. Levine, "Aging and Its Relationship to Health Knowledge and Medication Compliance," *The Gerontologist*, 22 (April 1982): 384–387; Robert Kendrick and J. Ronald D. Bayre, "Compliance with Prescribed Medication by Elderly Patients," *Canadian Medical Association Journal*, 127 (November 15, 1982): 961–962.

8. Klein *et al.*, "Aging and Its Relationship."

9. Kendrick and Bayne, "Compliance."

10. For additional information about medical care of the elderly, see "Clinical Geriatric Medicine," *The Medical Clinics of North America*, 63 (March 1983); and Laura B. Wilson, Sharon Simson, and Charles Baxter, *Handbook of Geriatric Emergency Care* (Baltimore: University Park Press, 1984).

8 Psychiatric Emergencies

Psychiatric emergencies are among the most challenging, complicated, and ambiguous cases that the social worker encounters, and he or she is likely to play a major role in evaluation and disposition of these problems. The role of the social worker in psychiatric emergencies will vary according to the nature of the emergency room, as will that of the psychiatrist. For instance, urban hospitals tend to see many chronic and well-known patients, while private and suburban hospitals, particularly at night, are likely to get true emergencies. Those social workers who are on duty during evenings and nights may also see the emergency room used as a "community dumping ground."[1] One study in a New York City hospital, for instance, showed that 70% of patients seen between midnight and morning were diagnosed as having psychiatric problems.[2] Some of these are the population discussed in Chapter 10; others are true emergencies in need of immediate evaluation and care. In some emergency settings, the social workers are the primary dispensers of mental health care and the most sophisticated psychiatrically of all the staff.[3] This is often the case where there is no attending psychiatrist immediately available and psychiatric residents rotate. In other settings, the social worker's role is seen as an ancillary one, and there may be rivalry among social worker, psychiatric nurse, and psychiatric resident. Sometimes it is necessary to stake out "turf" and to expend considerable effort in working out smooth and effective collaborative relationships. Whatever the relationship, the social worker is indispensable in this setting because of the expertise he or she brings in the understanding and coordination of outside influences and resources and their relationship to the patient's state of health.[4] If there are two treatment settings, separate medical and psychiatric emergency rooms, the social worker's responsibility may include reminding each that the patient still exists, so that referral to one does not mean that the other closes the case. One of the most important contributions the social worker can make, in fact, is to serve as a constant reminder that medical and psychiatric illness can co-exist and that one can cause the other. Another useful function is to make sure that valuable information from friends, relatives, or other accompanying persons is never neglected or underestimated. Case examples later in the chapter will illustrate ways in which this is done. Whatever the specific tasks of the social worker in regard to psychiatric emergencies, there is a body of knowledge that is essential to adequate job performance, and this chapter serves as an introduction to that material.

Problem Issues in Psychiatric Emergencies

Any social worker who deals with psychiatric emergencies has to be familiar with and have thought about certain problem areas. In order to fulfill the role of advocate and monitor, the worker needs to recognize the complexity and difficulty of issues such as the following:

Moral Judgments. Nowhere in medicine are "snap judgments" made so readily as in psychiatry. Psychiatrists are as sympathetic, as capable, as well trained as other physicians, but the unattractiveness and uncooperative nature of some patients, coupled with wide variations in symptomatology of similar conditions, makes inadequate diagnosis more likely than in some other specialties. As one psychiatrist has put it, the danger is "making a moral, instead of medical, judgment about the patient's conduct; defining the problem as disposition rather than care, thereby failing to consider more helpful alternatives."[5] It becomes the social worker's responsibility to circumvent the moral judgments, help the medical staff with a full history, and focus as much as possible on the fact of the patient's illness.

Underrecognition of Psychiatric and Social Problems in Patients with Medical Complaints. Studies have shown that large numbers of patients seen in emergency rooms have significant emotional problems.[6] Sometimes patients cannot articulate their problems. Sometimes the problems are the real reason for the emergency room visit but are not expressed because the patient feels the physician's unwillingness to accept and explore them. In small communities, there may be too much stigma involved in the acknowledgment of psychiatric symptomatology. "Respectable" members of the community may come in with complaints of pain that really reflect drug dependency, which may be appreciated but not dealt with by physicians. In all these, and in other cases as well, doctors tend to use an all-or-nothing approach; patients have either organic/physical or psychiatric disease rather than possibly a combination. Recognition of the emotional problems not only increases the chance of their being treated but also may alleviate other more clearly physical symptoms and the patient's handling of them.[7]

Underrecognition of Medical/Physical Problems in Patients Diagnosed as Having Psychiatric Illness. This is discussed more extensively in the section on organic brain syndrome. It has been stated that about 20% of psychiatric patients have undiagnosed medical illnesses.[8] Many conditions and illnesses, well documented, can present with "psychiatric" symptoms. History is of vital importance here, as well as a kind of instinct that develops over the years, and the social worker can often be responsible for helping to discover the true cause of the symptoms. A thorough medical screening should be part of any emergency room evaluation, even if the physician is sure that the illness is a purely psychiatric one.

The Role of Drugs and Medications. This issue is discussed in the next chapter and briefly in the section on organic brain syndrome. Probably about 50% of patients admitted as psychiatric emergencies are taking psychotropic drugs already.[9] They may be underdosed, overdosed, or in need of change or adjustment. Besides a psychiatric evaluation, there needs to be some contact with the treating person or clinic to get a fuller history and provide continuity. Some patients will be compliant and cooperative; others will abuse medication or take it erratically. Again, the social worker may be the one to ferret out this information. Street drugs, as discussed further on, may be responsible for organic brain syndromes that present as acute psychiatric emergencies. Some patients will complain of pain only to get drugs, and with certain chronic illnesses, it can be difficult to prevent and to interfere with drug dependence. Elderly patients may have extreme reactions to new medication or a change in medications, and a thorough recent medication history is very important. The family or doctor may be better sources than a confused and frightened patient. Along with alcohol, medications/drugs will be responsible for or linked to a large number of psychiatric emergencies and may also represent a substantial proportion of the disposition problems handed to the social worker.

   Chronicity.   In many ways, the most difficult patients are those with chronic psychiatric illness. Chapter 10 discusses the problems of caring for those no longer in custodial institutions, those not appealing to treaters, or those not amenable to treatment. Many emergency rooms have a large number of psychiatric repeaters. However, another group, or at least a subset of that group, do experience frequent crises and need acute treatment. It has been reported that this group, besides having more frequent hospitalizations than other psychiatric patients, tend to be more negativistic and to have greater difficulty establishing rapport.[10] Some elicit intense dislike from staff. Not surprisingly, they often have fewer social supports than other patients. They are described as more hostile, uncooperative, and suspicious than other patients, more impaired, less able to communicate, and more unrealistic in their expectations.[11] They use up an inordinate amount of time, often with poor results. Some of these patients will already have therapists or therapy centers and should be encouraged to return, rather than undermining treatment by seeking out new sources of attention. Others can be referred and on future visits urged to go back to the referral locations. Still others will use the emergency room as their therapist, and in fact, management there may keep them functioning.[12] And yet a final group will go from place to place and may be known to several emergency rooms in town. The social worker may have three different responsibilities in such cases. The first concerns the staff more than the patient: the staff must be helped to deal with their negative feelings about the patient, especially those who are so antagonistic and uncooperative that they elicit very strong emotions. Such behavior may be a learned response on the part of such patients and should be circumvented as much as possible by a calm, professional, concerned approach. The social worker, once aware of the nature of the situation himself or herself, can explain to other staff what is happening and help them modulate their reactions and their behavior. Second, the social worker is likely to be the coordinator of inquiries to and information from other facilities. This information will help in deciding what might work with this patient, what need not be repeated, and what is the most appropriate treatment location.

Third, it is likely to be the social worker who handles disposition when a patient cannot return to family, boarding home, or other setting, who cajoles or argues with a patient who refuses all recommendations, and who arranges whatever follow-up is indicated. All these tasks take immense patience and considerable detachment.

An additional problem with chronic patients is that visits to the emergency room may represent *other* people's distress and not their own. Not all visits are true emergencies. Sometimes a family member, friend, or caretaker just cannot tolerate the patient's behavior any longer; the patient may be quite unwilling to consider any intervention or change. The problem then becomes one of counseling and supporting the caretaker and, if the current system has clearly broken down, seeking another one. The other person's desperation may be so great that even a few days' wait while the social worker explores other possibilities is impossible. Some people will have had experiences with broken promises and will not believe anyone who asks them to hang on a little bit longer. The situation may become a pure disposition problem involving a difficult-to-place patient.

Evaluating and Handling Specific Patient Groups

The Mental Status Exam

The standard method of evaluating the level of impairment in a psychiatric patient is through a mental status exam (MSE). The MSE is a tool which contributes to diagnosis through identification of particular deficits and through the uncovering of impairment not readily apparent in some well-compensated individuals. Every emergency room social worker should be able to do a brief MSE. The best way to learn is through observation and supervision, either in the social work department or department of psychiatry.

A brief MSE will cover the following areas:

- *appearance and motor behavior:* neatness or dishevelment; agitation; psychomotor retardation; grimacing; posturing; tenseness; darting glances;
- *speech and thought processes*: loosening of associations; cognitive slippage; pressure of speech; flight of ideas; blocking;

- *mood and affect:* affect—appropriate or inappropriate; flat; labile; mood—anxious, sad; angry; euphoric; neutral;
- *content of communications:* hallucinations; delusions; ideas of reference; phobias; obsessions, areas of pre-occupation;
- *cognition:* oriented ×3 (time, place, person); recent and remote memory.

Some of the terms above may be unfamiliar to the social worker and should become part of the working vocabulary. The MSE can be very important, such as when the social worker screens all patients before referral to a psychiatrist, when the psychiatrist is on call and not immediately available, or when there is some question about the functioning of a particular patient. Even where the psychiatrist is in charge of evaluation and diagnosis, the social worker may want to do a brief, informal MSE if he or she sees the patient first in order to have as much information as possible for planning. The nature of the illness will have considerable impact on both short- and long-term plans.

The illnesses most commonly seen in true psychiatric emergencies are schizophrenia, major affective disorders, and organic brain syndrome. Although other conditions occur frequently, these illnesses in their acute phases need immediate attention. It is advisable that the social worker become acquainted with psychiatric diagnosis and terminology. This section will describe the conditions briefly but is merely an introduction, not a substitute for the learning that is necessary for adequate familiarity.[13]

Schizophrenia

Schizophrenia is a serious mental disorder involving significant and varied changes in mood, thinking, and behavior. Chronic schizophrenia results in severe personality disintegration and permanently impaired functioning that can be seen in some of the "burned-out" patients described in Chapter 10. A patient in an acute phase will show at least some of the following: bizarre delusions or delusions that interfere with thinking or behavior; hallucinations; incoherent or illogical thinking; flat or inappropriate affect; grossly disorganized or unusual behavior. In addition, there will be a noticeable deterioration in functioning, in terms of work, relationships, and self-care. Schizophrenia in its acute phase is usually treated with medications and hospitalization. Continued follow-up and family support are crucial in maintaining the patient's improved status, and the social worker will play a substantial role in arranging these.

In evaluating schizophrenia, it is useful to find out whether the particular episode is the first one or not. If not, there may be well-established pathways to help already available.[14] In any evaluation it is important to find out whether treatment relationships already exist. If so, the goal will be to strengthen them, not to disconnect the patient and send him or her elsewhere. One example of this occurs when a patient, even one with a less serious condition, seeks help in an emergency department during a "therapy crisis."[15] Perhaps there has been a painful breakthrough in therapy, or the therapist is away, or the patient is angry or upset for any one of a hundred reasons. It is not always easy to learn whether the patient is in therapy, but the question should always be asked. If so, the patient should be supported and encouraged but also urged to return to his or her therapist to work out the conflict. Only if the patient refuses or if the evaluating psychiatrist feels that the treatment has not been adequate is it appropriate to make a new referral.

Major Affective Disorders: Manic Episode

A manic episode occurs in a person experiencing a predominantly "elevated, expansive, irritable mood" which may exist alone or become alternatively or intermittently depressed. Symptoms may include increased activity; increased talking or pressure to talk; flight of ideas or the feeling that thoughts are racing; inflated self-esteem, sometimes to a delusional level; decreased need for sleep; distractibility; and unwise and uncontrolled activities such as spending sprees. The physical, financial, and relationship dangers of a person in a manic phase (that is, a person who "cannot stop") are such that treatment must be instituted immediately. Again, medication and hospitalization are the treatments of choice. Some patients experience bipolar illness, episodes of both mania and depression throughout their lives.

Major Affective Disorders: Depressive Episode

This condition is characterized by a persistently dysphoric mood, loss of pleasure and interest in all or most pastimes and activities. Anxiety and anger may also be present. Symptoms may include marked changes in weight and appetite; sleep disturbances (especially early morning awakening); agitation or physical retardation; loss of energy and feelings of fatigue; feelings of guilt, worthlessness, self-reproach; impairment in ability to concentrate; recurrent thoughts of death or suicide. Here, too, the potential hazards, including suicide (discussed in the next section), require immediate treatment which may take several forms and may be involuntary.

The Suicidal or Potentially Suicidal Patient

Suicide is no small matter in the United States: in 1980 there were about 400,000 attempts and 28,000 completed suicides.[16] Suicidal or potentially suicidal patients often elicit considerable anxiety in emergency room staff. This group includes those brought to the emergency department for serious suicide attempts, those who threaten or contemplate suicide in a way that is not merely manipulative, and those whose depression is so severe that suicide becomes a possibility. While these patients are best dealt with by psychiatrists, the social worker should also be involved with them and their families and can serve a number of very useful functions.

The social worker can first help family and staff understand the powerful and desperate feelings behind much suicidal behavior, which may occur "as an expression of intense feelings when other forms of expression have failed."[17] The family or other involved people will need immediate help in understanding the nature of these feelings and in dealing with their own feelings of guilt, anger, and despair. They should be allowed some privacy and not be kept sitting in the waiting room. The social worker or the psychiatrist, depending on time available or on allocation of roles, needs to let them know of the patient's condition, whether or not there was indeed a suicide attempt, and what the recommendations are for treatment. The family may be able to say whether these recommendations are feasible. They also may need recommendations for themselves in dealing with the patient. When there has been a completed suicide, the family may need a great deal of help and should be allowed to stay as long as necessary, calling whomever they wish for assistance (see Chapter 5). Although a physician will need to speak with them to verify the fact of death and answer questions, the social worker can take on the major supportive and counseling role. Besides the feelings already expressed, the families of some very difficult patients may be experiencing relief which increases their distress and which they cannot acknowledge. The sensitive social worker can be aware of this and deal with it as appropriate in this encounter. The family may also need help with concrete issues, such as requirements of the medical examiner, burial, and notification of various people. In addition, they should be referred for follow-up to help them deal with their own feelings and changed family pattern. There may be some families which the social worker decides to follow-up by phone for a few weeks. There are also self-help groups for families who do not want a more formal kind of follow-up.

Not all suicidal patients are immediately identifiable, and the social worker, as well as the rest of the staff, should be aware of high-risk groups: older white men; depressed and/or schizophrenic patients (often in their twenties); substance abusers; psychiatric patients with many emergency room visits; professionals; the unemployed; the divorced and widowed; and those with a recent major loss. Obviously, the more factors present, the greater the risk. In addition, inner-city blacks and younger people show a higher incidence of suicide in recent years.[18] While not everyone who fits into these categories will be suicidal, it is important to keep them in mind and occasionally to remind other staff that a particular patient is in a high-risk group. The other major factor is previous suicide attempts; as many as 60% of completed suicides have been preceded by earlier attempts.[19] In a busy emergency room without a psychiatrist immediately available, it may be the social worker who elicits information about previous suicide attempts from either the patient or the family. In these settings, the social worker may take the history and be responsible not only for the evaluation but for communicating the urgency of the situation to other staff. Some social work departments have developed criteria for evaluating whether a patient is suicidal; important questions, for instance, involve the presence of the following: past attempts (chronic or acute, that is, history of repeated suicide attempts and gestures, or of suicide attempts only in response to especially stressful situations); means now available and their lethal nature; specific plans about suicide; recent loss as the patient would define it; resources and supports available to the patient; other people who are concerned and willing to help; previous psychiatric hospitalizations; or a history of alcohol. In addition, the patient's affect and ability to communicate are significant in assessing the total picture.[20]

Many of the suicidal patients who come into emergency rooms are difficult to deal with and unappealing; it is always tempting to evaluate them in a perfunctory manner and send them out. This is one group of patients, however, who must be treated with great care. Even though they contribute to their own rejection and abandonment by others, social workers must try not to become involved in this vicious circle and to try to keep others out of it. The most unlikable patients may need the most help and may not want to take it; however, if they are actively suicidal, the decision is no longer theirs. If the crisis is over, they must still be treated with as much kindness and tolerance as humanly possible, without allowing excessive manipulation on their part.

Other patients with severe depression may be rejected because of rapid and uninformed judgments by medical staff. The following example illustrates such a case and successful efforts by social workers to get the patient into treatment:

Case Study

Ms. O was brought in by police who found her crying on the sidewalk. She was a disheveled woman in her 30s who communicated minimally and appeared extremely depressed. The psychiatric resident concluded that because of certain family happenings the patient was suffering from a reactive depression, in addition to a character disorder, and would not be an appropriate candidate for inpatient care. On the basis of her appearance and lack of cooperation, he concluded that she was primarily a "street person" and should be discharged.

The social worker felt uncomfortable with the proposed disposition and consulted a supervisor with considerable clinical psychiatric experience. In the meantime, the worker had slowly obtained additional information from the patient and was able to talk with people who knew her. It turned out that the patient had a stable home life, two school-aged children, and a boyfriend who was very much concerned and described her condition as very different from anything he had ever seen before.

The patient refused to see or talk with her boyfriend, children, or best friend, who offered her a place to stay. She was adamant about not returning home, stating repeatedly that she was of no use to anyone, that no one cared about her, and that she had no place to go. The supervisor felt that she was seriously depressed and should be hospitalized immediately. She gently suggested to the resident that, in view of the additional information obtained (some of which contradicted his history), the initial impression might have been misleading. He persisted in his opinion that she was suffering primarily from a character disorder and should be discharged.

Shortly after, the patient roused herself to say that she had to call in sick to work, and it was discovered that she had a very responsible job in a bank (and undoubtedly good insurance coverage). A picture emerged of a woman with apparently no psychiatric history, warm and stable relationships, and a good employment history, who was in the midst of an acute depression. The social workers decided that one way or another she had to be hospitalized. They consulted a colleague on the inpatient psychiatric floor who told them that his unit was not accepting admissions but that he would speak with the chief resident. The chief resident reported that he knew the psychiatrist who was doing evaluations at the local crisis center and would give him a call. The patient agreed to go there and was sent in an ambulance, with a note to the evaluating physician. She was admitted immediately and began treatment.

In this case, without the intervention of concerned and persistent social workers, Ms. O would have been discharged and probably escorted out as an "undesirable." It is likely that she would have sustained harm, if not self-inflicted, then as a victim while on the streets. In addition, her job would have been threatened and her condition might have deteriorated much more before she obtained the necessary medical attention.

Another area where family or close friends may need help is in trying to understand the reason or meaning for a suicide attempt. Speculating with the family on what the patient may have been feeling can bring out significant information and can contribute to the development of useful approaches and interventions. For instance, dependent people who have suffered a change in a relationship or the loss of an important person may fear abandonment and the terrifying prospect of being alone. Those who measure their self-worth by external successes may be devastated by perceived failures. Some may feel totally cut off from others and unable to communicate or to cope. Some may feel angry and desirous of hurting others by killing themselves. Adolescents do not always understand death very well and may see it as a peaceful, nurturing state much to be desired. And some patients are so severely depressed that their unrelenting feelings of hopelessness drive them to suicide.[21]

Obviously, motivations are often mixed and sometimes not very clear at all. A skilled social worker can elicit ideas from family members and assuage their guilt by helping them to plan realistically for the short-term future. Those who have reached "the end of their rope" need additional support and help in making plans.

Follow-up is sometimes inadequate for those who are no longer actively suicidal. Some will be hospitalized and will agree to remain in the hospital. Others will be sent home with follow-up arrangements that may or may not be appropriate. Studies have shown that between 25% and 40% of this group do not go for follow-up.[22] Other research shows a much higher incidence of completed suicides for psychiatric emergency room patients than for the general population.[23] Obviously, follow-up must be carefully arranged and suitable to the patient's needs and capacities. Referral should ideally be negotiated with the patient during the course of the interview, with a specific appointment made with a specific person, involving only a short wait until the appointment. Cooperation from family and friends should also be enlisted, wherever possible. They should understand that certain patients are best given small supplies of medications and need to be seen frequently for further prescriptions.

The Violent Patient

Violent patients are usually brought to emergency rooms against their will and can create serious management problems in units not ready to handle them. While patients who present an immediate danger to others can often be hospitalized involuntarily for a short time, initial attempts to evaluate them can lead to harm to staff and hospital property if not competently done. The social worker, as part of the team responsible for evaluation, management, and disposition, should be as knowledgeable as possible about this group. This section does not deal with those patients who are disruptive and aggressive but not psychiatrically disturbed. They may not be able to be treated and may have to be ejected by security or turned over to police.

Certain groups of patients appear to have a greater propensity to dangerousness than others, and a full and complete history, from the family as well as the patient, may contribute much to the assessment. Those who have been so identified include the intoxicated, both by drugs and alcohol; those experiencing withdrawal from either, especially when efforts in the emergency department to obtain new supplies have failed (patients in DTs can be extremely assaultive); those with organic brain syndrome and who are acutely delirious; the acutely psychotic, especially manic, who may swing from "good" to violent behavior; paranoid characters; borderline personalities; and anti-social personalities, especially in withdrawal.[24] Past history is also important, particularly previous or current arrests, previous violent incidents resulting in serious harm to someone else, and family history of violence.[25] Those with negative histories are less likely to be violent, but positive histories should alert the staff to the possibilities of assaultive or violent behavior. Patients who are able to be interviewed should be asked directly about arrests and injuries to others. Those identified as potentially dangerous should be treated with great caution but firm control.

While some patients are brought in already excited and violent, others become so during the course of the interview. If there is any question about the patient's ability to control him/herself, he or she should be seen as soon as possible, without any waiting. He or she should also be allowed to seat him/herself, that is, as close to or as far away from the interviewer as possible. The patient who can maintain his or her own distance is likely to feel less boxed in and threatened. Ideally, the interviewer should be between the patient and the door, which should be left open. The room chosen for the interview should be one that affords privacy but is visible to others in the unit, so that an interviewer's signal will bring someone running.

The patient should not be left alone or close to other noisy, disturbed, or badly injured patients. Offering food, drink, or the opportunity to use restrooms shows interest in the patient and may help him or her relax. It is important to get the patient to try to relax, and talking softly, asking how he or she needs help, giving support, and expressing interest can all contribute.[26]

During the interview, certain behavioral clues may signify danger. Increased tension is likely to precede violent behavior and may be seen in posture (for instance, gripping the chair, clenching the hands, "combat posture"); loud and strident speech and a series of accusations; threats, which should always be taken seriously; descriptions of violent fantasies and dreams; and increased motor activity.[27] A high-risk patient who cannot sit still represents an emergency and a need for immediate intervention.[28]

Too much intervention can cause as much harm as too little. Verbal intervention should be effective in controlling most aggressive behavior. The interviewer has to make clear to the patient that he or she and the emergency room staff will maintain control and will help the patient maintain control as well. The importance of talking cannot be overstated. One writer suggests a statement such as the following: "Look, let's set some ground rules right now. You want to tell me how angry you feel. You can tell me. But you sit down and talk about it. I'm not here to be intimidated, that's not my function."[29] Others say very bluntly that "I'm going to stop you from losing control."[30] Those who are easily intimidated should avoid taking the interview or evaluating role in these situations. Showing fear can undermine a patient's control. If there is no choice, a worker who is afraid of the patient can ask family, police, or hospital security to remain.

Besides emphasizing the need for and expectation of control, there are other ways of defusing a potentially violent encounter. The social worker or other interviewer should be ready to admit fault, such as insensitivity or saying the wrong thing. He or she must emphasize to the patient that the anger is acceptable and that alternate ways of expressing it are available and can be taught. The issue of control is always present, whether implicit or explicit. Encouraging verbalization is always critical.

When verbal management does not work, it is more sensible to restrain a patient than to risk assault and destruction. A pre-existing code that summons security allows them to appear without warning the patient and thus inciting him. Security should stand by so that the patient can see them and decide not to act. Only if the sight of them does not calm him down should physical restraint be used.

An emergency room that sees violent patients with any kind of regularity should have a protocol for dealing with them. Any program for physical restraint should be well rehearsed, with staff members taking consistent and manageable parts. The goal of an effort to subdue a patient physically is safety for everyone, and that is best assured by planning ahead.[31]

Violent patients are generally hospitalized and/or committed briefly. When they are transferred to another hospital, the social worker may be in charge of making the transportation arrangements and must make sure that they are adequately safe and secure, both for the patient, the driver, and the person accompanying the patient. The social worker may also have to deal with puzzled and bewildered family, to help them come to terms with the behavior and plan for the future.

"Dangerousness" is not easy to predict, even in high-risk patients, and psychiatric projections of highly aggressive behavior are usually short-term ones, involving the immediate future. Sometimes there is disagreement among staff about certain patients, and the social worker needs to be vocal and assertive if he or she feels that an acutely assaultive patient is being discharged. In this kind of case, it is better to be too conservative. Those who can be sent out need the same kind of well-arranged and coordinated follow-up as described in the section on suicidal patients. Family or close friends also need to be involved in medication schedules and should know whom to call if the patient becomes uncooperative.

Organic Brain Syndrome (OBS)

Organic brain syndrome is one of the more complex, misleading, and sometime dangerous constellations of symptoms seen in the emergency room because of the high incidence of misdiagnosis. It is a disorder of orientation, memory, intellect, judgment, and affect and is the leading cause of confusional states leading to hospitalization.[32] It includes altered states of consciousness, usually lethargy or somnolence but sometimes excitement, and confused thinking with generally abnormal behavior.[33] Sometimes these behaviors include agitation, belligerence, and psychosis and bizarre actions, and the patient is immediately labeled a psychiatric patient and referred without adequate evaluation.[34] Symptoms can vary in individual patients to such an extent that the diagnosis may go unrecognized. Acute OBS, however, (as opposed to chronic, which is longstanding) can result from a serious medical condition that may be life-threatening without treatment. In addition, treatment of the medical problem may reverse the OBS. Again the major problem here is hasty and inadequate evaluation leading to premature and erroneous diagnosis. As the American Psychiatric Association has stated,

> . . . all behavioral emergencies should be viewed as having an underlying organic basis until proven otherwise and should be considered as potential threats to the patients themselves as well as to others, including the staff. Until the physician determines otherwise, the patient should be prevented from leaving the area.[35]

While this statement has broader application than OBS, it is particularly relevant here. A nasty, belligerent, confused patient from the street may have OBS (from drugs) yet may be thrown out by an impatient staff; an elderly person with no past psy-

chiatric history and acute anemia or acute renal failure may be
shuttled off prematurely to a psychiatric floor. The following is
an example of hasty conclusions that could have cost a patient's
life.

Case Study

P, a young college student, was brought into the emergency room
by police, kicking and struggling. Police said they had found him
lying on the sidewalk a few blocks away. He was belligerent,
uncooperative, and confused, and the busy and tired physician in
charge concluded that he had no medical problem and consequently ordered him out of the emergency room. The social worker,
however, knew many of the students on campus, was familiar with
this young man, and was sure that something organic must be
underlying such unusual behavior. The worker, who had an excellent relationship with the physician, expressed his concerns in
the strongest terms and pleaded for further evaluation, even without the patient's cooperation. A more aggressive evaluation, mostly
against the patient's will, revealed a head injury that could have
had serious consequences. The patient had been mugged and left
for dead. His behavior was organically determined and of course
reversed by medical treatment. The alertness and assertiveness of
the social worker and the physician's willingness to listen to others
may have saved this patient.

This is only one example of the social worker's potential
usefulness in helping to identify organic brain syndrome. The
worker should be familiar with the condition, or more accurately,
the constellation of symptoms, and should himself or herself be
able to do basic screening. Hospitals in urban areas with large
concentrations of both elderly and substance abusers tend to see
a greater incidence of OBS and should develop protocols for
evaluation, diagnosis, and treatment. In one major urban hospital,
for instance, a psychiatric nurse screens for OBS through use of
the following four categories:[36]

1. *Disorientation:* This is demonstrated by the patient's
    inability to state where he or she is and what the time
    and date are. This may be an early indicator of OBS and
    is usually progressive. The patient should be able to
    identify day, within two days; month; year; place; city.
    Two or more errors means a positive finding in this
    category.

2. *Clouding of Consciousness:* This is basically a loss of awareness and/or inability to sustain attention. These are often misinterpreted as lack of cooperation or simple sleepiness. In some cases, the patient may be stuporous.

3. *Age of More than 40 without Previous Psychiatric History:* When family bring in a patient and explain with great concern that all of a sudden the patient stopped acting like himself or herself or just "flipped" out, the social worker, nurse, and physician should take this communication very seriously.

4. *Abnormal Vital Signs:* Blood pressure, pulse, temperature, and respiration outside normal limits.

This protocol provides for a brief mental status exam when the patient meets one of the screening criteria. With a finding of cognitive impairment (such things as loss of recent memory, loss of recall, and other elements), a presumptive diagnosis of OBS is made and appropriate physical testing undertaken.

OBS can appear in nearly all segments of the population but is particularly common in substance abusers, particularly black males, and in the elderly. Sometimes the organic condition precipitating the behavior is not immediately recognizable until it progresses to a point where the patient's life is in serious danger. Iron-deficiency anemia, renal failure, congestive heart failure, and drug intoxication from prescription or over-the-counter drugs are only a few of the many possible causes.[37] The social worker must contribute as much as possible to a thorough history of the patient's previous medical condition and treatment, health and eating habits, and behavioral changes over the last few days. When the patient is not elderly, the worker must immediately think of alcohol or illicit street drugs, and as in the case example, must make sure that prejudice and sometimes justified dislike do not interfere with evaluation.

This discussion has dealt primarily with acute organic brain syndrome, which is due to an organic condition or injury needing immediate treatment. Acute organic brain syndrome is mostly reversible; that is, the patient returns to his previous level of functioning. In modern psychiatric parlance, it is known as *delirium.* In contrast, *dementia,* or chronic organic brain syndrome, tends to involve more lasting changes. Although an organic causative factor or group of factors may be present, it may also be chronic and have been treated or ignored for a long time. An important differentiating factor is that in dementia there is no clouding of consciousness. There are, however, impairments of cognition, judgment, and other mental and intellectual functions.[38] Dementia may occur as part of the aging process in some people, in schizophrenics, in long-term alcoholics, and in others. These groups will generally not receive acute medical care and will become disposition problems for the social worker. A particularly dangerous set of circumstances arises when a demented person or a person with a previous psychiatric illness develops an acute organic brain syndrome, as from acute renal failure. The risk of premature categorization and judgment that completely ignores the acute organic brain syndrome and thus the critical underlying condition is a very high one. Again, the social worker should take upon himself or herself a substantial part of the evaluation with particular attention to past history and recent changes.

Other Psychiatric Conditions in the Elderly

Elderly patients brought in as psychiatric emergencies are often people with no previous history of emotional disturbance. They are more likely to express their complaints in somatic terms than are younger patients and may not seek help until their symptoms are well advanced.[39] As in the previous section, the social worker may elicit a history of "sudden changes in relatively stable people."[40] The patient, experiencing a state of confusion and intellectual/cognitive deficit, may also be faced with a psychiatric label and staff attitudes much less supportive than are given to a patient with a readily identifiable acute medical condition.[41] This first encounter with psychiatric medicine may be frightening and aversive. The social worker can provide support and reassurance to both the patient and family and encourage other staff to do so as well.

While a substantial percentage of elderly patients will have organic brain syndrome, other conditions may also occur. There is a high incidence of affective disorders in the elderly, for instance, that may go unrecognized. When somaticization occurs —that is, expression of the depressive affect in physical complaints—physicians may begin a battery of unnecessary and possibly risky diagnostic tests without recognizing the underlying cause. Depression should generally be included in the differential diagnosis of elderly coming in without acute, life-threatening physical emergencies. Depressed patients who do not need hospitalization may need help with treatment recommendations, home care, community supports, education of family, and the development of other resources.

It is also important to remember that elderly people may have fewer emotional resources and may respond dramatically to losses and to stresses such as new illnesses, medication adjustment, environmental changes, and even increased poverty. Catastrophic illness in a well-functioning elderly person may lead to psychiatric illness. A heart attack, for instance, may lead to depression in a formerly active, independent person. Similarly, a person with previously compensated psychiatric illness may have an exacerbation as a result of minor physical problems.[42] It is likely to be the social worker who, before the patient is relegated to the ranks of the psychiatrically disabled, remembers to assess his or her nutritional status and whether there is heat in the home. A referral to a program such as a meals-on-wheels program, if it is available, may be as helpful as medication and psychiatric follow-up. Whatever the initial or final diagnosis, however, it is important to remember (and perhaps important for the social worker to remind other staff of this) the high incidence of undiagnosed medical issues in older psychiatric patients and the many ways in which medical conditions can be masked by resulting psychiatric symptoms.[43] The following is a case example of a not-unusual situation.

Case Study

Mr. Q, aged 67, was brought into the emergency room by a concerned family who described him as becoming increasingly depressed over the last few weeks. They speculated that the recent death of a close relative might have precipitated the depression. He was lethargic and communicated very little except that he felt tired. Evaluation led to a diagnosis of depression, and he was about to be admitted to the psychiatric floor. The social worker, however, in taking a history from his daughter, learned that Mr. Q had been on thyroid medication for much of his life but had not taken any for some time. She asked the physician cautiously whether that information might be relevant. Mr. Q was admitted, thyroid function tests were done immediately, and he was found to be suffering from severe hypothyroidism. Treatment was begun quickly, and the depression cleared up.

Psychiatric Emergencies in Children

Psychiatric emergencies in children are situations in which the life of the child or someone else is in danger or the child is at high risk for a catastrophic trauma.[44] The growing incidence of suicide and suicide attemtps in young children and adolescents makes the recognition and treatment of severe emotional stress more imperative than ever before. The social worker plays a major role in the assessment of child psychiatric disturbance because of the importance of the history. Such things as suicidal behavior in a parent or relative that the child may be mimicking;[45] previous accidental (or otherwise) injuries; history of severe trauma or multiple hospital stays; chronic physical illness; a series of separations, losses, or deprivations; and physical or emotional abuse all put a child more at risk.[46] The social worker must be gentle and supportive even with uncommunicable or uncooperative parents and elicit all the relevant history possible. In addition, he or she can learn a great deal from observing the family interactions. If a psychiatrist is there, he or she will want to examine the child, as will an attending physician, but the social worker will also have impressions to share, particularly if the child is in a very withdrawn or excited state.

One physician has categorized psychiatric emergencies in children as follows:[47]

1. Suicidal, self-destructive, extremely depressive behavior, including extreme withdrawal, suicidal thoughts, self-harm;
2. harmful and destructive behavior to others, including loss of control, threats, fire-setting, serious antisocial behavior (with 75% of child psychiatric emergencies in this study in these categories);
3. abuse and neglect;
4. phobic and extremely anxious behavior, including school refusal;
5. psychotic behavior;
6. runaways, who are at high risk for emotional disturbance, as well as external harm;
7. medical-psychiatric emergencies, such as severe anorexia or noncompliance with critical medical regimens (it is not uncommon for emergency rooms to see diabetic adolescents repeatedly brought in comatose because of refusal to take insulin);

8. drug, alcohol, and other substance abuse;
9. other, such as family crisis.

In all these situations, the family will need a tremendous amount of help, absorbing the shock if there have been sudden developments, trying to understand the situation, dealing with their guilt, and figuring out how to interact with their child during the immediate crisis. The social worker may also suggest long-term follow-up and the need for the family's cooperation so that the idea is not an unfamiliar one at discharge. In fact, the social worker's initial assessment and description of the family's behavior at the time of crisis will be extremely helpful to the treating person as well as whoever provides follow-up. When the social worker feels that dangers in the home need to be assessed more thoroughly and monitored, such as possible abuse, alcoholism, mental illness in a relative, or severe and unremitting stress, questions need to be raised as questions, not hypotheses, and direction given to the treating person for more exploration, to avoid treatment in a "vacuum" which will then return the child to the same intolerable situation.

Commitment

Patients determined to be severely mentally ill and dangerous to themselves or others or so incapable of self-care that they are at high risk are the groups usually appropriate for commitment. State laws vary considerably in specific procedures and criteria for commitment, but in nearly every location it is possible to commit someone on an emergency basis for a short period of time, usually a matter of days. The rationale behind such a system is that, in the opinion of those who have observed the patient, generally including someone trained to make these assessments, the immediate danger to the patient outweighs any interference with his or her rights. After the initial stay, a hearing is necessary to decide whether the patient must continue to remain in the hospital. It is these hearings that make many physicians reluctant to recommend an emergency commitment at all. They are unwilling to take the risk of being called to testify at a later hearing, often with good reason because of the time involved. In addition, while some mental health systems work smoothly, others are cumbersome, frustrating, and often not helpful to patients.

When it becomes clear, however, that a patient is in danger or is a danger to others, commitment must become a possibility. The social worker, along with the rest of the team, needs to be thoroughly familiar with the applicable state law and how it is interpreted locally. For instance, there is a considerable difference between an overt act and a threat and a threat supported by some kind of activity. The first might be taking an overdose; the second, threatening to do so; and the third, threatening but also hoarding pills. Which of these is adequate grounds for commitment when there is a real belief in suicidal potential is a critical factor in planning for the patient. Whether the law allows commitment to prevent further debilitation, such as in a manic patient who is exhausting himself or herself physically, spending the family's money, and ruining close relationships, is also an aspect to be explored. In many locations, interpretation of the law is as important as the letter of the law.

Commitment, however, is never the first issue to be considered. First of all, the psychiatrist involved must decide whether the patient needs hospitalization. Only then does the question of whether the hospitalization is to be voluntary or involuntary arise.[48] A voluntary admission is almost always preferable. A sympathetic and patient social worker may be able to help a patient accept voluntary admission rather than go through the stressful and often degrading process of an involuntary commitment—especially if the intent of the emergency room staff to provide for hospitalization, one way or another, has been clearly communicated. The social worker will help to evaluate the context in which the patient has been functioning—family support, family exhaustion, past experiences, living situation—which contributes to the decision about commitment. The social worker may be the contact person with the local office of mental health and may be responsible for certain routine aspects of the commitment. If he or she has actually witnessed the behavior that suggests danger, he or she may be expected to testify at a later hearing. In the meantime, once an emergency commitment is arranged, the social worker may be responsible for transportation to the accepting facility. If police or municipal ambulance do not provide such service, the social worker will have to find alternatives. Anyone who has been committed cannot be transported alone, so that arrangements such as taxicabs are not appropriate unless the patient is not a management problem and can be accompanied by a responsible person. Otherwise, an ambulance with a trained attendant is probably the most suitable mode.

Notes

1. Judith Healy, "ERs and Psychosocial Services," *Health and Social Work*, 6 (February 1981): 36–43.

2. Ibid.

3. Gerald W. Grumet and David L. Trachtman, "Psychiatric Social Workers in the Emergency Department," *Health and Social Work*, 1 (August 1976): 113–131.

4. See Andrew E. Slaby, "Emergency Psychiatry in the General Hospital: Staffing, Training, and Leadership Issues," *General Hospital Psychiatry*, 3 (1981): 306–309.

5. Charles Shagass, "The Medical Model in Psychiatry," *Comprehensive Psychiatry*, 16 (September–October 1975): 411.

6. Peggy H. Jacobsen and Robert J. Howell, "Psychiatric Problems in Emergency Rooms," *Health and Social Work*, 3 (May 1978): Grumet and Trachtman, "Psychiatric Social Workers."

7. Troy L. Thompson, Alan Stoudemire, Wayne Mitchell, and Richard Grant, "Underrecognition of Patients' Psychosocial Distress in a University Hospital Medical Clinic," *American Journal of Psychiatry*, 140 (February 1983): 158–161.

8. Slaby, "Emergency Psychiatry." See also David A. Gross, "Medical Origins of Psychiatric Emergencies: The Systems Approach," *International Journal of Psychiatry Medicine*, 11 (1981–82): 1–24. This paper provides an extensive listing of medical conditions presenting with psychiatric symptoms.

9. Stephen M. Soreff, "Psychiatric Emergencies: Principles and Practice," *Drug Therapy*, 13 (April 1983): 73–86.

10. Ellen Bassuk and Samuel Gerson, "Chronic Crisis Patients: A Discrete Clinical Group," *American Journal of Psychiatry*, 137 (December 1980): 1513–1517.

11. Ibid.

12. Ibid.

13. Schizophrenia, major affective disorders, and other psychiatric illnesses are defined and described in the *Diagnostic and Statistical Manual of Mental Disorders III (DSM-III)*, 3rd ed. (Washington, DC: American Psychiatric Association, 1980).

14. David A. Soskis, "Behavioral First Aid" (teaching materials for Behavioral Science Course at Temple University Medical School, 1979–81).

15. Andrew E. Skodol, Frederic Kass, and Edward Charles, "Crisis in Psychotherapy: Principles of Emergency Consultation and Intervention," *American Journal of Orthopsychiatry*, 49 (October 1979): 585–597.

16. Herbert Brown, "Recognizing and Helping Others Who May be

Suicidal," *Harvard Medical School Health Letter*, 6:12 (October 1981): 3.

17. Donna C. Aguilera and Janice M. Messick, "Situational Crises," in *Crisis Intervention: Theory and Methodology*, (St. Louis: C.V. Mosby Co., 1978).

18. *Harvard Medical School Health Letter*; James R. Hillard, Dietolf Ramm, William W. K. Zung, and Jacqueline M. Holland, "Suicide in a Psychiatric Emergency Room Population," *American Journal of Psychiatry*, 140 (April 1983): 459–462.

19. *Harvard Medical School Health Letter.*

20. Edith Groner, "Delivery of Clinical Social Work Services in the Emergency Room: A Description of an Existing Program," *Social Work in Health Care*, 4 (Fall 1978): 19–29.

21. Aguilera and Messick, "Situational Crisis"; *Harvard Medical School Health Letter.*

22. David J. Knesper, "A Study of Referral Failures for Potentially Suicidal Patients: A Method of Medical Care Evaluation," *Hospital and Community Psychiatry*, 33 (January 1982): 49–52.

23. Hillard *et al.*, "Suicide."

24. William R. Dubin, "Evaluating and Managing the Violent Patient," *Annals of Emergency Medicine*, 10 (September 1981): 481–484.

25. Pang L. Man, "Are 'Dangerous' Patients Dangerous?" *Legal Aspects of Medical Practice*, (March 1979): 46–48.

26. Dubin, "Evaluating and Managing"; Soreff, "Psychiatric Emergencies."

27. Dubin, "Evaluating and Managing"; Bruce L. Danto, "Homicidal Psychiatric Patients: Techniques of Survival," Roche Report: *Frontiers of Psychiatry* (December 1982).

28. Dubin, "Evaluating and Managing."

29. Danto, "Homicidal Psychiatric Patients."

30. Dubin, "Evaluating and Managing."

31. See John R. Lion, "Acute Intervention in the E.R," in *Evaluation and Management of the Violent Patient* (Springfield, Ill.: Charles C Thomas, 1972).

32. Frank R. Purdie, Benjamin Honigman, and Peter Rosen, "Acute Organic Brain Syndrome: A Review of 100 Cases," *Annals of Emergency Medicine*, 10 (September 1981): 455–461.

33. Ibid.

34. William R. Dubin, Kenneth J. Weiss, and Joseph Z. Zeccardi, "Organic Brain Syndrome; the Psychiatric Imposter," *Journal of the American Medical Association*, 249 (January 7, 1983): 60–62; Howard M. Waxman, Erwin A. Carner, William Dubin, and Melissa Klein, "Geriatric Psychiatry in the E.D.: Characteristics of Geriatric and Non-

geriatric Admissions," *Journal of the American Geriatrics Society*, 30 (1982): 427–432.

35. "Need for Psychiatrists in Hospital ERs Increasing," *Psychiatric News* (May 21, 1982): 6.

36. Dubin *et al.*, *op. cit.*

37. Ibid.; *Purdie et al.*, "Acute Organic Brain Syndrome."

38. See *DSM III*.

39. Ellen L. Bassuk, Sarah Minden, and Robert Apsler, "Geriatric Emergencies: Psychiatric or Medical?" *American Journal of Psychiatry*, 140 (May 1983): 539–542.

40. Waxman, *et al.*, "Geriatric Psychiatry."

41. Bassuk *et al.* feel that this is not necessarily so and that this group of patients may elicit considerable positive feeling.

42. Charles H. Weingarten, Lois G. Rosoff, Susan V. Eisen, and Mollie C. Grob, "Medical Care in a Geriatric Psychiatry Unit: Impact on Psychiatric Outcome," *Journal of the American Geriatrics Society*, 30 (December 1982): 738–743.

43. Ibid.

44. Mohammed Shafii, Russell Whittinghill, and Mark H. Healy, "The Pediatric-psychiatric Model for Emergencies in Child Psychiatry: A Study of 994 Cases," *American Journal of Psychiatry*, 136 (December 1979): 1600–1601.

45. Stephen P. Herman and John E. Schwalter, "Depression, Suicide and the Young Child," *Emergency Medicine*, 13 (September 30, 1981): 61–62, 67–68.

46. Ibid.

47. Shafii *et al.*, "The Pediatric-psychiatric Model."

48. Alan Stone, "Recent Mental Health Litigation: A Critical Perspective," *American Journal of Psychiatry*, 134 (March 1977): 273–279.

For an excellent discussion of collaboration between social workers and residents in a psychiatric emergency setting, see Kermit B. Nash, "Social Work in a University Hospital," *Archives of General Psychiatry* 22 (April 1970): 332–337.

9 Alcohol and Drug Abuse

The social worker in the emergency room sees the results of alcohol and drug abuse every day. Although patterns of use vary among individuals and generalizations should be made with care, there are several important points to bear in mind. First, abuse and physical dependence are not necessarily the same. For instance, a man may stop by a bar every payday and drink with his friends until he is heavily intoxicated. That is alcohol abuse and not alcoholism. He could do it three times a week, and it would still be abuse *as long as he retained control over the drinking*. Similar, although not the same, parallels can be made with drug abuse and drug dependence. Consequently, it is important not to jump to premature conclusions in the diagnosis of drug and alcohol abusers. *Abuse* refers to excessive use, beyond what is healthy or has been prescribed; *dependence* refers to a craving, physical or psychological, which interferes with the individual's control over taking or not taking a particular substance or group of substances.

Although drug and alcohol abuse are discussed separately in this chapter, they do not necessarily exist separately. Data from federal government studies reveal that 23%—perhaps the biggest single group—of all drug abuse episodes in one recent National Institute on Drug Abuse's sample are combined with alcohol.[1] Drug Abuse Warning Network (DAWN) studies funded by this agency sample large urban hospitals, so that the figures do not necessarily mean that alcohol and drug use are characteristic of the same population. Although most alcohol abusers will not be using drugs, most polydrug users (those who use many drugs—

or any drug) will at some time abuse alcohol.[2] The risks and the problems are both much greater with the combination, and treatment is much more complicated.

Finally, social workers and other ER personnel need to be aware of the importance of denial in drug abuse and, even more, in alcohol abuse. In alcoholism, at least, it is part of the illness and interferes with acknowledgment of the condition and the harm it is causing. Anger, hostility, judgmental remarks, and accusations are useless. Powerlessness is very difficult for staff to handle, yet it will be their experience in many contacts with this population. Doing a good job with substance abusers means being able to make small, positive interventions and helping them know where to go when they are ready.

Alcohol Abuse

It has been estimated that alcoholism is the most ignored public health problem in America, involving 5% to 10% of the adult population.[3] More than 200,000 deaths a year in the United States are estimated to be alcohol-related. Half of traffic deaths; one-third of traffic injuries; one-third of suicides; one-third of crimes; and more than two-thirds of drownings are all related to use of alcohol.[4] Studies in emergency rooms consistently show that a large percentage of patients have been drinking heavily, even when their presenting complaints are not related to alcohol. For example, one study of more than 700 patients at a large teaching hospital's emergency facility found that 40% had consumed alcohol and 32% had high blood levels.[5] Apart from physical indications, recent heavy use of alcohol was inferred from four signs: alcohol on breath; slurred speech; abnormal motor co-ordination; and red conjunctivae.[6] While the social worker may not feel comfortable assessing the last criterion, the previous three are often not difficult to evaluate. The specific nature of these signs is important for recording, as a notation of "has been drinking" or "intoxicated" without supporting observations is useless and may even be mistaken. The reasons why a patient is presumed to have been drinking should always be stated.

Another study of 200 consenting subjects during day (8 A.M.–4 P.M.) and night hours (12 P.M.–8 A.M.) in an emergency room found 20% of them to be alcoholic. The day and night figures varied considerably: 11% during the day, but 29% at night.[7] The diagnosis of alcoholism was made through the presence of three of the following criteria:

1. Alcoholic withdrawal, medical complication, binge drinking, alcoholic blackout;
2. cannot stop drinking, before breakfast drinking; non-beverage alcohol consumption;
3. arrest, fights, or work trouble because of drinking;
4. patient, family, or others thinks patient drinks too much.[8]

Patients were asked about these, and the presence of two indicated probable alcoholism. These two studies are included here as examples because the indicators of "intoxication" and "alcoholism" used in them are transferrable to the social work evaluation and interview. In addition, they are typical of current findings on the role of alcohol abuse in many medical emergencies. While the conclusion of alcohol abuse may not be difficult given certain physical signs, the diagnosis of alcoholism is more complicated. If there is any possibility at all, the history should include use of the criteria above and the questions in the next section.

The diagnosis of alcoholism is often associated with other psychiatric diagnoses, most commonly affective disorders (see Chapter 8), antisocial personality, and drug abuse. This is a group at high risk for suicide, criminal activity, assault, and other harm to themselves and others. In fact, in one of the studies cited, the chief complaint for 63% was trauma or injury, although whether others had also been harmed was not indicated.[9] Another 23% came in with unexplained dizziness and fatigue. Hardly anyone came in for treatment of alcoholism, and that, of course, is one of the problems. One can only speculate about the number of trauma patients who came in unconscious and unable to be interviewed, but whose injuries were clearly alcohol-related.

Given the high percentage of intoxicated patients at night, nighttime social work services should be available in busy emergency rooms if they expect to make an impact on this problem. Some hospitals with detoxification units admit patients at all hours of the night and have a social worker available to take part in the admission and to begin immediate work on discharge planning. A few hospitals have separate alcohol emergency units. In a setting such as this, treatment and planning can be intense and specialized and the possibility of undetected alcoholism in emergency patients decreases.

Screening for Alcohol Abuse

The idea that alcoholism may be ignored or missed in emergency room patients comes as a surprise to many staff who see a large population of suspected alcoholics make their way through the hospital. Chapters 7 and 8 discuss the dangers of assuming that certain symptoms are a result of problem drinking or alcoholism without a thorough medical screening. And yet the opposite also happens: physicians completely miss the diagnosis of alcoholism in patients where it might be very clear with proper screening.[10] Many people come in with complaints apparently unrelated to drinking behavior, where diagnostic detective work is necessary to obtain full information. This is an area where social workers can be extremely helpful in assessment and diagnosis. Screening for alcoholism in general medical cases by asking questions about drinking habits, medical complications of drinking, and arrests or work trouble associated with drinking[11] can reveal information crucial for further evaluation and correct treatment. One authority suggests a very nonthreatening approach, with the introduction first of questions regarding cigarette and coffee use; then prescription drugs such as sedatives and tranquilizers; then wine, beer, and liquor; and finally down to illegally obtained drugs, if appropriate. The reasons for use of the various substances and the results obtained are also highly relevant.[12] Although such screening will not be done routinely, when there is any question of alcohol-related illness or injury, or even when there could be any question, there should be an attempt to obtain as much information as possible about drinking behavior and drug use. Otherwise, the patient's treatment may focus on the immediate problem without touching the underlying disturbance.

Alcoholics who pass unrecognized through the emergency room once or twice are likely to be back. They will be car accident victims (or the drivers); victims of major trauma; victims of self-poisoning; patients suffering from seizures, intracranial bleeding, gastrointestinal bleeding, ulcer disease, emphysema, diabetes, and numerous other life-threatening conditions.[13] They may also suffer from malnutrition, exposure, and various infections. The family may be despairing and exhausted or may long since have withdrawn. The explicit diagnosis of alcoholism, however, may help the family to acknowledge what they have hidden from themselves or not been able to face.

Where an allegedly intoxicated patient has been involved in an automobile accident, police may be present in large numbers in the emergency room asking for medical information, particularly about blood alcohol levels. Since several states have recently passed strict drunk driving laws, police may be more active than in the past and have less discretion in their dealings with the patient. The social worker should not give out any information about the patient other than the standard report on nature of injuries and condition. The police have appropriate channels for obtaining other information about the patient and should be encouraged to use them. In addition, the patient should not be discharged to the police if there is any question about the seriousness of his or her medical condition. Far better is a period of observation, with a police guard, if necessary. This should be the standard procedure for any patient under arrest or otherwise in police custody. The patient should be discharged only when he or she is no longer in need of immediate medical care, unless the social worker knows that there is an adequate prison hospital unit and the patient is indeed going there.

The patient who is clearly intoxicated, whether alcoholic or not, will still need a medical screening to make sure that other medical problems do not need attention. Often in the emergency room the staff's goals are only to get the patient sober, then get him or her out. The social worker should always encourage a period of observation when there is any question about other medical problems or the patient's readiness (as opposed to willingness) to leave. An intoxicated patient who is physically very ill, or is very young, or one who has pending DTs (delirium tremens) is likely to be admitted (but not always—in some emergency rooms it is not unknown for some patients to be given money for a drink or two to prevent alcohol withdrawal and DTs). Others are simply discharged, and it is often up to the social worker to find them a place to go. Even more difficult is the belligerent, hostile, intoxicated patient who refuses to consent to examination or treatment, who may have been brought in by police, and sometimes also who refuses to leave the emergency room. In this situation the social worker must collaborate with nurses and physicians to assess first whether the patient's judgment is so impaired that he or she really cannot make an informed decision to forego treatment, and second, whether leaving the emergency room without treatment will result in the likelihood of immediate harm. Sometimes it is just not possible to tell the extent of illness or injury in a person who does not cooperate, and important information may be missed. If possible, a person who seems intoxicated and *may* have a medical problem should be kept and observed for a while unless he or she insists on leaving. Many patients who are angry and belligerent can be calmed down and, while not immediately amenable to examination, will sit for a few hours in a comfortable spot in the emergency room. This is not the same as encouraging people to come in for refuge; rather, it is a safety measure to avoid discharging a patient medically but not visibly in need of treatment. Social workers can talk to patients about staying, can sit with them if they cannot be alone, and can obtain information not previously available. In addition, they can call family and ask them to come in and occasionally will get the opportunity to do on-the-spot family counseling in a setting which makes denial of the patient's condition practically impossible.

The intoxicated patient who is clearly very ill or badly injured may have to be treated over his or her objections. This is a complicated issue and may involve many people, including hospital administration.When the social worker has any doubts about the patient's judgment, cognition, or decision-making ability, he or she should take the part of those who urge treatment in a medical emergency and a period of holding, as mentioned, in questionable situations.

Handling Discharge

The most difficult problem for the social worker is what to do with the patient who is ready to leave the emergency room and is not being admitted to a hospital. General issues of disposition are covered in Chapter 10. Those patients who do not by history appear to be alcoholic may respond well to a discussion by the physician of the physical dangers of alcohol abuse and suggestions by the social worker of other ways to deal with stresses, pressures, disappointments, and anger.

For those who are indeed alcoholic, the first step is to say so, to tell the patient gently that he or she is an alcoholic, and needs treatment for that illness. It is important to be quite sure before telling the patient. It is also more helpful to hold this conversation with some family member(s) present.

Given the magnitude of the denial in this illness, the negative responses should not be surprising. However, there will occasionally be a patient who has just been waiting for outside corroboration of what he or she already knows and is ready to try a treatment program. These patients will be appropriate candidates for whatever inpatient detoxification and treatment facilities are available (detoxification being the gradual reduction and elimination of physical dependence). Outpatient treatment possibilities abound, although their records are mixed. The best known and most successful is Alcoholics Anonymous (AA) which has thousands of chapters all over the country. They are ready to offer immediate help to a person who asks for it. In addition, Women for Sobriety (WFS)[14] is geared to women with drinking problems as well as alcoholism. These programs provide peer support, counseling, and necessary confrontation in a setting that shows success to be achievable. There are many other treatment programs using different approaches and methods, and the social worker should be acquainted with the ones in his or her area and if possible should get to know some of their personnel.

If the programs available do not provide any service on a walk-in basis, they should be encouraged to do so, since someone who finally summons the courage to seek help may not be able to maintain his or her resolution without immediate attention. In attempting to make a referral, the social worker can identify the problem to the patient, suggest treatment possibilities, provide literature, and help with phone calls. The next steps are up to the patient. Someone who is not yet ready to take any action may pick up folders, which should be available in both the social work office and in the waiting room.

Whatever the patient's needs and desires, the social worker can offer a great deal of help and support to the family. Besides identifying the problem and informing them of special programs for the family members of alcoholics such as Alanon and Alateen (for children), he or she can also provide brief counseling. If the patient is unwilling or unable to seek help, the issue of what is best for the family arises, and the social worker may have to begin the difficult process of helping the family—particularly a spouse or parent—focus on his or her own needs. If there are young children, the spouse may be in conflict about obligations to both them and the patient and too paralyzed by guilty rage to take much action. The social worker can present counseling as helpful and encouraging rather than exhortatory and guilt-evoking and can then refer the family for further services.

Drug Abuse and Dependence

There are many patterns and types of drug abuse to be seen in an emergency room. Some patients, for instance, may come into the ER with either genuine or exaggerated symptoms primarily in order to obtain drugs. Others may be brought in with overdoses, drug-related illnesses, or other illnesses or conditions where drug dependence is not immediately apparent. Still others may have become inadvertently addicted to pain medication, for instance, amphetamines for weight control, or sleeping pills. They may not be aware of or understand their physical addiction and may be coming in for relief of symptoms whose origin they cannot understand.[15] Another type of drug abuse involves suicide attempts and is primarily a problem of girls and women. For instance, other recent DAWN studies reveal that when sex is reported, 54% of drug abusers are women.[16] These studies deal not only with "street drugs," where figures might be quite different, but with all drug abuse, defined as "nonmedical use of a substance for psychic effect, dependence, or suicide attempt/ gesture." When motives are provided, 47% of cases involve suicide or attempt (59% F, 32% M); 25% dependence (35% M, 16%F); and 23%, psychic effect (27% M, 20% F). In other words, two-thirds of use by men in these studies were what is commonly considered "drug abuse," but only a little over one-third by women, who tend to use drugs more heavily for suicide attempts and gestures. Of all users in these studies 68% were white, 26% black, and 6% other. A substantial proportion were young, those in their teens and twenties. Lower life expectancy may explain the smaller proportions above that age. At any rate, drug dependence should probably be part of the differential diagnosis for certain population groups in that age range. Keeping this information in mind may help the social worker and others to prevent signs of drug abuse from being overlooked.

Other DAWN studies provide useful information on overdose from numerous hospitals throughout the United States. This material is included here to help the social worker understand the different needs of patients who have overdosed on various drugs. For instance, there appears to be growing evidence of increase in acute overdose with tranquilizers and various sedative-hypnotic drugs.[17] Of the patients identified in one particular study, many were highly visible and might have been predicted to present with an overdose sooner or later. For instance, 47.3% had had prior overdoses, with 22.6% having taken three or more prior overdoses. Nearly half had had continuing, repeated contacts with emergency rooms. Nearly 40% had been involved in some kind of psychiatric treatment or counseling over the past year, but the rest had not.

Those who use "street" drugs are also more likely to be admitted to ER with physical complications, such as endocarditis and other cardiovascular complications, pulmonary complications, malnutrition, exposure, various infections, and hepatitis. In fact, in some hospitals up to 90% of admissions for hepatitis are a result of parenteral (by injection—other means include snorting and ingesting) drug abuse.[18] Another danger is AIDS (auto-immune deficiency syndrome) which is an illness with a virulent course, many complications, and no known cure, and may be spread by contaminated needles.

Drug abusers also have higher incidences of gonorrhea, syphilis, and other venereal diseases. In addition, since 80% of female drug abusers are of childbearing age, a pregnancy test should be done, and the woman counseled if it is positive. Both continued drug use and sudden withdrawal can inflict severe harm on the fetus, and the woman should be encouraged to enter a treatment program if she wants to continue the pregnancy.[19] (The same holds true for women of childbearing age who abuse alcohol; a pregnancy test should be done, and if it is positive, the woman should be urged to enter a treatment program in an effort to avoid the devastating fetal alcohol syndrome.) Women who are noncompliant should at least be encouraged to obtain prenatal care, or to come for delivery at that particular hospital, where someone knows them.

Screening for Drug Abuse and the Underlying Problems

While the nurse and physician will have the primary responsibility for diagnosis, the social worker can observe such gross indicators as needle marks and can also note behavior and appearance very carefully. If the medical staff is busy with emergencies and the social worker sees the patient first, his or her observations may be invaluable to the physician in formulating a diagnosis. History-taking is crucial, especially when a patient is not known to the staff. If the patient's appearance and condition do not elicit suspicion, he or she may be misdiagnosed, as in the case that follows:

Case Study

Mr. R, a young man whose pregnant wife accompanied him, was treated for viral gastroenteritis in the emergency department. After treatment he became agitated and belligerent and complained of being hot. As they were leaving, he collapsed. The social worker checked the chart and found noted there that he was a former drug abuser. She then asked his wife about drug use and discovered that he had injected speed within the last five days. The physicians, on receiving the additional information, reexamined the patient and found that he was indeed suffering from a drug reaction.

The kinds of drug abuse the social worker sees will vary tremendously, as will treatment recommendations and resources available.

A certain group of drug-dependent patients are not above harming themselves physically to produce symptoms which will need medication. A patient who comes into the ER asking for a specific abuse-prone medication is to be viewed with suspicion. Once emergency room staff are reasonably certain that a patient is a drug abuser and visits the emergency room primarily for the purpose of obtaining drugs, such information can be communicated to others who are likely to be treating him or her. For instance, if the social worker keeps a card file on repeaters and problem patients, the card can indicate that the patient is a known or suspected drug abuser and list one or two reasons for that conclusion. The patient's name can also be included on an emergency room "problem list" available to all staff who are working there. A notation on the patient's chart, again with reasons, is also appropriate. In one hospital, emergency room staff took these steps in regard to a patient who visited frequently with various ailments and injuries and asked persistently for medication. When the patient found he was on the list of problem patients and that his chart labeled him as a "known drug abuser," he sued the hospital for defamation and lost. The court recognized that hospital personnel had a duty to communicate their opinions and findings to treating physicians.[20] Consequently, staff should not hesitate to make such information available to those who will be examining and treating the patient—as long as their conclusions are based on observations which are also recorded.

This patient, like many other drug abusers, had several genuine physical complaints, some of them quite unrelated to drug use. The social worker, as advocate of the patient, will sometimes have to encourage physicians and nurses to perform the necessary medical examination. It may also fall to the social worker, either alone or with the physician, to confront the patient and explain why he or she will not receive the medication he or she seeks. This should be done as gently as possible but, even so, may elicit suprise and indignation from the patient, especially one who has not acknowledged drug dependence. Rather than simply refusing to give medications, the physician can suggest other means of symptom relief and should be requested to do so by the social worker. In addition, the patient who is facing the issue for the first time should receive support and sympathy for having to deal with such a difficult problem and suggestions for follow-up. He or she can be invited back for further medical care and sessions with the social worker, with the understanding that there will be no more drugs.

On the other hand, certain groups of patients, such as those with sickle cell anemia, may need large amounts of pain medication during crises. Some do become addicted and exaggerate the magnitude and frequency of their symptoms in order to get drugs; many, however, do not and are often unjustly maligned by doctors and nurses who tend to generalize about them and their condition. An example of such an attitude in one emergency room follows:

Case Study

Reverend S, who suffered from sickle cell disease, had a large urban parish which included University Hospital. He was a well-known and respected member of the community and had held the parish for many years. Occasionally, when he was in a sickle cell crisis and his own doctor was not available, Reverend S would seek treatment in the University Hospital emergency department. On one such visit he noticed a parishioner, who also had sickle cell disease, in the next cubicle and went over to see him, without his coat and clerical collar. The physician, glancing at the two men, shouted loudly to the nurse, "Get those two junkies out of here!" Not wanting to make a scene, Reverend S left quickly but later complained bitterly to the social worker.

Patients who overdose on sedatives or related drugs are likely to be clinically depressed or suicidal. Nearly half have been drinking at the time of drug ingestion, with significant blood alcohol levels. Many have histories of systematic, long-term abuse, and well over half have obtained the drugs used in the overdose from nonmedical sources. Drugs prescribed by physicians, however, are far more likely to be from nonpsychiatrists.[21] It may be that psychiatrists prescribe more appropriately and monitor abuse more effectively. Treatment plans following overdoses, discussed in the next section, should always include ongoing psychiatric care. Street drug users, such as heroin addicts, may enter the ER with one of the physical illnesses mentioned, after an overdose, or in connection with some kind of criminal activity. Medical evaluation is most likely to reveal the particular agent. Polydrug abusers, those who use many agents, including alcohol, singly or in combination, can be identified by medical evaluation and by history. This group is one of the hardest to help. It has been speculated that the approach that is most effective for alcoholics is not at all helpful for this group.[22] The alcoholic, if and when he can achieve the desired goal of abstinence, usually has some sources of support such as family and workplace or at least can cultivate them again. The polydrug abuser's drug use, unlike alcoholism, is not a disease but rather a symptom of underlying psychosocial problems. His or her family background is usually disorganized and capable of little or no support. Discontinuance of one drug may lead to dependence on another. Consequently, evaluation focuses not only on the patient but also on new potential sources of support which are available in the community.

Handling Discharge

Discharge plans and recommendations vary according to the type of drug abuse. Patients who are depressed and overuse sedatives should be referred for continued psychiatric care. Family members, if available, should be enlisted for support and monitoring. Physicians whose patients have overdosed on their prescriptions should be so informed, and physicians whose primary business is the prescribing and dispensing of drugs for many should be reported to state and federal authorities. The social worker can play a useful role here by trying to elicit as much information as possible and coordinating the various contacts. It is important to remember, and to make sure that other staff are aware, that a patient who has taken an overdose should be presumed to be a continuing suicidal risk until information to the contrary is available. If the patient will not enter treatment, attempts should be made to limit his or her supplies (through prescribing physicians, for instance) and to inform significant others of the continuing danger. As with families of alcoholics, the social worker may provide the most help by encouraging the families to explore their own options and take care of themselves.

Standards of patient protection are the same as with alcohol abusers. Patients should not be discharged to police or sent out on their own until they are medically cleared. A period of observation is usually the best course if there are any questions about the patient's status.

Those who are open to treatment can be referred to inpatient programs and methadone maintenance programs, which are available in some areas and will be successful for a very small group. Others may improve after several hospitalizations; still others enter detoxification programs to bring their level of drug dependence down to a more manageable level financially. A good inpatient program must have a highly structured follow-up program as well. Because of the high level of disorganization and the absence of any real sources of support in the lives of many abusers of hard drugs and polydrug abusers, a treatment program must offer new and lasting supports. In addition, someone whose days have been organized around the need for and obtaining of drugs must be offered a highly structured living style, such as that in a halfway house.

Many outpatient programs are also available, as well as programs such as Narcotics Anonymous, modeled on AA, which has chapters all over the country. Any program in the treatment of drug and/or alcohol abuse with federal, and usually state, support is required to have stringent confidentiality guidelines. The participant has well-defined protections against disclosure of his participation, addiction, or other factors, and this aspect of treatment should be emphasized for those who are otherwise hesitant. Living arrangements are a major issue because of the dangers of sending a patient back to the drug culture from which he or she came. The social worker may have to spend considerable time and effort in looking into and developing possible resources for moving people not only out of a drug-saturated setting but into a new setting offering a high level of organization and social interaction. Whatever the social worker can do with the resources available, he or she should remember that the best possible treatment is one that "promotes supportive group membership in a drug-free environment."[23]

Notes

1. National Institute on Drug Abuse, *Statistical Series, Quarterly Report, Provisional Data* (October–December 1981): 5. (Department of Health and Human Services; Public Health Service; Alcohol, Drug Abuse and Mental Health Administration.)

2. George E. Vaillant, "Alcoholism and Drug Dependence," in Armond M. Nicholi, Jr., ed., *The Harvard Guide to Modern Psychiatry* (Cambridge, Mass: The Belknap Press of Harvard University Press, 1978).

3. Ibid.

4. "Alcoholism" (Chicago: Blue Shield Association, 1979).

5. S. Holt, I. C. Stewart et al., "Alcohol and the Emergency Service Patient," *British Medical Journal*, 281 (September 6, 1980): 638–640.

6. Ibid.

7. Douglas A. Rund, William K. Summers, and Michael Levin, "Alcohol Usage and Psychiatric Illness in Emergency Patients," *Journal of The American Medical Association*, 245 (March 27, 1981): 1240–1241.

8. Ibid. Neither "alcoholism" nor "intoxicated" is defined in this chapter, but the studies discussed do present their own practical definitions.

9. Ibid.

10. G. H. Jones, "The Recognition of Alcoholism by Psychiatrists in Training," *Psychological Medicine*, 9 (1979): 789–791.

11. Rund et al., "Alcohol Usage."

12. Sidney Cohen and Donald M. Gallant, *Diagnosis of Drug and Alcohol Abuse*, Vol. I, No. 6 of *Medical Monograph Series* (State University of New York, Downstate Medical Center, 1981).

13. Ibid.; Holt *et al.*, "Alcohol and the Emergency Service Patient"; Frank R. J. Purdie, Ben Honigman, and Peter Rosen, "The Chronic Emergency Department Patient," *Annals of Emergency Medicine*, 10 (June 1981): 293–301.

14. Located in Quakertown, Penn., Women for Sobriety has many of the same goals as AA but also focuses on development of self-esteem for women. There are chapters throughout the country.

15. Cohen and Gallant, "Diagnosis."

16. National Institute on Drug Abuse, Statistical Services, "Sex and Race Differentials in Acute Drug Abuse Episodes 1980." (Topical Data from the Drug Abuse Warning Network (DAWN), Department of Helath and Human Services; Public Health Service; Alcohol, Drug Abuse and Mental Health Administration.)

17. National Institute on Drug Abuse, "Emergency Room Study for Sedative-Hypnotic Overdose: A Study of the Issues, 1982," *Treatment Monograph Series.* (Department of Health and Human Services; Public Health Service; Alcohol, Drug Abuse and Mental Health Administration.)

18. Cohen and Gallant, "Diagnosis."

19. Ibid.

20. Griffin v. Cortland Memorial Hospital, Inc., 446 N.Y.S. 2d 430 (Sup. Ct., App. Div. 1981).

21. National Institute on Drug Abuse, "Emergency Room Study of Sedative-Hypnotic Overdose: A Study of the Issues, 1982," *Treatment Monograph Series.* (Department of Health and Human Services; Public Health Service; Alcohol, Drug Abuse and Mental Health Administration.)

22. Vaillant, "Alcoholism and Drug Dependence."

23. Ibid., 577.

10 Problems in Disposition, Discharge, and Transfer

The hardest patients for the emergency department social worker are those whom the rest of the staff want out. Their unwelcome status can be due to a number of reasons: they may be medically cleared or treated but not leaving quickly enough; they may not need treatment at all; they may be known to the staff as chronic abusers of the emergency room or seen as unworthy of much time or effort (street people, chronic psychiatric patients, alcoholics, addicts, "space cases"); or they may be in need of treatment but indigent and consequently not viewed as an appropriate admission to this particular hospital. They may also be people who, regardless of physical condition, just have no place to go. If they are elderly, chronically ill, or clearly unfortunate in some way, staff may feel guilty and uncomfortable about not being able to help and redouble their efforts to get the patient to leave—out of sight, out of mind.

The social worker in such cases is often caught between duty to the hospital, the employer, and duty to the patient, which is really the primary responsibility. The issues, however, are complicated ones. What if there is really nowhere for some of these patients to go? What if it is winter and very cold and there is no available shelter for an elderly person? The problems are exacerbated on weekends, when for many people with no other place to turn, the emergency department becomes a multipurpose social agency, particularly in poor urban areas.[1] Some of these people are sophisticated enough to know that "the way to get attention is to couch their complaints in medical terms." Others just wander in, and still others are brought in by police who know very well that medical attention is often not the primary need but have no other resources to use for them. In difficult economic times, emergency health care may be the only service available to some people, whose physical condition may be deteriorating as a result of stress, poor nutrition, and postponed medical care. Once treated, they return to the same situation.

The major questions are, first, should the emergency department be a place of refuge, not for everyone, since that way leads to bankruptcy, but for those vulnerable to abuse, those with inadequate links to other helping systems, or those in unmistakable danger of further harm or deterioration if sent out immediately? Second, what is the hospital's responsibility, and how far should it extend? Hospitals vary in their responses to these questions. Many "rich" private hospitals have more resources yet less tolerance; they do not want to invest in these unremunerative people, nor do they want to expose their more desirable patients to them. Some of these hospitals are relatively inaccessible and consequently do not have to face the issues, but others discharge, transfer, or dump in very irresponsible ways. Not all private hospitals act in this way, and some, in fact, do make major contributions to the poor of their communities. The hospitals that handle the most cases, and tend to show the most concern, are those that can least afford it. They are generally easier to get to and have a long tradition of helping the unfortunate and impoverished; in addition, other hospitals transfer, sometimes anonymously, their unwanted patients to these.[2] These public or community hospitals are also the ones most likely to have social workers in their emergency departments because of the large volume of patients in need of social services.

The major point in this chapter is that "the social worker's primary responsibility is to clients."[3] Hospitals are businesses as well as community agencies, and the social worker's responsibility to the hospital often conflicts with the needs of the client. The social worker must serve as advocate, negotiator, facilitator, and resource coordinator, with the goal of not exposing someone to further harm by premature or unassisted discharge. Whether this goal is met depends on hospital attitudes, both administrative and medical; community resources; the social worker's skill, knowledge, and influence; and sometimes on the patients themselves. Sometimes the goal cannot be met; some patients exhaust sympathy, tolerance, and available resources. This chapter will discuss some of the different patient groups and approaches and resources for dealing with them.

Psychiatric Patients

Chapter 8 deals with the needs and problems of patients with acute mental illness or those with conditions generally considered treatable by psychiatrists. There is a very large group, however, who are "burned out," or for whom no known treatment seems to work, or who have overused and abused the system, or who need custodial care which is no longer available. In the 1970s, to put it briefly, the trend in mental health changed from "warehousing" to "dumping." Patients who had previously been housed in large state mental hospitals, often without much treatment or recreational or therapeutic activity, were discharged into the "community," but what the "community" was supposed to be was never made clear. States and localities whose expenditures for mental health went down because of these wholesale discharges were satisfied with the reductions and not interested in committing the money for aftercare. Patients were discharged to boarding homes or hotels which were often filthy and inadequate and where some of them were abused, starved, robbed, and beaten. Many were lost to view. Others now roam the streets, embarrassing those in more genteel neighborhoods and providing likely victims in rougher areas. Their visibility makes them no less neglected, and national policy at this point seems bent on continuing this neglect, as any social worker will discover who tries to get one of them back into a hospital.

This group, in summary, have minimal social competence and limited problem-solving ability, which dooms them to a marginal adjustment at best with marked social isolation, and sometimes antisocial behavior.[4] Their families tend to have disappeared from view or to be totally exhausted and unable to help or even tolerate the patient any longer. Such patients periodically patronize emergency rooms, brought in by police because of bizarre behavior, walking in on their own, or "referred" by another hospital or agency wanting to get rid of them. A typical example follows.

Case

Mrs. T, aged 48, is brought to the emergency room by the police who were called because she was stealing food from patrons of McDonalds. Considerable investigation reveals that she was recently discharged from the state mental hospital, after a 10-year hospitalization, and was placed in a boarding home. The boarding home owner will not take her back. She claims Mrs. T has stolen

from her, provokes arguments with other residents, and has struck
other residents although none had been injured. The boarding
home owner says arrangements had not been made with the BSU
(base service unit) for aftercare. Mrs. T is on psychiatric medications. She has no money.[5]

A psychiatric evaluation is a standard part of the emergency
department's response to this group of patients, but they elicit
little interest from psychiatric residents or attendings and are
almost never admitted. Generally, they are given additional
medications and discharged back to the base service unit (community mental health center) for continued follow-up. The social
worker is then responsible for disposition. There will be an
occasional patient who the worker feels very strongly should be
admitted, either because he or she is extremely deteriorated,
seems acutely depressed, is more actively psychotic than usual,
or shows some symptomatology that suggests the need for active
treatment. (See Chapter 8 for a discussion of hospitalization.)
Many of these patients desperately want to be in the hospital and
never wanted to be discharged in the first place. Some, like
Mrs. U., quickly learn how to be admitted. When all efforts at
showing how ill she was failed, she began hitting a waiting
stranger in the emergency room—and was promptly committed
as dangerous to others. It is unlikely that she was allowed to stay
more than a few days, but at least she obtained a brief respite
from the outside world and further evaluation.

The social worker must, first of all, consider where the
patient will live. If there is family, they may be willing to
provide shelter and care, but exhausted families are often pushed
too far and too hard by agencies with limited resources and
many withdraw completely. The family that is willing to take
the patient needs support and follow-up beyond the lip service
that is often provided. Day hospitals, medication clinics, respite
care, whatever is available should be tried repeatedly until the
family can no longer cope.

Those hospitals with adequate boarding homes in the neighborhood may be able to place some of these patients, particularly
if there is a regular source of income, such as SSI or public
assistance. Relationships with boarding homes will be discussed
later in the chapter. The boarding home operators must be able
to tolerate unusual and disruptive behavior and must be able to
cooperate with medication, treatment, and follow-up programs.
In return, they know that they will be able to bring the patient

back to the emergency room if he or she proves unmanageable. Because of the rootless and disorganized lifestyle of some of this group, the social worker may have to investigate financial resources and figure out what, if any, sources of income exist and where checks have been going. Some patients will need new applications for different kinds of financial assistance, and fortunately, in a few cities, there are even specially funded or volunteer legal programs to help with problems such as SSI or SSD terminations.

If the city or locality has placement resources, some patients may be assisted through them or through missions, shelters, or religious, voluntary, or charitable programs. Various shelter possibilities are discussed later in the chapter. The major goal for this group is to keep them housed, fed, followed if possible by the appropriate agency, and free from abuse and exploitation. No one social worker is responsible for finding the answers to a chronic social and economic problem such as this one, but he or she can at least not be a part of the wholesale abandonment of this group. Commitment to helping these patients is not always easy, as they can be nasty, manipulative, and endlessly demanding. Although chronic psychiatric patients are presented here as a separate group, it is clear that a large proportion of patients in other categories who become disposition problems also suffer from mental illness or alcoholism.

The Very Dependent, Rejects, and Transients

Nearly every emergency department has an identifiable group of patients who are viewed by medical staff as inappropriately in the hospital. They have varying characteristics: some are regulars, using the emergency room as their usual source of medical care in spite of efforts to steer them elsewhere, or use the ER as their umbrella social agency because they know it will be open when others are closed and that they are likely to be seen because of legal requirements. Some are just lonely. Metropolitan emergency rooms tend to see these people at all times of the day but are almost assured of their presence during evening, nights, and weekends, particularly in cold weather. In winter some may be suffering from the results of exposure and may actually come or be brought in asking for a place to stay.

The regulars may be homeless—"street people"—or have places to live. All these groups may overlap; street people may be regulars or intermittent or infrequent visitors. They may have major medical problems or may be quite healthy, considering their life-style. Alcoholism and mental illness are often present but not always obvious. Some observers have commented that "these patients [become] the responsibility of the ED [emergency department] by default because alcoholism or mental illness prevent[s] their compliance with any therapeutic program."[6] Some of this group are pathetic, dependent, inadequate; others are crafty, resourceful, and relatively successful at manipulating their environment. Whatever their medical needs, this is an unpopular group in the emergency department, as terms such as "dirtball" and "gomer" (Get Out of My Emergency Room) demonstrate. They are often filthy and unkempt and resist efforts to clean them up. A few become popular among the staff or are treated almost as pets because of particular personality characteristics. Many of this group overlap with the chronically mental ill previously discussed.

The third subgroup here is the population of those who are just difficult and uncooperative. Medicine, social work, and other helping professions are starting to deal with the fact that there truly is a group of difficult people who may be at least partly responsible for their isolation and difficult situations. The reasons for their behavior may be inaccessible to understanding, but the reactions they elicit are often strong and disturbing. As one physician has noted,

> What is it about the patient 'everybody hates' that compromises . . . workaday skills? It is probably the additional burden of having to deny or disarm the intense, hateful feelings kindled by the dependent, entitled, manipulative, or self-destructive patient.[7]

A typical example follows.

Case Study

Ms. V, aged 79, appeared several times in the emergency department over three days and then refused to leave. No one could ascertain where she had come from, although she did have accessible family. She was cleared medically and psychiatrically in spite of a leg ulcer which she refused to have examined. Throughout the three-day period, the ulcer seemed to be getting worse under the bandage and began to smell.

The social worker did not want to send Ms. V out without a specific destination. She was allowed to sit in the emergency department and was fed while the worker tried to develop alternative disposition possibilities. Ms. V's family flatly refused to take her because of "obnoxious behavior." A friend with whom she insisted on living and had lived with in the past also would not take her. Further investigation revealed that Ms. V had been moving from boarding home to boarding home. Her leaving was a result not only of her behavior but also of her reluctance to sign over her checks. She had with her in the emergency department several bankbooks and an undetermined amount of money. Finally she was given three options: (1) admission to a boarding home; (2) transportation to a destination of her choice; or (3) escort out of the hospital. She refused all planning and insisted that she should not have to pay for housing. Staff felt uncomfortable about having her forcibly ejected, and she continued to sit.

Eventually, Ms. V left on her own, reportedly taking a cab. Staff heard later that she was admitted to another hospital. The assumption was made that she had finally allowed examination of her leg. Since there was no question of her competency, the discharge problems would still remain to be solved by the admitting hospital.

This group of patients also includes the hostile intoxicated person who refuses to consent to examination or treatment and has been brought in by police. Often the best course of action is to keep the patient under observation until he or she is capable of more communication or is determined to be well enough to leave. It is *not* a good idea to send out alone an intoxicated person who may be driving a car, and the social worker will have to find family or friends who will be responsible for taking the person home or may have to send the patient home in a taxi. In unusual cases, the police may have to be summoned if an intoxicated person insists on driving home.

This group can best be dealt with by acknowledging and accepting negative feelings, reaching agreement among the staff as to what should be offered, making limits clear to the patient, and then sticking to these limits. Only when it is clear that patients truly are not responsible for their behavior should the worker make exceptions and begin efforts to find some kind of protective services.

An emergency department that has an identifiable group of rejects or transients (or "regulars" or "street people" or "difficult patients," however they are characterized) should have a file accessible to all staff.[8] The social workers are the most appropriate keepers of the file, which should contain name, vital statistics, brief medical history, medications, usual complaints, usual contacts or supports, agencies, past efforts in the emergency department, help to be offered, help not to be offered, and other relevant information. Such a file is particularly useful in a very busy emergency department or one with new staff. Although there may be names and agencies listed under contacts and supports, the social worker should not expect too much from these, as this population eventually exhausts the patience and resources of family, friends, and volunteer and professional helpers. In addition, as with "space cases" and other chronically mentally ill, much work may already have been done in vain. Besides being physically distasteful, many emergency department regulars evoke negative feelings in staff through serving as constant reminders of their inability to do anything for these patients.[9] Even so, the medical staff should be encouraged by the social worker to do a thorough physical exam, since familiarity can sometimes result in a perfunctory evaluation which misses significant medical problems.

In planning for each of these patients, the social worker must ask three questions: (1) What harm is likely to occur without social work intervention? (2) What does the patient need to prevent this harm, and how has the patient used this service if it has been given in the past? (3) What are the resources available right now (night, weekend, winter)? Every emergency department social worker should have the following:

1. Knowledge of available in-home services: friendly visitors, daily phone calls, alarm systems, visiting nurses, home health aides, meals-on-wheels, handyman services, and others. He or she should know just how available they are and for what income and insurance levels, and how long they take to implement.

2. Knowledge of adult day care programs, their requirements, and transportation needs.

3. Supplies of clothing, food, and means of transportation, and/or a petty cash fund (see Chapters 2 and 11). Social workers who have trouble obtaining these can explain to administration that they are a very cost-effective investment, as they help to get people out of the emergency department.

4. Links to the Travelers Aid Association or similar agency. Some transients truly are on their way from one place to another and run short of money, are robbed, become ill,

or suffer some other interference. A person with willing relatives in another location may be able to receive travel assistance.

5.   Knowledge of and links to shelter resources for different populations (families, mothers with children, adolescents, single men), such as Salvation Army, missions, municipal and county shelters, church-sponsored shelters, low-cost hotels, local boarding homes, and others. The worker should be familiar with the various rules and entrance requirements of each. Some emergency department social workers have been able to make arrangements with acceptable local boarding homes, whereby the proprietor agrees to take an indigent patient "on trust" or with a small down payment from the social work department until the next check arrives or a regular source of income can be arranged. Emergency department social workers should look into such agreements; sometimes the hospital can offer services to the boarding home that strengthen the relationship.

With all these patients, the help to be offered depends on their needs and the available resources. Those who visit the emergency department regularly may still continue to do so but may become more compliant with a medical regimen through supportive services. Those who have made a very precarious adjustment in their own homes or elsewhere out of the hospital may be helped considerably by whatever home-care or day-care services exist, though they are precious few in some communities. In small communities and rural areas, visiting nurse service may be available, and telephone contact may keep some people going. Obtaining telephones for those without them should be a high priority. Support and encouragement are equally important. Some emergency department visitors are recently discharged patients who feel frightened and inadequate at home. They need support and often concrete assistance, as with medications.

Those who live on the street may want to return to the street, although no one should be sent out in snow or cold weather. Temporary or permanent shelter; opportunities for regular financial grants, where they are possible; rehabilitation programs; and medical care are what can be offered and should be offered at each visit, except to patients who clearly do not want them. The social worker, as well as the medical staff, must be careful not to let frustrations and annoyance blind him or her to current complaints and needs and must make sure that retaliatory measures, even subtle ones, are not directed against these patients.

Discussions of the homeless usually refer to transients, but in the 1980s a new population is appearing: the long-term unemployed, formerly self-supporting and at least moderately successful, who may now be without homes, insurance, or hope for the future. Often health care has been neglected until family members appear at the emergency room in a deteriorated state of health. Health care is not something to be deserved, and yet this group deserves all the attention, support, and concrete assistance that can be mustered. The social worker should do everything possible to make sure that health care is provided regardless of ability to pay, that other family members are taken care of, and that the family is connected to whatever resources exist in the community. If many families in this predicament appear in the emergency department, the social worker should consider providing some documentation to local government and community groups to illustrate the magnitude of the problem.

Some of these people may be strangers in the area, having traveled with or without their families in a fruitless search for work.[10] Whether they are native or not is irrelevant.

Helping the New Poor and Homeless

No hospital or group of hospitals can pick up the slack in different economic times. Although hospitals, particularly on weekends, may function for some people as multipurpose social agencies, there is a limit to what they can provide, even those dedicated to the idea of community service. A community where there is high unemployment, recent disaster, or some other widely distributed problem may quickly overtax emergency rooms, not only because there may be no other place to go but also because many people, through stress, inadequate nutrition, and inability to obtain routine medical care, will actually experience a deterioration in their health. Chapter 2 discusses some of the concrete services, even including food, that a social worker may be providing in the emergency department. Every hospital has to make a decision as to what extra services it will provide and in what form. There will always be a few hospitals that turn their backs on the community they are serving, but most are willing to make some contribution, particularly in collaboration with other hospitals. For instance, in Multnomah County, Oregon, during high unemployment, Project Medishare was developed through the efforts of 450 hospitals, physicians, and pharmacies.[11] The program's goal is the provision of nonemergency care to the jobless before the need for expensive hospital care develops. Obviously, such a program takes the burden of providing for this group out of the emergency department. A similar program in the seven-county Greater Detroit area, Project Healthcare, has been set up to serve as many as 500,000 people who qualify.[12]

Other communities have given even farther and have set up places of refuge, particularly for transient or homeless families. There exists a critical shortage of emergency housing, particularly in areas such as the Sun Belt with large influxes of newcomers.[13] These places, for instance, have few old, inexpensive center-city hotels. In a number of cities,[14] Travelers' Aid has taken the initiative and either independently or as part of city-wide coalitions developed systems of emergency shelter, which take people in for anywhere from a few days to a month and a half. The systems vary according to location but usually include purchase or lease of their own building; use of public housing units; and vouchers to selected hotels, restaurants, and grocery stores. Generally families, couples, and single women are accepted, but not single men.

Wichita, Kansas, has involved the private sector in a huge effort to provide resources for the city's poor and unemployed.[15] The largest landlord in the city has set aside 25 of its 2000 apartments for short-term emergency housing and is subsidizing the rent in 25 more for poor tenants. The hotel/motel association has made 500 rooms available for emergency shelter. Supermarkets contribute food for the needy. Apparently a large number of volunteer hours as well as concrete services are what make this program as effective as possible.

An example of a comprehensive city-sponsored program is that developed by Philadelphia,[16] where the goal is that no one be without shelter during the cold winter months. Besides emergency food, fuel, and clothing arrangements, there are two kinds of shelter arrangements. These are in addition to the existing facilities, such as the Salvation Army, various church-sponsored missions and shelters, and a city shelter for homeless families, as well as soup kitchens around the city and programs of assistance funded by private foundations.

The first shelter is a Drop-In Center for those who are "chronically homeless but who at times seek temporary shelter."

Nearly every social worker has had the experience of making painstaking arrangements for someone who bounces back shortly after, in need of the same services all over again. Mr. W is a typical example: Having come into the emergency department on a cold winter day dressed practically in tatters, he was medically evaluated, fed, dressed (with coats and shoes being none too plentiful at this time of year), and finally sent to an appropriate shelter. One week later, in even worse weather, he was brought back by police who saw him wandering outside—coatless, shoeless, and no longer welcome in the shelter.

The Drop-In Center was set up with this kind of person in mind. He can wander in, bathe, get deloused, get clothing, eat, and sleep for a night or two out of the cold. The system protects his anonymity and asks nothing of him. The shelter sleeps up to sixty people, with additional dining space and a sitting room that can sleep forty more in the worst weather. Not surprisingly, the center is often jammed to capacity. Emergency department social workers in Philadelphia know that if a person is medically cleared—and most hospital staff try to be careful about clearance, not wanting to jeopardize the system—he or she can be directed to the Drop-In Center and will likely be accepted there.

The second shelter is an Adult Evaluation Center, which is for people not immediately placeable but awaiting placement. Referrals here must be made through the Adult Services Division of the City Department of Welfare; that is, people must be accepted to the Center. Since this means going through ordinary bureaucratic channels, the process is longer and more complicated than sending someone to the Drop-In Center. Even so, it provides a great deal of help to social workers unable to place patients. Once in the Evaluation Center, the patient spends several days getting cleaned up and medically and socially evaluated until a placement can be located. Those in need of in-or outpatient medical care are sent to certain hospitals, which accept them because they know the Center will take them back.

Finally, the city has opened a Psychiatric Boarding Home for those who can live in the community in a "semistructured environment" but tend to do poorly in ordinary boarding homes or other placement settings.

This is a welcome, ambitious program which has undoubtedly saved the lives of many people who might otherwise have died of exposure and in addition has preserved hospital resources that might have been fruitlessly expended by admitting people without medical necessity or devoting staff time to find scarce or nonexistent placements. Even so, the program cannot keep up with the increase in homeless people, especially the new group of young homeless.

Runaways

Hospitals in large metropolitan centers or in university communities supporting "youth ghettos" of young drifters who flock to the area may see an occasional runaway. Most will either go without health care or take advantage of whatever formal or informal resources exist in the street or neighborhood, but occasionally, an adolescent will break away from whatever system he or she is in or, worse, will be in such poor physical condition that frightened companions bring or dump him or her at the hospital. Those who reach the hospital are lucky; many are abandoned and left to die by companions or by the adults who use and abuse them. About one million American children a year run away from home; many thousands of others are kidnapped or snatched by parents in custody disputes.[17] Although a discussion of runaways is beyond the scope of this chapter, it is important to remember that children run away for many reasons, including neglect, abuse, and intolerable stress at home. There is a beginning collection of literature on the types of runaways and the reasons for their actions.[18] Some of these children are taken up by unscrupulous adults who put them into service as prostitutes; others enter into similar activities on their own in order to survive. Generally, only older teenagers have any chance at all of making a safe and healthy adjustment; others are greatly at risk, and the longer they are away from home, the less chance they have of surviving. Consequently, any child of any age who comes into the emergency room alone, with another child, or with an adult who does not seem to be the parent should be evaluated as a possible runaway. The worst approach is to provide medical treatment and send him or her out. Runaways need support, acceptance, and kind and gentle treatment.

While many runaways, perhaps most, will not admit to the status, there are a number of things that can be done. First, the social worker can try to get the child admitted by explaining to the medical staff the urgency of the situation. Second, he or she can check *The National Runaway/Missing Persons Report*,[19] which is issued periodically and has pictures and descriptions of missing children. Every hospital and emergency department should receive it and keep it accessible. Third, the social worker should call, or should encourage the child to call, at a later time, the National Runaway Switchboard at 800-621-4000, which is a 24-hour, toll-free hot line. The child should understand that even if he or she does not want to be located, he or she can call the number and have a message relayed to his family that he or she is safe. Through the hot line he or she can also receive other kinds of help at any time. Fourth, the social worker should be knowledgeable about teen and runaway shelters in the area. Many metropolitan and university areas have such shelters which accept runaways with no questions asked. An emergency department which sees more than an occasional runaway should have a relationship with one or more shelters. Finally, since the Federal Bureau of Investigation now has a computerized system of missing persons which includes reported runaways, the social worker will have to consider whether to involve law enforcement. In some situations, such as when a child is unconscious or badly injured, such notification may be appropriate. Even the emergency department that rarely sees a runaway should be ready for those who come; the emergency department that can expect to see them more often or that serves an area with many drifting youth should strive to present itself as a place where runaways will be better off, not worse off, for their visit. As a representative of the society that has been rejected, the emergency department can create either a very positive or very negative impression on a lost and lonely child.

The "Space Cases"

"Space cases"[20] refers to a specific group of patients, mostly young adult males, who are chronic former mental patients and who have experienced repeated "revolving door" treatment in psychiatric facilities. Unlike ordinary street people, if such a category exists, they are shunned or tormented by their peers, being seen by other street people as delusionary, unpredictable, and unreliable. People who have studied this population claim that it has grown enormously and will continue to grow throughout the 1980s.

The major problem, from the social worker's view, is the limited or nonexistent nature of the skills for coping and living in this group. They have often had longstanding problems, including repeated psychiatric hospitalizations and minor brushes with the law, and may have been seen as too crazy to lock up. In fact, police may often bring them into emergency rooms hoping that some kind of treatment will be available. They are not trusted by other street people. They tend to be unskilled and to have poor judgment and management abilities, relying on human services programs or "resorting to the most debasing means of survival." Some are violent and destructive and show a pattern of criminal behavior that is more marked by the symptoms of mental illness. Most are isolated and dependent but are unwilling to cooperate with social agencies insofar as such cooperation means giving up the anonymity so prized on the street. The following is an example of a patient who probably falls into the category of "space case:"

> Mr. X is a 32-year-old retarded man brought into the emergency department by his mother, who says he is recently out on bail after being jailed for "throwing stones." The mother's landlord insists that she get him out of her home, and residents of their housing project have threatened to kill him if he appears there again. He has no funds, having been cut off from SSI. In addition, he has a letter from a nearby hospital stating that he has "bad blood" (syphilis).

In this particular case, investigation revealed that the syphilis was not active and had been treated. The social worker felt that the mother as well as the son was withholding much relevant information. Both were uncooperative, and, in fact, the mother did end up taking the son back home. If she had left him at the hospital, or if he had been brought in alone by the police, it is likely that he would either have been "streeted" or sent to a short-term local shelter if one existed. Nothing else would have been available.

The major problems in working with this group are, first, that a great deal of effort may be expended for nothing, since they often wander from place to place and reject scarce placements; second, friendly and helpful resources, such as neighborhood boarding homes, do not want or need this population and will quickly be alienated by being referred too many of them. Some of this group, especially those getting older, do respond positively to efforts to secure them financial support. SSI is increasingly difficult to get, but some will be eligible; others might be able to obtain local income grants. Otherwise, medical screening and treatment, food, clothing, if available, and referral to a place to sleep may be the most that can be done.

The Ill and Impaired But Not Admitted

One of the most difficult groups of patients to help are those who are brought in by concerned relatives, neighbors, or landlords because their physical condition has deteriorated to the point where they are incapable of self-care. Some are elderly people living alone, but others have families who are worn out emotionally or financially or both or cannot stay home from work to care for them. With both private and public insurance payments more restrictive, hospitals cannot afford to admit patients who need custodial rather than acute medical care. Sometimes social services have already been provided, but the assistance obtained is inadequate, as in the following example.

Case

An 86-year-old bedridden, incontinent total-care female is brought to the emergency room by the police. The patient had been living with her granddaughter and her granddaughter's seven children. The granddaughter has been having problems coping with providing the care and twice weekly receives homemaker services. These services had been arranged by the hospital social worker after a previous visit to the emergency room. An application had also been submitted for nursing home certification, but approval has not been obtained. The granddaughter did not accompany the patient to the hospital but told the hospital staff that she absolutely can no longer handle the 24-hour care required by the patient and will not take the patient back. There are no other family or friends willing to take the patient. Although the patient does have medical problems, she does not require admission to the hospital.[21]

Other elderly patients may be mentally impaired and in need of supervision that cannot be provided at home, as in the following example.

Case

A 74-year-old man is brought to the emergency room by the police who found him wandering on the street. The man has a leg laceration which is treated, and he has no other conditions which require admission to the hospital. The gentleman is very disoriented. After much effort, his landlady is contacted. She tells the social worker that the man does not have a history of psychiatric problems but is "senile." Furthermore, he has no family or friends who can give him support. The landlady says the man cannot return to his rented room since he has not paid the rent in three months, the room is untidy, and she has received complaints from other renters about the man's poor personal hygiene. The man left the room three days ago, and since then she has packed all his belongings in boxes, and upon his return she had planned to ask him to leave. The gentleman is ambulatory and physically able to do his activities of daily living if reminded. The landlady tells the worker that he is occasionally incontinent of urine. He has no money. His SSI check is due the following week.[22]

Other patients may be "dumped" by nursing homes who have provided inadequate care or may be sent by responsible homes with which the hospital has a transfer agreement.

Options are very limited for this population. Sometimes the social worker can exert pressure on the family or landlady or nursing home to take the patient back, but that is at best a temporary solution. The availability of in-home and respite services, such as homemaker, home health aide, meals-on-wheels, and others can make a tremendous difference in the success of this option. Much depends on financial resources. (See Chapter 7 for a discussion of this subject.) On return, the patient's condition may have deteriorated enough so that admission is now warranted. The hospital may have its own extended care facility where a bed or two is reserved for such cases. The hospital may have an agreement with one or more nursing homes, where in return for a certain number of private patients, the homes agree to take indigent patients, sometimes on an emergency basis, if beds are available. Occasionally a social work department will have funds to pay a nursing home until some kind of financial coverage is obtained. However, the areas with critical shortages of nursing homes may have no resources whatever for this group of people. Even when facilities exist, some patients will not want to go, and the social worker will be faced with the dilemma of helping to plan for someone who cannot care for himself or herself but still wants to go "home." There will be times when the worker opts for the principle of self-determination and with great misgivings sends the patient home, with whatever supports the community provides.

Some municipalities do provide emergency placement and will find a bed either in a privately run home or a city institution. This is a rare service and can be a great blessing, but relief at removal of responsibility should not keep the social worker and his or her colleagues from continued monitoring of the quality of these placements.

Occasionally, all resources are exhausted, the patient is still in the emergency room, and something now has to happen. A good rule of thumb here is to sit down and think about the patients' deficits and what will happen if they are not remedied or ameliorated. If it is clear that the patient will suffer immediate harm—because of total inability at self-care, disorientation, or other problems—the worker will have to remember once again that his or her primary duty is to the client, not the hospital. Consequently, every effort must be made not to send the patient out. As discussed in Chapter 2, the worker may have to plead for an administrative admission, in which a patient is admitted for other than medical needs and the hospital agrees to take at least a partial loss. The worker's credibility and reputation will be a major issue here; also previous discussions may have set the stage. If the hospital adamantly refuses admission, the worker can at least decline to make arrangements for the patient to leave, saying that it is poor social work practice and against his or her conscience. Such a position is not easily taken in a time of limited job opportunities and cannot be a frequent occurrence, but social workers who command respect in the emergency department are occasionally able to force an admission in this way.

The problem may be considerably alleviated if the emergency department has an observation or holding ward, so that the social worker has an extra day or two to make plans with the patient.

Transfers

Although transfers are usually based on medical necessity, some are done for reasons of convenience, such as sending an indigent patient to a public hospital. The emergency department social worker in some hospitals may find himself or herself in the uncomfortable position of being asked to arrange transportation for a patient whose medical condition is unstable and who should probably not be moved. Not being familiar enough with medical decision making, the social worker may not know what to do. If other physicians and nurses in the emergency department question the advisability of the transfer, the social worker should do whatever possible to delay or prevent it. Checking with an attendant if a resident has made the decision is one way; asking the advice of protesting doctors and nurses or the social work supervisor is another; just plain stalling on arranging the transportation is yet another. Hospitals in which inappropriate transfers take place frequently tend to be private hospitals and are unlikely to have social workers in their emergency rooms in the first place, but a social worker in such a hospital should scrutinize as well as possible with an untrained eye all patients being transferred out for admission to other hospitals. Transfers made only on the basis of financial evaluation can be life-threatening to patients.

Some wealthy private hospitals go to extraordinary lengths to keep noninsured or underinsured people away. They provide maps and directions to public and university hospitals[23] (the latter are often not subsidized and are in no better financial position than the offending hospitals to accept these patients, and yet they do); they send patients to other hospital emergency departments without notification or even put them in paid-for taxis; or they request transfer but misrepresent the reasons. Some of these hospitals may have continuing federally mandated obligations that require them to provide emergency care for all who seek it, and yet they ignore these obligations until community groups or the federal government insist on compliance.

The hospitals who receive these patients tend to be those with a history of commitment to the poor, generally public, university, or certain community hospitals. With the continuing closing of city hospitals, other hospitals find themselves receiving more unexpected and unwanted transfers, commonly known as "dumps." In today's world, no hospitals, especially those in the inner city, can afford to accept all who come, but those who are transferred from one emergency room to another will nearly always be seen. The social worker in the receiving hospital will have numerous extra tasks related to the transfer, such as trying to find financial resources, disposition planning if the patient is not to be admitted, and sometimes just trying to discover his or her identity. It is important for someone in the emergency department to keep track of suspicious transfers and to make sure that the administrator of the hospital knows about them. While this person is more appropriately the physician, the social worker may have to provide the encouragement for the actual reporting. Suspicious transfers in which, as sometimes happens, the patient has been harmed by the move, should be investigated, by the social worker if necessary.

The Joint Commission on the Accreditation of Hospitals has provided explicit instructions for when to transfer:

Unless extenuating circumstances are documented in the patient's record, no patient shall be arbitrarily transferred to another hospital if the hospital where he is initially seen has the means for providing adequate care. The patient shall not be transferred until the receiving hospital or facility has consented to accept the patient, and the patient is considered sufficiently stabilized for transport. Responsibility for the patient during transfer shall be established, and all pertinent medical information shall accompany the patient being transferred.[24]

Although the standard requires that hospitals retain emergency patients for which they are able to provide care, many hospitals which otherwise follow JCAH prefer a lesser standard: a patient can be transferred if he or she will not be harmed by the transfer and the other facility agrees to accept him or her. According to this view, an indigent patient can be transferred solely on the basis of financial need as long as another hospital will take him or her.

Many transfers, after the patient is stabilized, are beneficial, such as when patients are transferred to burn centers, children's hospitals, or psychiatric facilities. The social worker may be responsible for arranging transportation and sometimes for letting families know where the patients are actually located. Some appropriate transfers may be difficult to arrange; for instance, there are cities where no service—neither ambulance, taxi, nor vehicle—will carry a person with active tuberculosis. Transfer becomes practically impossible.

A different situation is inability to admit an emergency patient because there are no beds. Some hospitals prepare for this eventuality by setting aside a certain number of beds for patients from the emergency room. Others set up an observation unit right in the emergency room where patients can stay until an inpatient bed opens up.[25] Such units allow observation on short-term treatment for a few hours and provide beds for those who just cannot be discharged immediately. They prevent inappropriate discharge; allow observation time; enhance the quality of patient care by allowing medical staff adequate time to get together relevant information; keep patients comfortable yet out of the way, improving patient flow; provide temporary space during bed shortages; and take into account "human/social considerations where delay in discharge may not be medically indicated but is in the interests of patients."[26] Physicians and nurses have been reported as being quite satisfied with such an arrangement, which lets them follow through with patient care more than usual. Like many of the other efforts described in this chapter, the observation ward represents a compromise in which the needs of the patient are acknowledged even when they are not strictly medical, and yet the extent of the hospital's giving is not a serious economic threat. The social worker is always striving to find that balance.

Notes

1. Carole W. Soskis, "The Weekend Emergency Room: The Only Game in Town," *Health and Social Work*, 5 (August 1980): 37–43. See also Judith Healy, "Emergency Rooms and Psychosocial Services," *Health and Social Work*, 6 (February 1981): 36–43.

2. Emily Friedman, "The Dumping Dilemma: The Poor Are Always with Some of Us," *Hospitals*, 56 (September 1, 1982): 51–56. For a study of nursing home-to-hospital transfers that did not show evidence of dumping, see Muriel Gillick and Knight Steel, "Referral of Patients from Long-term to Acute-care Facilities," *Journal of the American Geriatrics Society*, 31 (February 1983): 74–78.

3. National Association of Social Workers, *Code of Ethics*, passed by the Delegate Assembly, 1979. Implemented July 1, 1980. *Social Work*, 25 (May 1980): 184–187.

4. Ann T. Slavinsky, Judith D. Tierney, and Judith B. Krauss, "Back to the Community: A Dubious Blessing," *Nursing Outlook*, 24 (June 1976): 370–374.

5. Case example is from Myra Wall, *Study of Emergency Health Needs in Philadelphia* (Philadelphia Health Management Corporation, 1980). Funded by Philadelphia General Hospital Research Fund.

6. Frank R. J. Purdie, Ben Honigman, and Peter Rosen, "The Chronic Emergency Department Patient," *Annals of Emergency Medicine*, 10 (June 1981): 298.

7. James E. Graves, "Taking Care of the Hateful Patient," *New England Journal of Medicine*, 298 (April 20, 1978): 301.

8. Purdie *et al.*, "Chronic Emergency."

9. James M. Mannon, "Defining and Treating Problem Patients in a Hospital ER," *Journal of Medical Care*, 14 (December 1976): 1004–1013.

10. "Homeless Represent Major Health Problem," *Hospitals*, 57 (January 1, 1983): 21.

11. "Medical Aid for Jobless Organized in Cities Hit Hard by Recession," *Hospital Week*, 18 (December 31, 1982): 3.

12. "The Hard-Luck Christmas of '82," *Newsweek*, 100 (December 27, 1982): 12–16.

13. *Models for Emergency Shelter in Travelers' Aid*, (Travelers' Aid Association of America, Des Plaines, Ill.: 1981). Programs discussed are in Houston, Texas; Long Beach, California; Salt Lake City, Utah; Denver, Colorado; and Chattanooga, Tennessee.

14. Ibid.

15. "Medical Aid."

16. *Human Services Crisis System*, Office of the Managing Director, City of Philadelphia (October–November 1982).

17. "A Nation of Runaway Kids," *Newsweek*, 100 (October 18, 1982): 97.

18. See, for example, Albert R. Roberts, "Adolescent Runaways in Suburbia: A New Typology," *Adolescence*, 17 (Summer 1982): 387–396.

19. *The National Runaway/Missing Persons Report*, Search: Central Registry of the Missing, 560 Sylvan Avenue, Englewood Cliffs, N.J. 07632 (issued monthly).

20. Steven P. Segal and Jim Baumohl, "Engaging the Disengaged: Proposals on Madness and Vagrancy," *Social Work*, 25 (September 1980): 358–365. The concept of and discussion of "space cases" in this chapter have been derived primarily from this important paper.

21. Case example from Wall, *Emergency Health Needs*.

22. Ibid.

23. Friedman, "Dumping Dilemma."

24. Joint Commission on the Accreditation of Hospitals, *Accreditation Manual for Hospitals* (Chicago, 1982).

25. Roy G. Farrell, "Use of an Observation Ward in a Community Hospital," *Annals of Emergency Medicine*, 11 (July 1982): 353–357.

26. Ibid.

11 Setting Up a Social Work Emergency Service

All hospital emergency departments need—and should have—social work services immediately available. The discussions in the previous chapters about the changing role of and demands on the emergency room, and the many services a social worker can provide there, make it clear that the question for most social work departments is not whether services must be provided, but how. This chapter addresses that question, outlining first how to assess the need for social work services and how to justify to the administration the positions recommended. We will discuss briefly a list of possible alternatives for smaller departments and hospitals, then go on to a set of directions for actually setting up a hospital emergency department social work program.

Assessing the Need

Preliminary Steps

The best possible beginning for a department considering the provision of social work services in the emergency room would be to go through all the steps suggested in this chapter for its assessment. For those whose time and resources are limited, suggestions are provided for a less exhaustive survey.

The specific approach to assessing need in a particular hospital will depend partly on the relationship between the emergency department staff and the social work department.

For instance, it is not uncommon to have numerous complaints from physicians and nurses in the emergency room that social work services are never available when they need them. These same people may never avail themselves of the opportunity to talk to a social worker on call. One hospital, for instance, where the name and number of a social worker was available to emergency room staff day and night, had numerous complaints about never being able to get hold of a social worker. Yet the worker on call was never sought out for advice or assistance. An investigation of the complaints revealed that over a period of several months there were only four cases where the staff had wanted social work help that was not "available" (though it might have been, on the other end of a telephone).

This example suggests two things: first, developing a positive relationship between the emergency room staff and the social work department is a prerequisite to any other action. And second, it is inadequate to rely on other health personnel for referrals.[1] The first step is to approach the administrator(s) and medical director of emergency services and to explain that in view of the growing and changing nature of emergency room populations, it is a fair conclusion that a sizable proportion may need social work services. The social work department would like suggestions as to how to be more helpful. That same conversation should include a description of the services social workers actually can provide to avoid misconceptions about what is actually being offered. Previous to this discussion, the social work department should have reached some kind of agreement about call, since it would then be a wise move to offer the emergency room staff a list of social workers to call about problem patients. It would have to be emphasized that this first phase is a combination of evaluation/service so that workers called in the middle of the night would provide over-the-phone assessment, support, advice, and resources but would not necessarily come into the hospital.

After these initial conversations come a series of contacts with physicians, nurses, physicians' assistants, aides, admitting clerks, and other personnel. They, too, should be told of the services social workers can provide and asked for their suggestions and descriptions of problems. They can be provided with the on-call list and, in addition, asked to mark the chart of every patient they would like to have referred to social service but did not. The elaborateness of this beginning assessment may depend only on time and resources. One hospital, for instance, spent a month evaluating perceptions of social work needs in the emergency room by asking doctors and nurses to fill out a questionnaire attached to each patient admission form. Not surprisingly, few of the patients in the would-have-referred category, which was about 14% of all patients seen, actually did get referred.[2]

We have now to come back to the second point coming from our earlier example, which is that it is inadequate to rely on other health personnel for referrals.[3] Since no other group sees with the eyes of a trained social worker, it is safe to assume that a substantial number of patients requiring social services will slip by the medical and clerical staff, in spite of acute need and serious interference with medical treatment and follow-up. Consequently, the best way to find out what the needs for social work are in the emergency room is to go there and see.

Part of the evaluation, including some of the observation (although not all, since an experienced eye will see what others miss) and some of the work on the log, would make an excellent student project. The student(s) involved could contribute to the recommendations and be involved in setting up and staffing the ensuing emergency room social work program. Adequate supervision is particularly important here, not only to help the student clarify and express his or her perceptions but also to provide quality control for the recommendations the Social Work department will be making.

The process of establishing a social work emergency service is a long and exhaustive one, and the discussion that follows presupposes an administration with little or no interest in providing social work services in the emergency room and a social work department with little experience in or knowledge of emergency services. In situations where the hospital administration is receptive to or even introduces the idea of social work in the emergency room or where the social work department is already familiar with or provides services to the ED, the kinds and amount of information needed will be much less. Social work departments already flooded by requests for help in the emergency room will not need to approach emergency department directors in such an unstructured manner. They know about the need; how to fill it will become a mutual problem. In other hospitals, administrators concerned with readmissions, overstay days, and community relations may suggest to social work directors that they set up a program in the emergency room. Here, too, assessing the magnitude of the need is the goal. Justification will not be so necessary.

Observing the Emergency Room

The social worker conducting the evaluation should first become familiar with the emergency room and its workings. Look at physical layout: Is the waiting room spacious and provided with enough chairs, or is it crowded and stuffy, with many people having to stand? Do the staff have room to work without bumping into each other? Do the patient rooms or cubicles afford privacy or the possibility of privacy? Are there easily accessible restrooms? Is there any place for a social work interview? Look also at staffing patterns and try to relate them to length of wait. Are the physicians "independent contractors" hired by the hospital to set up a practice in the emergency room? Are they salaried employees of the hospital? Are members of the hospital medical staff obliged to rotate through the emergency room? Do residents work in the emergency room? If so, in what specialties? A few hospitals have residencies for physicians specializing in emergency medicine. In these settings, the evaluating social worker should ask permission to attend some of the training lectures for residents—and to give one. The nature of the physicians' association with the hospital may give clues as to their views of and interaction with patients, in addition to their expertise in the field of emergency medicine.

Watch a few intake procedures. Notice what kinds of questions are asked and how they are asked. What is the attitude of the admissions clerk toward various minority groups, those who have language difficulties, the elderly, those on medical assistance, those brought in by police, those who are disturbed or disruptive? Is there any real triage? (Triage is a battlefield term referring to the separating of casualties into groups according to the immediacy of the need for treatment.) In some emergency rooms a nurse quickly assesses each person for this purpose; in others, any triage is done by untrained clerical personnel, sometimes with disastrous results.

Finally, look for specific characteristics of the emergency department. Some examples might be emphasis on speed and efficiency; a highly medical technical approach; a "soft spot" for or prejudice against certain patients or groups of patients; uses of humor; good or poor relations with police and fire rescue personnel; interest or lack of interest in particular illnesses, problems, or conditions.

Just this first cursory examination will provide a tremendous amount of information about the hospital's emergency room and may already suggest different kinds of social work intervention. Besides the level and adequacy of medical care and the prejudices, attitudes, and interests of the staff, it will now be possible to identify specific populations who may need extra attention or support and whose needs may have to be emphasized to the staff. The physical layout gives clues to the quality of the wait, which in places with limited staff may already be very long. Overcrowding, lack of privacy, resentment, and exhaustion may prevent many patients from fully articulating their complaints, from understanding medical advice and instructions, and from complying with medical recommendations. The same factors may also lead to fatigue and irritability in hard-working staff. In such cases the social worker can be a useful buffer and mediator. Already it may be quite obvious as to what a social worker could begin doing in the emergency room.

Studying the Emergency Room Log

For a more comprehensive assessment of potential need, look at the emergency room log, in which patients' names, ID numbers, dates, initial complaints, final diagnosis, disposition, and sometimes other information are recorded. Skim the log for the previous year or past few months and estimate the average number of patients per day. (The total number of visits to the emergency department the year before will already provide one estimate of the average number.) On which days were the most patients seen? Is there any consistent pattern? Using other sources if necessary, try to relate these busy days to particular times, events, and seasons—winter cold and storms, summer heat waves, holidays, factory layoffs, weekends, local happenings.

Next, glance at every third or fourth day for a few months to see when the busiest times are. If the busiest hours of the day are between six and nine P.M., an eight-to-four social worker will be providing limited assistance. Finally, look at the entries for times and days already identified as particularly busy to see what the more frequently mentioned presenting problems are. Note what the dispositions are for these problems. In the more structured interviews with staff, ask about certain of these presenting problems and their recorded dispositions to assess the levels of sophistication, satisfaction, frustration and willingness to collaborate that will have to be confronted.

This work on the log, while it may be time-consuming and tedious, can provide a sense of what goes on in the emergency room that might otherwise require weeks of observation. In addition, these concrete figures and specific examples of problems can be useful in presenting an objective proposal to the administration about the need for social work services in their particular emergency room.

Interviewing Staff

Having come so far, learn still more from a few structured interviews with one representative from each staff group having contact with patients—physician, nurse, aide, clerk. Make sure that different times and days are included in the various shifts. If students are available, they may want to interview one representative from each shift. Ask the following questions:

1. In your experience, what are the busiest times in the emergency room?
2. Which do you find the most difficult patients to deal with in the emergency room? Why?
3. Which resources do you find least available to patients you see in the emergency room?
4. Have you requested social work help in the emergency room? If so, how often? What for?
5. Do you see a need for social work services (or a social worker) in the emergency room? For which times? To provide which services?

If the emergency room has patient representatives (discussed in Chapter 2), it is important to learn as much as possible about the patient representative's role, ties to the community, and perception of social work needs. An effort to communicate honestly and fully at this point will prevent rivalry and duplication later on and will lead to a harmonious collaborative relationship, which recognizes that there is more than enough work for everyone.

Identifying Patient Groups in Need of Social Work Help

The final step in the assessment process is a series of direct observations. During several shifts and days, those workers doing the study should spend time sitting near the intake worker and the waiting area and walking around the treatment area. Certain groups of persons may appear to need social work help: the elderly, living alone or suffering sudden or severe impairment; children and adolescents with chronic conditions and their families; suspected victims of physical or sexual abuse; families of seriously ill, injured, or disturbed patients; families of patients who have died; frightened or angry patients and families; patients without family supports; patients who make multiple visits either without physical complaints or without the ability to follow medical recommendations; victims of accidents or crimes; emotionally disturbed; those in need of concrete services (money, food, clothing, transportation, medications, help with dependents); patients with multiple health problems. Others who are likely to need social work support or services are those who have difficulty communicating their presenting problem, through language differences, anxiety, or impairment; those whose behavior makes them disruptive to the emergency room and consequently unpopular with the staff; those brought in from other institutions; those for whom there is a disposition problem; and those whose problems are a mixture of medical, social, and psychological elements. Observation will undoubtedly suggest which of these groups are most likely to be encountered in a particular emergency department, what strengths and weaknesses the staff displays in working with them, and what resources will be needed in coping with the problems.

The results of this survey will be a tabulation of the busiest days and times in the emergency room and possible relationships to local, seasonal, or other kinds of events; staff perceptions of what problems and patients they need help with; and social work observations of specific groups or types of patients where social work intervention could be helpful. From this material it should be possible to designate the days and hours where full-time social work coverage is necessary or to conclude, in the case of some larger hospitals, that complete coverage is the answer twenty-four hours a day, seven days a week. Where that is not the case, decisions need to be made about using on-call social workers within the hospital at less busy times or developing a roster of social workers who will be called at home.

Explaining and Justifying the Need for Services

At this point the social work department may be pleased with its design and findings, but selling them to the administration is a different matter entirely. Depending on the hospital, the patient population, the fiscal situation, and other issues, a reluctant administration needs to hear about the advantages to the hospital of an emergency room social worker in terms of finances, more appropriate use of medical personnel, and community relations. It may be necessary to develop a projection as to how many or what proportion of indigent patients whose care is not paid for or is paid for at a very low level could be prevented with proper counseling, referral, and follow-up from making unnecessary repeat visits. Based on information obtained about admissions from the emergency department, project the number of un-compensated overstay days that might be avoided if social-family evaluation and discharge planning were begun immediately on admission through the emergency room. Project, but do not promise. While money always tends to be the bottom line for new projects or services in the hospital[4] and the possibility of curbing expenditures will make the administration more recep-tive to any proposals, remember to point out that while you hope to be able to reduce unnecessary or prolonged patient visits, this first phase of delivery service is an exploratory one. In addition, emphasize the emotional drain on medical staff of trying to serve patients whose problems are only partially or minimally alleviated by medical attention and the role that the social worker can play in saving staff time, easing frustration, promoting better use of resources, and raising morale. Finally, point out that, as the interface between the neighborhood and the hospital, the emergency room has a crucial role in shaping community atti-tudes toward the hospital. The social worker's combination of skills in providing support, counseling, advocacy, and related services can not only help to improve the relationship between the community and the hospital, but it can also lessen patient dissatisfaction and avoid neglect of the "quiet" yet critical emer-gency, thus diminishing the hospital's risks of liability.

Staffing the Social Work Emergency Service

The hospital's financial situation, the commitment of the social work department, and the administration's attitudes will play an important part in the decision, but the best possible arrangement for a busy hospital is to have a social worker actually present in the emergency room at all times. Shifts may be the same as those used for the nurses (7 A.M.–3 P.M., 3 P.M.–11 P.M., 11 P.M.–7 A.M.)

in order to promote a team feeling or may be those used by the social work department. Complete coverage would involve one worker for each shift five days a week, plus other full-time or part-time workers to cover not only the remaining shifts but also the times (usually Friday, Saturday, Sunday, and/or Monday) where two social workers may be needed.[5] Since social workers, unlike nurses, are not conditioned to expect to work nights and other off hours, most hospitals with full coverage would undoubtedly require rotation through all shifts. A social worker who covered only nights would become an accepted and valued part of the nighttime team but would be completely isolated from the social work department. In most hospital settings there is at least a quiet conflict in loyalties between a worker's medical service and the social work department. This split in loyalties, which is different from anything that a physician or nurse might feel, can be constructive in bringing new perspectives to both the service and the department. In fact, part of a social worker's value in a medical setting is his or her ability to present a nonmedical, nonparochial view. This ability would tend to be diminished in a social worker whose contact with nonmedical colleagues was limited to written memos and notes in the chart.

If it is clear that only one worker can be hired for the emergency department, a decision will have to be made as to how best to use that person's time. In a hospital with particularly busy weekends, for instance, four ten-hour days, Friday through Monday, 10 A.M. to 8 P.M., might be the best possible arrangement. In a case like this, workers in other services could rotate on-call assignments for Tuesday, Wednesday, and Thursday and would have to check in at the emergency room on those mornings to see if there were any cases pending.

Another alternative is to have a regular five-day-a-week worker in the emergency department and to hire a part-time person for the two weekend days. A former employee of the social work department who is now pursuing an advanced degree or wants part-time work because of family obligations might be a perfect match. This can be a very successful arrangement. The Monday-through-Friday social worker would be particularly helpful in hospitals whose emergency rooms adjoin walk-in clinics. Such clinics siphon off those patients with medical needs that are not true emergencies and, when working, will ensure that emergency room resources will not be misallocated but that patients who feel an urgent need for service can obtain it. The same worker might easily be available to provide coverage in both settings.

These are by no means the only alternatives, and a creative department will come up with other possibilities. It is important to remember that the emergency room is one of the more draining and exhausting settings in the hospital and can rapidly produce burnout in a zealous and committed individual. For that reason, whatever the staffing arrangements, alternate workers must be available to allow the emergency department social worker occasional time away from the demands of the job.

Those social work departments which recognize and document the need for emergency room social workers but are unable to get the necessary funding will have to develop a call system and an understanding with the medical staff as to when and for what social workers will be available.

This particular scenario, where the social work department attempts to provide service on a piecemeal basis, requires complete and careful documentation. Here, particularly, a protocol for referral for social work services is the basic instrument in a social work program. Specific populations or patient groups might require their own protocols. Some departments have developed a series of protocols to cover every kind of conceivable referral situation.[6] Some of these will be included in the Appendixes.

What is crucial, however, is that physicians, nurses, and others have explicit and understandable guidelines as to when to call in a social worker. Having developed such guidelines, the social work department then must respond, even at the cost of reduced service to other areas. A beeper system is likely to increase availability and reduce response time. A period of careful record-keeping about the number of calls, number and types of patients served, time spent in the emergency room, and time lost to other services will result in the development of a cogent argument for social work staff and emergency staff to bring to administration together.

Another way of handling the situation, in which both the social work department and the director and staff of the emergency room agree on the need for service, is to refuse to respond at all to emergency department requests for help (that is, to take on additional responsibilities) without additional staff. If the medical director and the administrator of the emergency room clamor for an additional social worker, the chances of getting one would be considerably better.

Where no additional workers can be hired and the current workload is not so burdensome as to prohibit any flexibility, a system of coverage which uses all workers is probably quite feasible. For instance, during every week each worker (and student) could work an evening or a weekend day, thus providing coverage for all times except nights.[7] Those who wanted a particular assignment could cover the same time period every week; for others, a rotation schedule would avoid any real hardship. Departments which have instituted this kind of program report that a social worker is then available to talk with working relatives of inpatients, to deal with in-hospital emergencies (such as unplanned discharges on weekends or a family crisis involving an inpatient), and to be generally available for any urgent inpatient social work needs.

What of the small hospital with only one or two social workers to handle all patient social service needs? The reality is that while some of these hospitals appear to be meeting the obvious demands of their populations, others have little interest in or commitment to social work services. Their social workers, often minimally trained and experienced, are hired to deal with disposition problems, arrange transportation, and expedite the filling out of forms. Such hospitals are unlikely to be interested in providing social work services in their emergency rooms unless in response to specific problems. If such problems become obvious, they might provide a vehicle to educate the administration about social work and what it can do and to exert pressure for another worker. Some of these hospitals may want to contract out for emergency room social work services, and they do so at their own risk, since a familiarity with the particular patient population and a feeling for the specific hospital and its staff are important elements in a social worker's array of skills. In addition, innovative planning, informal resolutions, and "deals" with doctors and nurses tend to take place only in one's own hospital.

Developing Resources

With the social worker in place and somewhat acquainted with the setting and the characters, it is now time to set up a program. If there are other hospitals in the area with emergency room social workers, information on resources may be more easily available, although in areas with severe problems with disposition, overstay days, and uncompensated care, not all hospitals will encourage the sharing of limited resources. As much as possible, the new worker(s) should investigate and develop resources in the following areas:

1. Transportation: ambulance and taxi services; special facilities for retarded, handicapped, and other populations;
2. shelter: missions; emergency and other facilities provided by local government; people's emergency shelters; shelters for runaways; shelters for battered women; special populations; low-cost hotels; acceptable boarding homes; and sources of emergency housing grants;
3. concrete services: sources of cash, food, clothing, medication; church programs, welfare departments; and citizens' groups;
4. follow-up, maintenance, and supportive and rehabilitative services: homemaker and visiting nurse programs; call-a-day programs; programs for groups with particular handicaps;
5. psychiatric facilities;
6. children's services and programs;
7. special medical facilities and programs;
8. drug and alcohol rehabilitation programs;
9. sources of medical and rehabilitative equipment;
10. hospice programs;
11. resources in particular neighborhoods and communities, such as a community center for the local Spanish-speaking population or a day-care meal program for the local elderly population;
12. religious programs, resources, and people (for example, a church contact may be particularly important where there is a need for last rites or a refusal to consent to treatment based on religious beliefs);
13. groups with contacts with children, such as school nurses.

This is only a partial list and cannot be developed quickly, as the entries should ideally be checked out, either personally or through colleagues. Depending on the area and the population served, other needs will surface for which resources will have to be found or created. In addition, the workers should develop a good working relationship with the hospital's in-house counsel, if there is one, or with the administrator in charge of legal affairs. Questions involving consent, disposal of property, treatment of minors, and other legal issues (see Chapter 3) are always arising, and while the social worker will rarely have any decision-making responsibility or authority in these areas, familiarity with the issues and a way to get quick answers will help to avoid important omissions and to keep the hospital from making serious mistakes.

Listing resources, however, is only the beginning, since it is the development of a relationship with the people in charge that is critical. The emergency room social worker in a particular city or community will want to become part of an area-wide helping network that will also expect him or her to provide services to those sent or referred by other members of the network.

Critical Needs: People, Space, and Supplies

In the hospital itself, certain staff members and departments will become very important. Although the particular people and services will depend on the hospital itself, three examples will show the kinds of relationships that may be especially helpful. First, a good connection to the dietary department may mean that meals or snacks can occasionally be made available to patients at off times, even to those who are not being admitted. While no hospital wants to encourage the use of its facilities for rest, food, and shelter, an argument can sometimes be made for a particular patient that concrete services, such as food, are a part of his or her immediate short-term treatment program. Second, a friendly relationship with the medical records department may help to shortcut the usual procedures for obtaining records, particularly if the worker is willing to go down to pick up a record in person. "Lost" records can sometimes turn up this way. Third, the security personnel in the emergency department are a critical and underappreciated part of the team. In addition to keeping a protective eye on the social worker(s), who often see obstreperous and disoriented patients, they are an excellent source of referrals and often can point out unnoticed patients who are badly in need of attention. Finally a friendly relationship with a link to the psychiatry department can be invaluable when the evaluation or disposition of an impaired patient is in question.

Finally, in gathering together resources, it is important to lay aside, if at all possible, a store of concrete supplies. Small and safe amounts of petty cash are often necessary for emergency purchases, particularly on nights and weekends, and should be made readily available by the social work department as part of its budget. Particularly in colder climates, coats, jackets, socks, and shoes are often needed by poor or vagrant patients. Blankets, baby clothes, and other items of clothing are also useful to have on hand. In addition, a supply of nonperishable foods—canned and dried goods, juices—plus candles, matches, and shopping bags should be maintained to tide patients over while waiting for a check or other resources. Some departments will find innovative ways of obtaining these materials, such as by fund-raising events or business or volunteer donations, for instance. Whatever is collected should be stored carefully in a place accessible only to the social work department.

The emergency room social worker should have a private office or at least a cubicle where patients and families can speak in confidence and can cry, grieve, or pull themselves together without prying or interference. As discussed in previous chapters, however, the office is for these specific purposes and not a place for the social worker to hide.

Preparation and Training

The final preparatory step involves the emergency room worker— what kind of training should be required? First, the emergency room is not the place for a beginning worker, although it is a superb setting for a student placement, particularly for a second-year student with some background in a health care setting. The emergency room social worker should be a person of some maturity and experience, preferably with previous work in this or other hospitals. Either one of the social workers or a heavily involved supervisor should become part of the emergency department management, attending team meetings, planning policy and programs, evaluating care, and contributing suggestions and recommendations that are taken seriously. Such a role and relationship may take considerable time to develop in a setting whose staff are not used to collaborating with social workers. Eventually, formally or informally, social workers will find themselves educating the medical staff as to patient and community characteristics, resources needed and available, the effects of illness and injury on patients' lives, and other factors.

Training for the social workers themselves will depend on resources, time, costs, and expressed desire. Those hospitals who consider training a high priority develop complex and far-ranging programs. One hospital, for example, has described an orientation program that consists of ten classes and twelve shifts of practicum training under supervision. Not only do new workers begin coverage on their own with an armamentarium of skills, knowledge, and contacts, but also the setting is considered a major placement opportunity for students. Among the topics covered are the social worker's role, resources, DSM III (the current edition of the *Diagnostic and Statistical Manual*, which lists and explains psychiatric diagnoses), medical diagnoses, suicide evaluation, alcoholism, grief reactions, sexual assaults, domestic abuse, organic brain syndrome, psychotropic medications, drug abuse, ethical issues, and charting.[8] The number of workers, the arrangements for worker substitution, and the training program in this particular hospital suggest a program that can really promise comprehensive, available, adequate, and informed coverage. Even where the number of workers is limited, orientation and training can make a tremendous difference in the kinds of services that are eventually developed.

A training program might be designed like the one above, or it may include some or all of the following components (it is assumed that the worker has prior hospital experience):

1. Orientation to the hospital (including specific services and staff members that might be helpful, such as patient representatives, security, administrator for nights/ weekends);
2. orientation to the neighborhood and the patient population, demographic information, patient profiles, locales of particular interest or danger, and community resources;
3. definition of emergencies, and structure and function of the modern emergency room (see material from Chapter 1);
4. the role of the social worker in the emergency room;
5. major medical problems in the emergency room (including problems in medical screening that are sometimes unrecognized);
6. medications;
7. psychiatric problems in the emergency room, evalua-

       tion, diagnoses, resources, special problems (such as
       suicide attempts, substance abuse, and information on
       applicable laws and on resources);
8.   psychosocial problems in the emergency room or pop-
       ulations at risk, child abuse, domestic abuse, problems
       of the frail elderly, the sexually assaulted, and informa-
       tion on applicable laws and on resources;
9.   the bereaved family;
10. conflicts and ethical issues in the emergency room;
11. legal issues in the emergency room;
12. charting, obtaining information, continuity, and con-
       fidentiality.

In a city in which one or more hospitals maintain a residency program in emergency medicine, social workers might be allowed to attend relevant lectures and educational programs. In addition, they could themselves contribute to the teaching of residents and develop relationships that might be fruitful for later collaboration. If several hospitals have social workers in their emergency departments, the training program could be a joint project, repeated at intervals, at least in part, so that all workers can take advantage of the training. The information gleaned from the lectures can make up the bulk of an emergency room social workers' manual, which can be updated periodically as names and resources change. This book, too, is designed to serve as both a training manual and a guide to the initiation and delivery of services and should provide the nucleus for a collection of relevant materials.

While many hospitals will allow the social work department neither the time nor the resources to put together such a comprehensive training program, covering this material should still be a goal of the Social Work Department. An area-wide conference might be one way of exposing workers to a major educational program at least once and may provide the means for supervisors to go back to their hospitals and pass on the basics to new workers as they come in. At the least, whatever comprehensible written materials can be obtained should be made into a manual for the beginning worker to study with a supervisor. Even though a competent, highly motivated social worker may very well be able to function in the emergency room without any orientation at all, it can be a difficult and demoralizing enough setting so that he or she should begin work with all the tools available.

Notes

1. Helen Rehr, Barbara Berkman, and Gary Rosenberg, "Screening for High Social Risk: Principles and Problems," *Social Work*, 25 (September 1980): 403–406.

2. Margaret E. Gwinn, Patricia L. Ewalt, and Marilyn S. Janz, "On Call Is Not Enough: Social Workers in ED," *Hospitals*, 53 (December 1, 1979): 73–75.

3. Rehr et al., "Screening."

4. A program which charges fees for those who can pay without denying service to those who cannot is described in Edith Groner, "Delivery of Clinical Social Work Services in the Emergency Room: A Description of an Existing Program," *Social Work in Health Care*, 4 (Fall 1978): 19–29.

5. An extremely well-staffed and well-planned social work program in the emergency room is discussed in Joan Clement and Karil S. Klingbeil, "The Emergency Room," *Health and Social Work*, 6 (November 1981): 83S–90S. See also George Krell, "Hospital Social Work Should Be More Than a 9–5 Position," *Hospitals*, 50 (May 16, 1976): 99, 100, 102, 104, for a discussion of a special after-hours unit.

6. Clement and Klingbeil, "Emergency Room."

7. This arrangement is described by Margaret Jane Bennett in "The Social Worker's Role," *Hospitals*, 47 (May 16, 1973): 111, 114, 118.

8. Clement and Klingbeil, "Emergency Room."

Epilogue:
The ER Esprit de Corps

There is a special quality about working as part of an emergency room team, a characteristic esprit de corps that is familiar to those who have been significantly involved in this setting. Like other relatively intangible factors, it is often difficult to discuss in precise terms, but this does not lessen its contribution to the functioning of emergency rooms or to the lives of those who work in them. As the member of the team most concerned with psychosocial aspects of the emergency room, the social worker is in a good position both to evaluate and influence this process. What, then, are the relevant factors that can be specified?

In the broadest terms, the ER esprit de corps grows out of the efforts of the staff to cope as individuals and as a group with the special work experiences that they share. The most obvious special element is the regular, if unpredictable, occurrence of life-threatening medical emergencies. Although true medical emergencies may constitute a small proportion of the cases seen in an ER, they define its unique area of professional expertise; the morale and esprit de corps are apt to be low where true emergencies are infrequent. Conversely, morale and esprit de corps are often high in the presence of crisis conditions even when these impose severe stress on the staff and require long hours of uninterrupted work. During such crises, time goes by quickly, and the team pulls together.

The emotional excitement engendered by dramatic medical emergencies produces a kind of high. The staff senses itself as being in the front lines of important action. When major crimes, severe accidents, or natural disasters occur, staff know that the event in which they participated will be on tomorrow's local news programs and in the morning papers. Friends and family and sure to ask for the inside story. Consciously thinking about and enjoying and discussing this kind of glamorous excitement is often suppressed by ER staff either in an effort to play the role of the cool, seasoned veteran or because they feel it is unprofessional. Nevertheless, these are the events that make it all worthwhile; handling them well, professionally and personally, is the source of real pride.

Clearly, there are negative elements to these exciting crises as well. During them the ER staff is exposed to death, mutilation, the violent victimization of the innocent, and their inability to save the lives of some of their patients. Even in the most professional and well adjusted, these traumas touch areas of psychological vulnerability and mobilize defensive reactions. Under these circumstances, ER staff commonly turn to each other for sharing and support. Thus, the peak stresses of ER work tend to increase group cohesiveness and foster esprit de corps. These shared crises feed into a group memory and are retold and elaborated as the legends of each particular ER. These legends serve to socialize new staff members, prepare them for what they may have to face, and reassure them that even the most upsetting events can be mastered by the team they are now a part of.

By this point it should be clear that there are several models from different settings for the ER esprit de corps. The very terms "esprit de corps," "front lines," and "legends" suggest the most obvious: that of the combat group. This may explain why former medics and corpsmen often find the setting a congenial place to work. The concept of the buddy relationship is also a useful one in understanding the nature of interpersonal relations among ER staff members. The buddy relationship is forged under the stresses of combat where people of diverse backgrounds are thrown together in a life-threatening situation where they must depend on each other and work as a team in order to survive. Often a combat buddy is someone with whom one would never socialize under normal circumstances. Yet these relationships are frequently intense and long-lasting, based on memories that are unique, stress-filled, and shared—often memories that are impossible to share with anyone else—"You can't really understand unless you were there."

Several other analogies to combat experiences are relevant to understanding the ER. There is often a sense in both settings of being caught in the middle, between "them" (patients, the enemy) and "our people" (the rest of the hospital, the military command structure). This sense includes the knowledge that moral and material support from their own side might be unreliable. Under these circumstances the small group draws even more closely together; the only people you can really trust are your buddies. ER staffs can be brought closer together by these kinds of feelings when the hospital is full or when they are caught between the pressures of the community to provide ambulatory care for indigent patients and pressures from the hospital administration to avoid nonreimbursed cases.

The humor of the ER is also similar to combat humor in its often private and grisly nature. As in the combat situation and other high-stress settings, humor is often a necessary coping device to help distance those on the front lines from the traumas they deal with and form a shared culture for the stressed group. The movie and television series M*A*S*H provides a good example of this kind of humor and reveals the danger inherent in it of demeaning or depersonalizing both the professionals and their patients. The M*A*S*H crew is a surgical team, and operating room humor is clearly analogous in its nature and functions to that of the ER.

Another model for the ER esprit de corps is provided by policemen and women and firefighters—groups with whom the ER frequently interact around specific crises. Like them, the ER staff keep unusual hours and cannot choose their patients/clients. The necessity for regular night work can interfere with normal family and social life and tends to encourage a greater reliance on co-workers for meeting interpersonal needs. A chronically lonely person or one who has been recently separated, divorced, or bereaved frequently hangs around the station house or the ER even when his or her shift is done. Buddies are different from friends or family, but they can and often do fill a temporary void. At times this may interfere with the development of normal nonwork social ties, and it may be appropriate for the ER social worker to do some gentle counseling when this takes place.

A final analogy to police and firemen and women is in the relationship of the professional to those he or she serves. Like these groups, the relationship of the ER staff to patients is inherently brief and episodic. There is little motivation or opportunity to really get to know patients and experience the gratification of seeing them improve over time. Thus, whatever continuity of relationships one has is likely to be with other staff.

An understanding of the elements that contribute to the ER esprit de corps can help the ER social worker understand his or her own evolving adaptation to this special work setting. It can also help the social worker tolerate and even foster behaviors that might seem strange or unimportant to an outsider. Sharing a cold pizza and a cup of coffee, laughing at a grisly joke, sitting and talking with an intern who was unable to resuscitate an infant, for an hour after work, are the concrete personal experiences from which the ER esprit de corps grows. It is what can make a tough and often traumatic job livable and rewarding.

Appendixes

Appendix A: Emergency Room Log

SOCIAL WORKER			RESIDENT		DATE			SHIFT				DAY	NIGHT	
												PSYCHIATRIC ATTENDING		
														SW SUPERVISOR

CONTACTS										
SW NO.	PSY NO.	TIME	REFERRAL SOURCE	PATIENT NAME	HOSPITAL NUMBER	AGE	SEX	ASSESSMENT PROTOCOL	TREATMENT DISPOSITION	NO. OF 10 MIN. SVC UNITS

SOCIAL WORK PHONE TALLY
COMMUNITY INFORMATION

CONTACTS: Check according to who sees the patient ie: Social Worker or/+psychiatrist.

OF SERVICE UNITS: Service units will be counted in 10 minute increments. Keep track of all time spent in interviews, all telephone calls, charting, consultation, etc. An interview lasting 50 minutes would be 5 service units. Charting and phone calls covering an additional 35 minutes would comprise 3.5 service units for a total of 8.5 service units. Crisis intervention over 4 hours would comprise 24 service units.

Source: Social Work Department, Harborview Medical Center, Seattle, Washington.

Appendix B
Emergency Room Log Instructions

Social Worker:	Your name
Resident:	Resident Physician assigned to shift
Date:	Current date
Shift:	Current
Social Work Supervisor:	Individual who is responsible for clinical supervision and performance evaluation.
Psychiatric Attending:	Attending physician(s) assigned to cover days/nights.
Contacts:	Check according to *who* sees the patient, i.e., Social Worker and/or Psychiatrist.
Time:	Time patient checked in for treatment, i.e., 0400, 0910, etc.
Referral Source:	Indicate whether patient referred by medical staff, self, other.
Patient Name:	Name of patient for whom you have accepted responsibility for casework evaluation and intervention.
Hospital Number:	Assigned _____ number.
Age:	Patient's stated age.
Sex:	Male/Female
Assessment Protocol:	Indicate which protocol used, i.e., ER Psychiatric Evaluation, Domestic Violence, etc.
Treatment Disposition:	Indicate "Admit," "Home with friend," etc.
No. of Service Units:	Service units will be counted in 10-minute increments. Keep track of all time spent in interviews, all telephone calls, charting, consultation, etc. An interview lasting 50 minutes would be 5 service units. Charting and phone calls covering an additional 35 minutes would be 3.5 service units for a total of 8.5 service units.
Social Work Phone:	Social work telephone number.
Tally Community Information:	Log the number of calls to you during the shift from community agencies seeking general information, patients calling in crisis, etc.

Source: Social Work Department, Harborview Medical Center, Seattle, Washington.

Appendix C
Brief Contact and Assessment Form

Date: _____

Name: _____ Spouse: _____
    (Last Name)   (First Name)

D.O.B. _____ Hosp. #: _____ S.S. #: _____

Sex: M F   Marital Status: S M D S W

Religion: _____ Ethnic Group: _____

Address #1: _____ Phone: _____

Address #2: _____ Phone: _____

Doctor: _____

Diagnosis: _____

Recommended Medical Follow-up: _____

_____

Significant Others:

Name	Address	Relation	Phone
1)			
2)			
3)			
4)			

Medical Coverage: _____

Employer/DPA District: _____

Case #: _____ Worker: _____ Phone: _____

Financial Resources: _____

Patient admitted to: _____ Patient discharged to: _____
       (service)   (Bed #)

Is patient previously known to: E.D. _____ Social Work Staff ___

Psychiatry _____ Refer to ongoing worker _____

Other agency _____ Worker: _____

Social Work Assessment and Action:

_____

Source: Clifford Bell, M.S.W., Emergency Room Social Worker, Temple University Hospital, Philadelphia, Pennsylvania.

Appendix D
Recommended Occupation Description

Occupation Title: Emergency Department Social Worker

Department: Emergency Department

Reports to: Director of Social Work Department

Areas of Responsibility: Emergency Department, Walk-In Clinic

Summary of Occupation: The Social Worker in the medical setting is available to contribute to the total health care provided by the patient care team. The qualified practitioner for this position should be able to function satisfactorily in the following areas:

Duties and Responsibilities
1. Case Work
   1.1 Assist patient care staff with discharge planning.
   1.2 Coordinate the disposition of patients and their families (e.g., nursing home placement, shelters, and transportation).
   1.3 Maintain a patient file on all active patients and families with whom the Social Worker was involved and make this file accessible to appropriate Emergency Department Personnel.
   1.4 Provide follow-up of patient and families placed with resource agencies as needed.
2. Advocate
   2.1 Monitor the waiting room and the examination rooms to serve as liaison between the patient care personnel and patients and their families and to identify patients requiring social work assistance.
   2.2 Assist the patient care personnel in resolving difficult situations that might arise with uncooperative patients, families, and their friends.
   2.3 Evaluate completed Emergency Department Patient Questionnaires and follow-up areas requiring attention.
   2.4 Assist patients in preparing Medicare and SSI applications.
   2.5 Assist patients and their families in understanding and making constructive use of the patient care services available to them.
3. Education
   3.1 Identify to medical staff socioeconomic conditions and problems relevant to the health status of particular patients.
   3.2 Assist patients and their families in understanding the instructions at the time of discharge and the need for preventive medical care.
   3.3 Participate in ongoing continuing education program and meetings provided for Emergency Department Personnel.
   3.4 Participate on committees intended to enhance the quality of care for patients and their families.
   3.5 Supervise social work staff and students as assigned.

Recommended Occupation Description
  4. Referral
    4.1 Maintain a current resource file containing appropriate agencies and make this file accessible to Emergency Department Personnel.
    4.2 Coordinate all boarding home, nursing home, and other alternative living arrangement transfers.
    4.3 Assist patient care personnel in evaluating and reporting all incidents of suspected child abuse and sexual abuse.
    4.4 Refer and consult regarding patients who are admitted.
  5. Counseling
    5.1 Provide short-term supportive counseling to patients and families as needed.
    5.2 Provide vocational and job readiness counseling as needed.
    5.3 Provide crisis intervention to patients, families, and friends.
  6. Department Structure
    6.1 Be well versed in social work responsibilities regarding all "codes."
    6.2 Be aware of Emergency Department staff composition and the social worker's role.
    6.3 Be familiar with and participate in all disaster drills and plans.
    6.4 Be knowledgeable about all policies and regulations regarding the Emergency Department.

Education and Experience Required: The Emergency Department Social Worker should be a graduate of an accredited social work school with a Masters Degree in Social Work. This individual should have at least two years of full-time work experience, preferably in a medical human services area.

Source: Clifford Bell, M.S.W., Emergency Room Social Worker, Temple University Hospital, Philadelphia, Pennsylvania.

Appendix E
Minors' Consent to Medical, Dental, and Health Services [Pennsylvania] (35 P.S. 10101–10105)

§ 10101. Individual consent

Any minor who is eighteen years of age or older, or has graduated from high school, or has married, or has been pregnant, may give effective consent to medical, dental and health services for himself or herself, and the consent of no other person shall be necessary.
1970, Feb. 13, P.L. 19, No. 10, §1.

§ 10102. Consent for children with minor parents

Any minor who has been married or has borne a child may give effective consent to medical, dental and health services for his or her child.
1970, Feb. 13, P.L. 19, No. 10, §2.

§ 10103. Pregnancy, venereal disease and other reportable diseases

Any minor may give effective consent for medical and health services to determine the presence of or to treat pregnancy, and venereal disease and other diseases reportable under the act of April 23, 1956 (P.L. 1510), known as the "Disease Prevention and Control Law of 155,"[1] and the consent of no other person shall be necessary.
1970, Feb. 13, P.L. 19, No. 10, §3.

§ 10104. When consent unnecessary

Medical, dental and health services may be rendered to minors of any age without the consent of a parent or legal guardian when, in the physician's judgment, an attempt to secure consent would result in delay of treatment which would increase the risk to the minor's life or health. [emphasis added]
1970, Feb. 13, P.L. 19, No. 10, §4.

§ 10105. Liability for rendering services

The consent of a minor who professes to be, but is not a minor whose consent alone is effective to medical, dental and health services shall be deemed effective without the consent of the minor's parent or legal guardian, if the physician or other person relied in good faith upon the representations of the minor.
1970, Feb. 13, P.L. 19, No. 10, §5.

Source: Penna. Stat. Ann. tit. 35, §§ 10101–10105 (Purden's 1983).

[1]Section 52.1 et seq. of this title.

Appendix F
Medical and Social Work Protocol For Emergency Room/ Walk-In-Clinic Treatment Cases of Adult Abuse (Including Family Abuse)

Medical

1. Register victim as Alleged Adult Abuse.
2. Triage Nurse will notify social worker that the victim has been registered.
3. After victim has received medical treatment and has been medically cleared, Medicine/Surgery Service will notify the social worker that the patient is available for an interview.
4. If Triage Nurse determines that victim does not require medical attention, victim should be automatically triaged to social worker.
5. *All* cases of alleged Adult Abuse to be seen by social worker.

Social Work

1. Interview all alleged Adult Abuse patients.
2. Use Abuse folder.
3. After victim is medically cleared, interview victim to assess mental status, behavior, personal support systems, and need for additional services.
4. Assessment Categories:
   A. Subjective Distress
      - Anxiety/Fear/Anger
      - Depression
      - Social Isolation
      - Suicidal Ideation
      - Homicidal Ideation
      - Guilt/Blame
      - Denial of need for Therapeutic Intervention or referral
      - Minimization
   B. Behavioral Disturbance
      - Speech Disorganization
      - Agitation/Excitement
      - Reported Impulsivity
      - Interview-Belligerence
      - Inappropriate Affect, Appearance, Behavior
      - Report Overt Anger
      - Suicidal Behavior
      - Homicidal Behavior
   C. Chemical
      - Alcohol Abuse
      - Drug Abuse

D. Societal Role Impairment
- Wage Earner Role Impairment
- Housekeeper Role Impairment
- Student Role Impairment
- Mate Role Impairment
- Parental Role Impairment

5. Photograph patient for medical chart. Obtain consents for photography only if patient will be filing charges with law enforcement.

6. Provide patient with HMC form which explains how to file charges with law enforcement agency.

7. Complete Social Service Intake Report for battered woman patient.

8. Disposition
- Arrange for escort home, or other shelter if needed (Detox, if necessary).
- Give victim information and referral to legal and counseling services.
- Contact Children's Protective Service, if necessary.

9. Xerox medical workup and social work evaluation for Adult Abuse folder.

10. If patient is seen in Emergency Room, put folder in SAC drawer. If patient is seen in Walk-in-Clinic, put folder in Social Work drawer.

11. If patient wishes social work/counseling follow-up at Harborview Medical Center, please leave note for Emergency Room Social Worker.

Source: From "Adult Abuse Protocol" in *Protocol Manual*, Social Work Department, Harborview Medical Center, Seattle, Washington.

Appendix G
Adult Female Patient Protocol
Sexual Assault Center—Emergency Trauma Center

Information for All Involved with Patient

1. Triage immediately after the acutely ill or injured. Even though no severe physical trauma may be present, the psychosocial crisis present should be triaged as high priority.
2. Provide maximum emotional support. All effort should be made to minimize additional emotional trauma. Be gentle and empathetic. Explain what you are doing in a calm manner and voice. Take time to reassure the apprehensive patient.
3. Do not be judgmental or moralistic.
4. Allow the patient to feel as much in control of her body as possible.
5. Do not discuss sexual assault cases with anyone without the patient's specific consent.
6. The chart may become legal evidence. Statements made by the patient may be admissible in court. Be sure that all written statements made are objective, accurate, and legible.

Emergency Room Personnel

1. Sign victim in quickly. Do not keep the patient waiting in registration or other public space. Provide a private place for the patient (ER-9 or Quite Room) and complete registration there.
2. Only those *directly* involved with care should interact with the patient. Give your name and explain your role.
3. Contact ER physician immediately if evidence of moderate to severe trauma.
4. Contact social worker immediately.
5. If the assault occurred within the past 48 hours, contact the first available ER resident.
6. If the assault was more than 48 hours previously, the social worker will evaluate and either give the patient an appointment to the next available Women's Clinic or will request physician consultation earlier, as needed. In most cases, it is advisable to evaluate the patient medically during the ER visit, even though most medical-legal tests cannot be performed.

Social Worker

1. Assess immediate emotional needs of patient and family. Respond to questions and expressed emotions. Take as much time as necessary to respond to patient's emotional needs.
2. Confirm that the physician has been notified.
3. History: Obtain alone or in conjunction with the physician.
   a. Obtain information from persons accompanying patient before beginning the interview.

b. See patient alone or with support person of her choice.

c. Determine and use the patient's terminology for parts of the body and sexual acts. Use aids, e.g., books or diagrams as needed.

d. Obtain a directed history of the assault. Do not ask "why" or "how come" questions, e.g., "Why did you go to his house?" Phrase questions in terms of "who, what, where, when," e.g., "Who (how many) assaulted you? "Did the offender use oral, finger, penile, contact to mouth, vulva, vagina, rectum?" How long ago did it happen?" "Did penetration or ejaculation occur?" "What kind of force or enticement was used?" "What symptoms do you have now?"

e. When the physician arrives, present history and impressions (out of patient's hearing). Complete history-taking conjointly.

4. Explain to patient the reasons for questions asked, types of medical/legal tests needed, and possible treatment.

5. Assessment and counseling:

a. Assess behavior and affect. Obtain if possible some pre-assault history of psychosocial functioning as a baseline from which to evaluate present coping state. Note significant psychiatric history and any current counseling relationships.

b. Explain anticipated emotional problems, e.g., rape trauma syndrome, eating and sleeping disturbances, fears, flashbacks. Elicit (and respond to all) questions/concerns from patient. Give patient the Sexual Assault Center brochure (handout).

c. Encourage contact with the Sexual Assault Center.

6. Discuss reporting to police as patient's option. (Police may be contacted to come to the Emergency Room for an initial report.)

7. Obtain consents (in writing) for medical care and collection of evidence, photographs and release of evidence or information; specify to whom.

8. Record on Sexual Assault Report form (#0245) the following:

a. History of Sexual Assault

b. Patient's emotional state and orientation

c. Impression(s)

d. Plan
   - medical appointment for follow-up care in 5–7 days.
   - ongoing counseling and advocacy by the Sexual Assault Center.
   - referrals made to other social service agencies or the criminal justice system.
   - referral to Rape Relief (document advocate's name if possible).

9. Make three copies of Sexual Assault Report form (#0245) for SAC files. Complete Patient Profile for SAC file (no copy of this form is needed in the Medical Record).

10. Return completed SAC file and unused forms to SAC folder at ER social worker's station.

Physician*

6. Final Care
   a. Verbally express concern and availability for help as needed.
   b. Reinforce social worker information; reinforce that patient is physically intact and is not responsible for assault/abuse.
   c. Discuss medical problems which may arise and encourage patient to call as needed.
7. Final Diagnosis
   a. History of sexual assault. (Rape is a legal term, not a medical diagnosis.) Do not use terms such as "alleged," or "possible," assault.

---

*Nos. 1–5 omitted, for "Physician."

Source: Selected sections from "Adult Female Patient Protocol" in *Protocol Manual*, Social Work Department, Harborview Medical Center, Seattle, Washington.

Appendix H
Male Patient Protocol
Sexual Assault Center—Emergency Trauma Center

Information for All Involved with Patient

1. Triage immediately after the acutely ill or injured. Even though no severe physical trauma may be present, the psychosocial crisis present should be triaged as high priority.
2. Provide maximum emotional support. All effort should be made to minimize additional emotional trauma. Be gentle and empathetic. Explain what you are doing in a calm manner and voice. Take time to reassure the apprehensive patient.
3. Do not be judgmental or moralistic.
4. Allow the patient to feel as much in control of his body as possible.
5. Do not discuss sexual assault cases with anyone without the patient's specific consent.
6. The chart may become legal evidence. Statements made by the patient may be admissible in court. Be sure that all written statements made are objective, accurate and legible.

Emergency Room Personnel

1. Sign patient in quickly; do not keep waiting in registration or other public space. Provide a private place for the patient (ER-9 or Quiet Room) and complete registration there.
2. Only those *directly* involved with care should interact with the patient. Give your name and explain your role.
3. Contact ER physician immediately if evidence of moderate to severe trauma.
4. Contact social worker immediately.

Social Worker

1. Assess immediate emotional needs of patient and family. Respond to the questions and expressed emotions. Take as much time as necessary to respond to patient's emotional needs. Do not assume that sexually victimized male necessarily has a homosexual lifestyle.
2. Confirm that the physician has been notified.
3. History: Obtain alone or in conjunction with the physician.
   a. Obtain information from persons accompanying patient before beginning the interview.
   b. See patient alone or with support person of his choice.
   c. Determine and use the patient's terminology for parts of the body and sexual acts. Use aids, e.g., books or diagrams as needed.
   d. Obtain a directed history of the assault. Do not ask "why" or "how come" questions, e.g., "Why did you go to his house?" Phrase questions in terms of "who, what, where, when," e.g.,

"Who (how many) assaulted you?" "Did the offender use oral, finger, penile contact to mouth, penis, rectum?" "How long ago did it happen?" "Did pentration or ejaculation occur?" "What kind of force or enticement was used?" "What symptoms do you have now?"

    e. When the physician arrives, present history and impressions (out of patient's hearing). Complete history-taking conjointly.

4. Explain to patient the reasons for questions asked, types of medical/legal tests needed, and possible treatment.

5. Assessment and counseling:

    a. Assess behavior and affect. Obtain if possible some pre-assault history of psychosocial functioning as a baseline from which to evaluate present coping state. Note significant psychiatric history and any current counseling relationships.

    b. Explain anticipated emotional problems, e.g., rape trauma syndrome, eating and sleeping disturbances, fears, flashbacks, sexual identity issues. Elicit (and respond to all) questions/concerns from patient. Give patient the Sexual Assault Center brochure.

    c. Make a follow-up plan. Encourage contact with the Sexual Assault Center.

6. Discuss reporting to police as patient's option. (Police may be contacted to come to the Emergency Room for an initial report.)

7. Obtain consents (in writing) for medical care and collection of evidence, photographs and release of evidence or information; specify to whom.

8. Record on Sexual Assault Report form (#0245) the following:

    a. History of sexual assault

    b. Patient's emotional state and orientation

    c. Impression(s)

    d. Plan:

- medical appointment for follow-up care in 5–7 days to STD Clinic or private physician.
- ongoing counseling and advocacy by the Sexual Assault Center.
- referrals made to other social service agencies or the criminal justice system.

9. Make three copies of Sexual Assault Report form (#0245) for SAC files. Complete Patient Profile for SAC file (no copy of this form is needed in the Medical Record).

10. Return completed SAC file and unused forms to SAC folder at ER social worker's station.

Physician*

6. Final Care
   a. Verbally express concern and availability for help as needed.
   b. Reinforce social worker information; reinforce that patient is physically intact and is not responsible for the assault/abuse.
   c. Discuss medical problems which may arise and encourage patient to call as needed.

---

*Nos. 1–5 omitted, for "Physician."

Source: Selected sections from "Male Patient Protocol" in *Protocol Manual*, Social Work Department, Harborview Medical Center, Seattle, Washington.

Appendix I
Child/Adolescent Protocol
Sexual Assault Center—Emergency Trauma Center

Information for All Involved with Patient

1. Triage immediately after the acutely ill or injured. Even though no severe physical trauma may be present, the psychosocial crisis should be triaged as high priority.
2. Provide maximum emotional support to parents as well as to the child/adolescent victim. Do not be judgmental or allow your emotional responses (e.g., anger, outrage) to interfere with providing optimal care.
3. Only those *directly* involved in care should interact with the patient.
4. Do not discuss sexual assault cases with anyone without the written consent of the parent or legal guardian of the patient, if an adolescent.
5. The chart may become legal evidence. "Hearsay" statements from those who first see the child/adolescent may be admissible in court. All written statements should be objective, accurate, and legible.

Emergency Room Personnel

1. Provide private facilities for the patient (ER-9 or Quiet Room). Complete registration there.
2. Contact ER physician immediately if evidence of moderate to severe trauma.
3. Obtain consent for care from the parent(s) or legal guardian of all children less than eighteen years of age. If such consent cannot be obtained, contact the hospital administrator or the Juvenile Court for temporary consent. Examination of the adolescent should not be done without his/her consent unless a life-threatening emergency exists.
4. Contact social worker immediately.
5. If the assault occurred within the past 48 hours, contact the pediatric resident immediately.
6. If the assault was more than 48 hours previously, most legal tests cannot be performed. In most cases, however, the exam should still be done at this time. Rarely would it be more appropriate for the exam to be deferred. This should be determined by the social worker and doctor.

Social Worker

1. Assess immediate emotional needs of child and parents. Respond to questions and expressed emotions.
2. Confirm that the physician has been notified.

3. History: Obtain alone or in conjunction with the physician.
   a. Take as much time as necessary to respond to patient's emotional needs.
   b. Ascertain as much of the history as possible from parents or accompanying persons before interviewing the patient (out of patient's presence if possible).
   c. Evaluate whether patient should be interviewed separately from parent (i.e., embarrassment, blame, confidentiality issue).
   d. Determine and use the patient's terminology for parts of the body, sexual acts, etc. Use aids, i.e., anatomically correct dolls and picture books as needed. Questions should be appropriate for age and developmental level.
   e. Obtain a directed history of the assault. Do not ask "why" questions, e.g., "Why did you go to his house?" Phrase questions in terms of "who, what, where, when," e.g., "Did the offender use oral, finger, penile contact to mouth, vulva, vagina, rectum?" "How long ago did it happen?" "Did penetration or ejaculation occur?" "What kind of force, threat, or enticement was used?" "From whom did the patient seek help?"
   f. When the physician arrives, present history and impressions (out of patient's hearing). Complete history-taking jointly.
4. Explain to patient and parents the reasons for questions asked, types of medical/legal tests needed, and possible treatment.
5. Assessment and counseling:
   a. Assess emotional state and orientation, including response patterns of parent and child to each other. Ascertain support systems of patient and family. Do not return child home unless the environment is safe. Document changes in housing.
   b. Explain anticipated emotional problems, e.g., eating and sleeping disturbances, fears, regression. Respond to all questions of child and parents. Give patient and parents the Sexual Assault Center brochure.
   c. Encourage contact with the Sexual Assault Center.
6. Discuss reporting to police and Children's Protective Services. (Police may be contacted to come to Emergency Room for initial report.)
(No. 7 [Obtaining consents] omitted.)
8. Record on Sexual Assault Report form (#0245) the following:
   a. History of sexual assault
   b. Patient's/family's emotional state and orientation
   c. Impression(s)
   d. Plan:
      - medical appointment for follow-up care in 5–7 days.
      - ongoing counseling and advocacy by the Sexual Assault Center.

- Children's Protective Services referral, which is legally mandated.
- referrals made to other agencies as needed.

9. Make three copies of Sexual Assault Report form (#0245) for SAC files. Complete patient profile for SAC file (no copy of this form is needed in the medical record).

10. Return completed SAC file and unused forms to SAC folder at ER social worker's station.

Source: Selected sections from "Child/Adolescent Protocol" in *Protocol Manual*, Social Work Department, Harborview Medical Center, Seattle, Washington.

Index

Index